EVIDENCE OF SATAN IN
THE MODERN WORLD

LÉON CRISTIANI

EVIDENCE OF SATAN IN THE MODERN WORLD

Translated by Cynthia Rowland

SOPHIA INSTITUTE PRESS
Manchester, New Hampshire

Cover design: Updatefordesign Studio

Cover image: *The Angel Lucifer Exiled from Paradise Falls from Heaven* (Shutterstock 2149763061)

Unless otherwise noted, Scripture quotations are taken from the Douay-Rheims edition of the Old and New Testaments.

Nihil Obstat:
R. D. Dermitius Fogarty, D.D., L.C.L.
R. D. Kilianus Lynch, D.D., D.C.L., O.Carm.
Censores deputati

Imprimatur:
Cyrillus
Episcopus Southwarcensis
Datum Southwarci die 5a Junii 1961

The Nihil Obstat and the Imprimatur are ecclesiastical declarations that a publication is free of doctrinal or moral error, not a statement of the positive worth, nor an implication that the contents have the Archbishop's approval or recommendation.

Sophia Institute Press
Box 5284, Manchester, NH 03108
1-800-888-9344
www.SophiaInstitute.com

Sophia Institute Press is a registered trademark of Sophia Institute.

paperback ISBN 978-1-64413-846-5

ebook ISBN 978-1-64413-847-2

Library of Congress Control Number: 2022946100

First printing

CONTENTS

Introduction. 3

1. The Curé d'Ars and the Devil. 19

2. Satan at Lourdes. 49

3. Possession, Its Nature, Causes, and Treatment 83

4. The Particular Case of Antoine Gay [1790–1871] 99

5. Cases of Possession in the Nineteenth and Twentieth
   Centuries 125

6. Spellbound in Piacenza. 149

7. Magic in the Twentieth Century. 171

8. The Exorcisms 189

9. Satan in the Modern World 215

10. Satanism and the Devices of Satan 237

11. Lucifer and His Allies. 255

12. The Mentality of Satan. 277

About the Author. 289

EVIDENCE OF SATAN IN THE MODERN WORLD

INTRODUCTION

WHEN WE DECLARE that a certain statement is, or is not, Gospel truth, we are trying to say that it is, or is not, strictly credible.

Christ, to Christians, is the final authority to which we submit in all confidence, faith, and love. Even to unbelievers Christ is one of the most outstanding personalities in history. He is the personification of sincerity and truth, and is recorded as saying: "But let your speech be yea, yea: no, no: and that which is over and above these, is of evil" (Matt. 5:37).

We should therefore enquire what Jesus thought and said on the subject of Satan. Here the Gospel, as on all other points which concern man's spiritual life, is normative and definitive. Even if this should no longer be true for those who have lost their faith, it is nevertheless impossible to understand the mentality of previous centuries in France without reference to the Gospels. Those who had, or believed they had had, contact with the Devil, those who had endured his onslaughts, like the Curé d'Ars; those who were regarded as "possessed" and subjected to a more or less effective exorcism, have all interpreted their state in the light of the Gospels and the traditions derived therefrom.

Let us therefore see what the Bible has to say of Satan, and how it records cases of possession and the expulsion of devils. In particular we should note whether Christ himself believed in the existence of Satan.

THE TEMPTATION IN THE WILDERNESS

The first event to attract our attention is Christ's temptation in the wilderness, recorded in three Gospels. They show Christ and Satan meeting face to face. We should note, however, that there was no witness to this formidable encounter. The three Evangelists derived their account from Jesus Himself. He took care to inform His disciples of what had passed between the Devil and Himself. He wished them to know what He had seen, what it had meant to look each other, as one says, in the eye, to listen to Satan's attempts to subjugate Him, and make Him deviate from His path. In a word, Christ had wished to be tempted. And He was. He revealed to His followers what this temptation had been. Satan had shown Him all the kingdoms of the world, saying: "To thee will I give all this power, and the glory of them; for to me they are delivered, and to whom I will, I give them. If thou therefore wilt adore before me, all shall be thine" (Luke 4:6–7). The temptation therefore was no slight one, but on a world scale, on a scale Satan considered appropriate to his task.

Jesus, for His part, admitted Satan's predominance in all the kingdoms of the earth by thrice calling him "prince of this world" (John 12:31, 14:30, 16:11). Fr. Lagrange, speaking of these accounts of the temptation in the wilderness, compares them with the prologue of a classical tragedy, in which the theme of the forthcoming drama is announced and, as it were, prefigured. The battle in the desert between Christ and the Devil is such a prologue. It tells us everything about Christ's mission, which was solely to overthrow the dominion of Satan. St. John was to say in his first Epistle: "For this purpose, the Son of God appeared, that he might destroy the works of the Devil" (1 John 3:8). We might therefore expect the Gospels to be full of the work of Christ against Satan, and of Satan against Christ, and they are indeed so, to an astonishing degree. It is impossible to understand the Gospels without the certainty of Satan's existence and of his activity amongst us.

SOME EXAMPLES

It would not be possible to list every instance in which devils are mentioned in the New Testament, and we shall quote only some important examples.

Jesus began to preach in Galilee, and St. Mark writes that He "cast out many devils" (Mark 1:34). Before the Sermon on the Mount the crowds gathered round Him and St. Luke tells us why: "to be healed of their diseases. And they that were troubled with unclean spirits, were cured" (Luke 6:18). "And," says St. Matthew, "they presented to him all sick people that were taken with divers diseases and torments, and such as were possessed by devils, and lunatics, and those that had palsy, and he cured them" (Matt. 4:24).

In the case of Mary Magdalene, it is made clear that Jesus had cast out from her "seven devils" (Luke 8:2). When Jesus sends His apostles to preach in Galilee, He gives them power to cast out devils. When they return, He greets them joyfully: "I saw Satan like lightning falling from heaven" (Luke 10:18).

When Christ healed the woman "who had a spirit of infirmity eighteen years" and the ruler of the synagogue waxed indignant because it was the Sabbath, Jesus replied: "Ye hypocrites, doth not every one of you, on the sabbath day, loose his ox or his ass from the manger, and lead them to water? And ought not this daughter of Abraham, whom Satan hath bound, lo, these eighteen years, be loosed from this bond on the sabbath day?" (Luke 13:10–16).

There is also the casting out of the devil called Legion, because of the number inhabiting the possessed person. Legion asks to be allowed to pass into a herd of swine. Jesus permits this, and all the swine cast themselves into the lake where they are drowned. (The three Synoptic Gospels, particularly Mark 5:1–20.)

This element of burlesque is remarkably evocative, giving us an exact indication of demonic character and nature.

It reveals their "psychology," to which we shall return later, and what they do when in possession of a human being. "They introduce into, and maintain in, the possessed person," writes Mgr. Catherinet, "morbid disorders akin to madness; they possess an acute sense of discrimination, and know who Christ is; they prostrate themselves before him without shame, praying and begging him in the name of God not to cast them back into the Abyss, and in order to avoid this fate, beg to be allowed to enter into the swine and remain there. Scarcely have they entered into the swine than, with a vigor as astonishing as their versatility, they provoke the cruel and wanton destruction of the creatures they have been granted as a refuge. Fearful, obsequious, powerful, malignant, versatile and even grotesque, all these characteristics, so well-defined in this story, reappear in varying degrees in the other gospel accounts of the casting out of devils."[1]

To sum up, it is impossible for any serious historian, let alone for a Catholic, not to perceive that Christ is not merely using the phraseology of His times, that He has no intention of purely and simply accepting the ignorance and prejudice of His environment, but that He Himself believes in the existence and activity of Satan. He puts us on our guard, by His unremitting struggle against the

---

[1]   Desclee de Brouwer, *Satan, Etudes carmélitaine,* (Paris: Desclee de Brouwer, 1949), 319.

Devil, with the result that, finding Satan present to such an extent throughout the New Testament, we are forced to give urgent attention to the problem this creates.

WHY SO MANY CASES OF POSSESSION?

These stories are so frequent in the New Testament, the Devil is so constantly present, that one is inclined to wonder whether the whole business is not a little exaggerated. It is obvious that in ordinary life we do not encounter such a relatively large number of cases of possession as sprang up in the path of Jesus. Modern critics — or at least those who are pleased to call themselves "independent critics" — have not failed to suggest a certain improbability. According to them the majority of these "possessed persons" were either maniacs, or unbalanced, or more or less demented persons.

Even if it were so, even if Christ, in treating this type of "sick" person had merely been conforming to contemporary ideas of medicine, it is still none the less remarkable that He should, with a word, in the majority of these cases, have succeeded in freeing these unhappy persons from their infirmities and restoring them to their normal state. But where one considers all that has been said already, this method of resolving the problem appears a little summary. The Gospels distinguish quite clearly between the sick and the possessed. The latter show striking symptoms of the presence of an alien intelligence within them. This intelligence is hostile to Jesus and is what we describe as the intelligence of an evil spirit.

It would indeed have been astonishing if, after the vast prologue of the temptation in the wilderness, Satan had not intervened in the course of Christ's ministry, or had played only a secondary role. But this is not the case. Christ openly proclaimed His strength, saying He had come to break Satan's dominion over the world. Their struggle, it is true, took place mainly in the sphere of the invisible, the realm of sin and grace. And it will be thus until the end of the world. But by God's permission, this tremendous secular struggle has also its visible aspects, sometimes spectacular in nature. Yet such episodes are not the heart of the matter. We must remember this. Even if in this present book we dwell on these outer aspects, we have no desire to exaggerate their importance. What is at stake is the souls of men, the choice between Heaven and Hell, between bliss and damnation. It was therefore part of God's plan for men to make them aware of the powers of Satan, and to make this power yield to the Redeemer.

There is no reason to believe that the number of cases of possession quoted in the Gospels represent the normal number either at that period or today. It is possible, and even probable, that such cases would occur with extraordinary frequency in the neighborhood of Jesus. The union in one person of deity and human nature, as in Jesus, Son of Man and Son of God, would, by God's will, give rise to its counterpart in repeated manifestations of diabolism. Possession is, in a certain sense, a replica, a caricature, of the Incarnation of the Word. The pagan world, and even Judaism itself, were beginning to be undermined by that skepticism toward the supernatural which is one of the characteristics of the present day. The coming of Jesus and the countless cases of possession which occurred around Him were a striking revelation of the supernatural world, in its complementary aspects, the *City of God* and the *City of Satan*.

It is in this sense that we declared that the Gospel is *normative*. It sets up principles, provides illumination, establishes laws, and sheds over every age a light which is never to be extinguished. All that we know or believe on the subject of the Devil is rooted in the Gospels. Belief in the existence and maleficence of the Devil is part of Christian dogma. Our destiny is either demonic or angelic. We shall behold God, like the angels, says Jesus, or we shall be damned with Satan and all his host.

It was necessary to establish, or re-establish, this point before passing to contemporary facts. A rapid survey will be enough to trace developments from New Testament times to the present day.

We need, in general, to be on our guard against two dangers, of paying either too much attention to satanism, or too little. There have been centuries in which men saw the Devil everywhere, and others when he was not considered to be present anywhere — exaggerations which are equally false, equally deceptive, and both consequently inspired by Satan, the father of lies.

IN ANTIQUITY

It is not possible to say that there was any obsession with demonic activities amongst the early Christians. We could quote texts from St. Paul and St. Peter which are still relevant, and which should be taken as the expression of the strictest reality. We have to struggle against the Devil. Moral life is a constant struggle. There is more to life than flesh and blood. The Dragon is constantly at work. St. John, in his Apocalypse, said all there was to be said about the vicissitudes of Christian history, but it is undeniable that the Dragon has a part of primary importance to play within it. The periods of persecution which are so frequent in the history of the Church are pre-eminently diabolic. It is also certain the early Christians considered the pagan worship of idols as diabolic in inspiration. In their eyes the pagan deities were demonic.

This is not to say that the Fathers of the Church exaggerated. Augustine was well aware of the two Cities, which he described with lucidity and vigor and with all the breadth of vision of a spiritual genius.

Some find St. Augustine pessimistic. But if so, it is not induced by theological demonology. He does not ascribe all that is dark and somber in human action to the Devil alone. We have our own share of responsibility. On the contrary, he affirms—as we shall recall later—that "this dog is chained." The Devil can do nothing against us without our own will. His force comes from our consent, and his weakness from our resistance.

The most vivid stories of demonic activity handed down to us from Christian antiquity are those of the Desert Fathers. Anthony struggles at close quarters with the demon. The hermits of the Thebaïd, and monks of every order and of all ages, had their skirmishes with Satan. Nearer home, St. Martin had his own experiences. If, however, we make a brief survey of the Middle Ages, thumbing the in-folios of the great scholastic theologians, we are not overwhelmed by references to demonology. Authors who have made a special study of medieval literature on demonic possession or sorcery consider that the greatest masters, such as Albertus Magnus, Thomas Aquinas, and Duns Scotus, were inclined to discredit the alleged miraculous achievements of the sorcerers. In the fifteenth century Gerson and Gabriel Biel, the last of the Nominalists, disagreed on the question, the first asserting and the second denying the powers of devils over the terrestrial sphere.

A DANGEROUS DEVELOPMENT

Such was the position when, in 1486, there appeared a work destined to have the most widespread repercussions, and to influence a whole century toward the most obvious and deplorable exaggeration.

It was the *Malleus maleficarum*—*The Hammer of Witches*, written by two German Dominicans, Jakob Sprenger and Heinrich Institoris, the one professor at the University of Cologne, the other Inquisitor in Upper Germany. The work had an enormous circulation. There are known to have been twenty-eight editions in the fifteenth and sixteenth centuries. It was the handbook for the witch-hunt that followed and stimulated the production of a whole literature of demonology. There was no limit to the number of works, published for the use of inquisitors or confessors, dealing exclusively with sorcery and pacts with the Devil. The beginning of the seventeenth century saw a further crop of such works, giving impressive but repulsive details of "possession," of monsters, vampires, goblins, familiar spirits, and the like. In 1603 one author, Jourdain Guibelet, published a *Discours philosophique* whose academic title cloaked a treatise on *incubi* and *succubi*, that is, on sexual intercourse with demons.

The bibliography of Yves Plessis, dealing only with French works of demonology, lists almost 2,000 titles. Public opinion tended to regard all human ailments as signs of demonic activity. In his *Satan*, in the *Etudes carmélitaines* (p. 363), M. Emile Brouette reproduces a passage from Ambroise Paré, author of the much-quoted remark: "I tended him and God cured him," as follows: "I would say with Hippocrates, author and father of medicine, that there is something divine in all diseases, which men cannot explain.... There are sorcerers, enchanters, poisoners, all venomous, evil, cunning, deceptive, who have made a pact with devils who are their slaves and vassals, and by subtle, diabolic and unknown means corrupt the body, the understanding, the life and health of other creatures."

MORBID FANTASIES

Demonology in the sixteenth century led to an orgy of morbid fantasies. The Devil was to be found everywhere. Many stories of demonic infestation were utter fabrications. The anti-Catholic polemics of emergent Protestantism were dominated by satanism. The whole movement for Protestant reform was haunted from the beginning by the shadow of the demoniac. Although the hunt for sorcerers and sorceresses had begun well before Luther and Calvin, these men certainly did nothing to arrest it, and even quoted both Old and New Testaments as authority for intensifying it. "Luther, Melanchthon and Calvin," writes M. Brouette, "believed in satanism, and their followers, the fanatical preachers, only exacerbated the natural credulity of those converted to the new gospel."[2]

TERRIFYING FIGURES

The total number of accusations of witchcraft, quoted by the same author, are fantastic. It is true that he suggests that the figures given are "subject to great reservation, and need closer verification." "N. van Werveke," he writes,

> estimates that 30,000 accusations were heard in the courts of the Duchy of Luxembourg. L. Raiponce (*Essai sur la Sorcellerie*, p. 64) suggests the more modest figure of 50,000 executions for Germany, France and Belgium. A. Louandre (*La Sorcellerie*, p. 124), states that in Lorraine alone 900 sorcerers were sent to the torture in fifteen years; 500 in three months in 1515 in Geneva; 1,000 in the Diocese of Como in one year. According to J. Français, twenty-five persons were burnt for witchcraft in three years at Strasbourg. According to G. Save (*La Sorcellerie à Saint Dié*), the total number of cases of suspected sorcery in the St. Dié district reached 230, between 1530 and 1629. C.-E. Dumont (*Justice criminelle des Duchés de Lorraine*, Vol. II, p. 48), estimates that

---

[2] De Brouwer, *Etudes carmélitaine*, 367.

there were 740 trials for witchcraft between 1553
and 1669.

A complete list of all witchcraft trials would obviously be of considerable length.

Contrary to current belief, however much endorsed by eminent historians, the fury of the witch-hunt did not reach its climax at the end of the sixteenth century. Outbursts had been rare in the fourteenth century, becoming more frequent in the fifteenth, and numerous from 1530 onwards, that is to say, in the first half of the sixteenth century. The first half-century was in fact almost as sanguinary as the second half, that is from 1580 to 1620, which was the most ferocious of all.

There seems hardly any doubt that the major responsibility for the veritable explosion of demonological literature which occurred after 1530 can be assigned to Luther and Protestantism.

Such was the opinion of Mgr. Janssen, in his great history, *German Civilisation*.[3]

LUTHER AND THE DEVIL

It is certain that Luther, throughout his teaching, attributed much greater power to the Devil than had been done before his day. He claimed to have had personal evidence of this power. He himself, he declared, had seen Satan.

"Satan," he writes, "often appears in disguise: I have seen him with my own eyes, in the shape of a pig, a flaming wisp of straw, etc." He told his friend Myconius that the Devil had appeared to him at the Wartburg with the intention of killing him, and that he

---

[3]   French translation, Plon, Paris, 1902, Vol. 6, 432 et seq.

had often met him in the garden, in the form of a black boar. At Coburg, in 1530, he had recognized him one night in a star. "He walks with me in the dormitory," he wrote, "and he has ordered two devils to keep a watch on me: they are prying devils." He has given a detailed account of his conversation with the Devil. He quotes "very certain cases of satanic attacks" recounted by his friends. At Sessen three servants had been carried off alive by a demon; in the Marsch Satan had wrung the innkeeper's neck and carried off a soldier in a gust of wind; at Mühlberg a drunken fluteplayer had met the same fate; at Eisenach, another fluteplayer had been carried off by the Devil, although the preacher, Justus Menius, and several other ministers had kept a constant watch on the doors and windows of the house where he was staying. The body of the first fluteplayer had been recovered from a stream, the other was found in a hazel copse. And Luther vouches for all these happenings with some solemnity: "They are not," he writes, "idle stories, invented to frighten people, but indeed real happenings, truly alarming, and not childish rumors as some wiseacres would have it." He says further: "The devils that have been vanquished, humiliated and overcome become sprites and goblins, for there are such things as degenerate devils, and I am inclined to think that monkeys are of this nature."

This hypothesis seemed to appeal to him, for he returns to it: "Serpents and monkeys are more subject to the Devil than other animals. Satan dwells in them: he possesses them and uses them to deceive men and do them great harm. Demons are to be found in many countries, but particularly in Prussia. In Lapland, too, there are a great many demons and magicians. In Switzerland, not far from Lucerne, on a very high mountain, there is a lake called Lake Pilatus: there the Devil indulges in all kinds of infamies. In my country, on a high mountain called the Polsterberg—(goblin mountain)—there is a lake, and if you cast a stone into it, a storm arises and devastates the surrounding countryside. The lake is full of demons: Satan holds them imprisoned there."[4]

But it was not only in his private correspondence or table talk that Luther spoke thus. Demonology played an important part even in his teaching. In 1520, when he was still not entirely detached from the Catholic tradition, he declared that to attribute personal or public misfortunes to the activities of the Devil or of wicked men was to sin against the first commandment. But later he saw the Devil's hand everywhere. In his *Great Catechism* of 1529, which contains his most cherished beliefs, he states expressly that it is the Devil who provokes quarrels, assassinations, sedition, and war—a thesis which, as we shall show later, can be sustained—but the Devil also causes thunder, tempests, hail which destroys crops and animals; and he also spreads pestilence through the air. Presumably, therefore, the poisonous exhausts from modern cars are also his doing!

"The Devil," writes Luther, "is a constant menace to the life of Christians: he slakes his wrath by pouring down on them all kinds of evils and calamities. Hence the disasters in which so many unfortunates perish, some strangled, other driven mad: it is he who throws children into rivers, it is he who prepares those fatal falls."

According to Luther, the Devil has immense power: "The Devil," he writes, "is so powerful that he can cause death through a mere leaf. He has more drugs, more phials brimming with poison, than all the apothecaries in the world. The Devil constantly endangers human life by his activities; it is he who infects the air."

These are not rare or isolated quotations from Luther's works. Some of the assertions he makes are quite incredible. He is persuaded, for instance, that Satan sometimes has intercourse with

---

[4] All these texts are quoted by Mgr. Janssen, *German Civilisation* Vol. 6, 433.

young girls, who thereupon become pregnant; the children born of this horrid union are the sons of the Devil and have no souls. According to him they are only "heaps" of flesh, for the following rather summary reason: "The Devil can make a body, but he cannot make a spirit: Satan is therefore the soul of these children." And he concludes dogmatically, "Is it not horrible and terrifying to think that Satan can thus torture people and have the power to beget children?"[5]

AFTER LUTHER

One can imagine the effect of these repeated assertions, coming from such a man, on Protestant churches and Lutheran authors. The Devil figures in almost every Lutheran sermon, and popular literature swarmed with hosts of demons. Johann Nas, a Catholic writer from Germany, waxed indignant over this proliferation of satanic literature.

"In the space of a few years," he wrote in 1588, "so many books on the Devil have been published and circulated, books written in the name of the Devil, printed in the name of the Devil, bought and devoured in the name of the Devil: a great fuss is made of them, and their authors become famous amongst all the so-called servants of the Word."

"Formerly," he adds, "pious Christians forbade their children to name the spirit of Evil, or to describe him by one of his horrible names; it was forbidden to swear by the Devil, for Solomon has said: ... 'When the sinner swears by the Devil, he curses his own soul.' But nowadays we preach about the Devil, we write in the Devil's name, and it is all taken to be just and praiseworthy. And I

---

[5]   *German Civilisation,* 436.

can tell you why: it is because the grandfather of your 'evangelicals,' the 'holy patriarch,' Martin Luther, was the first to set an example."

In 1595, a "superintendent," that is to say, a Lutheran bishop, André Célichius, decided to satisfy public demand by publishing a complete treatise on demonic possession. And he left no doubt that he considered his work indispensable:

"Almost everywhere, afar and at home, the number of possessed persons is so great that it surprises and afflicts us, and this perhaps is the true plague by which our Egypt, and all its helpless inhabitants, is doomed to perish!"

In his own country, Mecklenburg, he estimated that there were at least thirty possessed persons, who were spreading fear and alarm everywhere. "Frail and weak creatures," he wrote, "women and girls, are greatly troubled by all they are constrained to see and hear. Many of them have renounced both faith and charity, for they have taken counsel of demons, which is anti-Christian and idolatrous behavior." He then described at length the ravages of demonology in his century!

But enough of these unhappy memories. In our own day such exaggerations are no doubt impossible. We shall now turn to look at symptoms of the presence of Satan in our modern world, and shall therefore pass at once to nineteenth-century France.

Can one still seriously speak of "witchcraft" in a period so close to our own? We shall endeavor to confine our answer to established certainties, avoiding all exaggeration.

∽ 1 ∽

THE CURÉ D'ARS AND THE DEVIL

A REMARKABLE CENTENARY

SINCE, AT THE time of writing, the whole Catholic Church, and more particularly the French Church, is celebrating the centenary of the death of the saintly Curé d'Ars, it is appropriate to begin by studying his life as evidence of the presence of Satan in the world. All his biographers have had to deal with this aspect of his life, and it is probable that at least twenty books on the subject will appear in the centenary year. The first was a brilliant study by Mgr. Fourrey, bishop of Belley, the diocese which includes the parish of Ars. Amongst the authors who have written, or are about to write on the subject, one should mention particularly the Abbé Nodet of Ars, who has made the most penetrating study of everything connected with the saintly Curé, and an expert of the quality of Mgr. Trochu, author of probably the most outstanding Life, from any quarter.[6] All agree that it is impossible to deal at all seriously with the life of the Curé d'Ars without mentioning the *Grappin*.

---

[6] Nodet, *Le Curé d'Ars* (Xavier Mappus, 1959); Trochu, *Le Curé d'Ars* (France: Emmanuel Vitte, 1925).

This is the name he gave to the Devil. In the dialect of his district and period, it means a three-tined fork or pitchfork. The Curé d'Ars no doubt chose this epithet as an indication that Satan is always trying to drive souls into Hell, just as one shifts dung with a pitchfork.

The life of the Curé d'Ars is so well known that it is hardly necessary to introduce him in detail before discussing the question of demonic infestation. We shall therefore content ourselves with a very brief introduction.

The son of a simple peasant family, he was born on May 8, 1786, at Dardilly, in the Diocese of Lyons and about five miles from that city. The Revolution was soon to break out, closing the churches and expelling the faithful priests. But faith lived on in Christian hearts in spite of the storm. Jean-Marie Vianney—for such was his name, though it has become customary to call him simply the Curé d'Ars—was brought up by his parents, and particularly by his pious mother, in the full Christian tradition. When he was still quite young, people would say: "He knows so many litanies, your Jean-Marie ought to become a priest or a monk." Yet this was not a very hopeful prospect, since religion seemed at the time to be on its deathbed.

But it was to experience a rebirth. Religious concord was re-established by Napoleon. The so-called "refractory" priests, who had, till then, suffered all the rigors of the law, resumed their duties. The churches reopened. The bells pealed out joyfully. Jean-Marie Vianney wanted to become a priest. But his memory was poor and unreliable. Latin made little impression on it, and theology and philosophy still less. The young man found his studies extraordinarily difficult. He worked and prayed and persevered. God gave him a tutor in the person of his Curé at Ecully, the Abbé Bailey, who devoted himself stubbornly to his task, interceded for him with the archbishop, and finally succeeded in getting him accepted for ordination. This was, no doubt, because of his extreme piety, and he was not immediately entrusted with the power to hear confessions. Yet God had destined him to become one of the great confessors of the century.

After a hardworking curacy at Ecully, he was appointed incumbent of Ars, a little village in Dombes, in 1818. Here Jean-Marie Vianney was to work until his death on August 4, 1859. Such was the priest whom we shall see at grips with the Devil.

But we should, first of all, deal with the objection which may be provoked by those very difficulties we have mentioned in connection with his studies. Some may object that we are dealing with a priest of such intellectual poverty that he was only accepted into the priesthood because he was good at reciting a Rosary, and because of the acute shortage of trained ministers at that period. This would perhaps detract from the value of his assertions that the Devil appeared to him, or tormented him, or gave other sensible evidence of his presence. If his learning was so restricted, it weakens the authority of his evidence.

Such, in fact, is the objection. It was, we shall see, often raised against the Curé d'Ars by his own colleagues. And we shall see the answer supplied by the facts. We shall have to question the doctors who knew him and were able to form an opinion of him. They will be able to show whether he was in any sense odd, or a victim of his nerves, or of his imagination.

For the time being, however, let us proceed to facts.

FIRST ONSLAUGHTS

The Abbé Vianney was thirty-two when he arrived at Ars. His little parish was poor, neglected, and apathetic, and he was consumed with the love of God and the love of souls. He resorted to prayer and fasting. He was, from the beginning, what he was to remain all his life, as the Church says in its prayer for his anniversary: a man of tireless prayer and continual penitence. All that he asked of God, in his ceaseless prayers and daily mortifications, was the conversion of his parish.

If there are enemies of the soul, which we call demons, they could not fail to be aware very soon of the young priest's ambitions; and it would be inevitable that they should wish to nullify his work. The young priest, in his first sermons, had raised his voice against the vices and disorders which disgraced the parish: drunkenness and dancing. As an obvious consequence the interests endangered by his attacks became vocal. The cabaret-keepers, the regulars in the bars, the dance addicts, the sabbath-breakers, felt endangered in their passions, their habits, and their sensual appetites. Yet in his parish he was observed to be so good, so gentle, so pious, and so fervent that he was already considered a saint. But the bad characters of the neighborhood, strangers to the parish, had no hesitation in spreading the most hateful calumnies against him. He lived like an angel, chastising the flesh every day, to tame it into docility, and to take his share in the burden of the Cross; yet his enemies dared to ascribe his pallor and his emaciated face to secret debauches. Scurrilous songs about him were current, he received anonymous letters, and insulting posters were stuck on his door.

"At this time," writes Catherine Lassagne, the most assiduous and reliable witness to his virtues, "he was slandered and despised. They would come and shout under his windows."

Without wishing to attribute all this to the exclusive activities of the Devil, it is permissible to see, in this odious campaign against his reputation and honor, the Devil's first onslaught on a faithful believer. And the attack did not fall far short of success. A witness at the process of canonization did in fact report: "He was so weary of the evil reports that were spread about him that he wanted to leave his parish, and he would have done so if someone had not persuaded him that his departure would only lend strength to these infamous rumors."

All that he could do was submit to the will of God, continue in prayer and penitence and, in particular, pray for his persecutors. Such was his first victory over Satan.

A HORRIBLE TEMPTATION

The Devil, however, was not so easily beaten, and his next onslaught was launched directly at his adversary. The Curé's very mortifications were perhaps the cause of a failure in health. Although endowed with a typically robust peasant constitution, he suffered from a nervous complaint during the first years of his ministry at Ars. This was no doubt due to what he called his "youthful follies," that is to say, the fasts and scourgings known only to God, that he had imposed on himself in his lonely presbytery. In the course of his illness he had attacks of discouragement and despair. He felt himself at death's door. Often he seemed to hear, coming from within himself, an insolent voice calling: "Now you'll have to go to Hell!" This is vouched for both by the Curé himself and by those who gave evidence at the process of canonization, and particularly by Catherine Lassagne, whom we have already mentioned. But yet at the bottom of his heart his faith was so strong that he could still proclaim his confidence in God, and by this means he promptly recovered that inner peace which he had almost lost.

So far, it is clear, the young priest was following the purest vein of the Christian apostolate, showing that he possessed the qualities of good sense, spiritual wisdom, and mental strength and stability.

Up to the present we have only been dealing with calumny and temptation, the customary method of procedure in cases of demonic interventions in our human destiny. We come now to demonic *infestations*, which are of quite another order, as we shall see.

SATANIC SKIRMISHES

There was a very obvious *crescendo* in Satan's struggle with the Curé. He seems to have passed through the same ordeal as was imposed, centuries before, on that saintly man, Job. Temptations were transformed into *infestations*. The Devil had obtained permission from the Master of our destinies to pass beyond the limits normally—and, incidentally, fortunately—imposed on his activity in our affairs. St. Augustine, recollect, spoke of the "chained dog" which cannot bite.

But the chain can sometimes, by divine permission, slacken a little. It did so for the Abbé Vianney in the winter of 1824 to 1825. He had been Curé of Ars for six years, and he was thirty-eight. There were strange phenomena which occurred only at night. Disturbing sounds prevented him from sleeping. Not naturally timorous, he thought at first it was due to rodents attacking the curtains of his bed. So he placed a fork beside his bedside to drive them off. But the more he beat the curtains to frighten the rats, the louder became the sound of their gnawing. In the morning, however, he would find no trace of any damage to the curtains. It did not occur to him to ascribe this phenomenon to the Devil. As the Abbé Toccanier, a priest who afterwards joined him as assistant, said later: "He was not credulous and was not easily persuaded to believe in extraordinary events."

Yet it seems reasonable to think that, as later developments would show, he was already being subjected to demonic attack. One author, Canon Saudreau, to whom we shall refer later and who is a great authority on demonic as well as divine mysticism, has explained the matter very lucidly:

"The Devil acts on man by tempting him.... No one escapes from his attacks. This is his normal way of working. In other, much rarer, cases, the devils betray their presence by vexing or distressing manifestations, which are more alarming than dangerous; they make noises, shake or move certain objects, upset and sometimes break them: this is called *infestation*."

He may have been thinking of the particular experience of the Curé d'Ars, but this was not the only one he had in mind.

But Satan, always, as we should remember, with God's permission, was to go even further. Soon, in fact, the young priest was to hear knocking on the door in the dead of night, and strange cries echoing through the presbytery. Still he never thought of demonic activity, but simply supposed that these sounds were due to burglars trying to get hold of the beautiful ornaments and other precious objects which the Vicomte d'Ars had given to the church, and which were lodged for safety in his attic. So he got out of bed, and went down into the little courtyard. He searched everywhere, in every hole and corner. Nothing was to be seen. Still he did not understand. And he decided to ask one of his parishioners to help protect him against his invisible assailants.

EYEWITNESS ACCOUNT

At that time, 1826, the village wheelwright was a robust young man of twenty-eight, who was to live long enough to be a witness at the process of canonization. His name was André Verchère. We shall let him tell his own story, taken from his deposition on oath, first on June 4, 1864, five years after the saint's death, and then again on October 2, 1876. "For several days," he said,

> M. Vianney had been hearing extraordinary noises
> in his house. One evening he came to see me and

said: "I'm not sure they aren't burglars.... Will you spend the night in my house?"

"Of course, Monsieur le Curé; I'll go and load my rifle."

That night I went to his house.... I was to sleep in his room, and he occupied the one next to it. I could not sleep. At about one o'clock I heard the handle and the latch of the yard-door shake violently. At the same time there were great hammer blows on the same door, and inside the house there was a thundering sound as if several carriages were driving through it.

I took my rifle and rushed to the window, which I opened. I looked out but saw nothing. The house shook for about a quarter of an hour. My legs were shaking too, and I felt the effects for about a week afterwards. As soon as the noise started M. le Curé lit a lamp. He came with me.

"Did you hear it?" he asked.

"You can see I did. That's why I got up and picked up my rifle."

"The presbytery was shaking as if there had been an earthquake."

"So you're afraid?" asked M. le Curé.

"No," I said, "I'm not afraid, but I feel my legs giving under me. The house is going to fall down."

"What do you suppose it is?"

"I think it's the Devil."

When the noise had died down, we went back to bed. M. le Curé came again the next evening and asked me to return to his home with him. I answered: "M. le Curé, I've had quite enough as it is!"

This story is confirmed by the Curé himself, who later recounted it at the Providence, a charitable institution he had founded, saying that his first watcher at the presbytery had been terrified: "Poor Verchère, with his rifle," he would say, laughing. "He was shaking all over. He'd even forgotten that he *had* a rifle."

OTHER WITNESSES

The wheelwright having cried off, the Abbé Vianney applied to the mayor, who sent two men to the presbytery, one his own son, Antoine, a stout fellow of twenty-six, and Jean Cotton, gardener at the Château d'Ars, aged twenty-four. Every evening for some twelve days they went to the presbytery to sleep. Here is their evidence at the process of canonization:

"We heard no sound," reports Jean Cotton, "but M. le Curé who was sleeping in the next room, did. His sleep was interrupted more than once, and he called out to us: 'My children, don't you hear anything?' We replied that no sound had reached us. However, at a certain moment, I did hear a sound like a knife-blade striking rapidly on a water-jug.... We had hung our watches near the mirror in his room. 'I'm very surprised,' said M. le Curé, 'that your watches aren't broken.'"

In spite of this, the Abbé Vianney did not yet venture to pronounce on the nature and origin of the unusual noises he had heard. But after a fresh experience the full light dawned on him.

The streets were covered in snow. It was mid-winter. Suddenly cries re-echoed in the night, coming from the yard of the presbytery.

Catherine Lassagne, who had the story direct from the Curé himself, said: "It was like an army of Austrians or Cossacks who were talking confusedly in a language he did not understand."

He went downstairs, opened the door and looked at the snow lying unsullied in the street. Not a footstep! Then all this hurly-burly, all these sounds of an army in transit, were only illusion. In any case, he thought, there was nothing human about it. But if it was not human, neither could it be the work of "good spirits." Now he knew fear. It was a presentiment of evil. His conviction was formed.

"I decided it was the Devil," he said later to his Bishop, Mgr. Devie, who was interrogating him, "because I was afraid: our good Lord does not make me afraid."

From then onwards he realized the uselessness of asking for human protection. He dismissed his guards and remained alone to face the Adversary.

THE GRAPPIN

The Adversary—for this is the meaning of the word "Devil" or "Satan"—was known to him, as we have said, by the name of *Grappin*, or pitchfork.

Once he was convinced of the true nature of the position, he adopted a very wise and prudent course.

"Sometimes I asked him," said his confessor, the Abbé Beau, in evidence, "how he warded off these attacks. He replied, 'I turn toward God: I make the sign of the Cross; I address some scornful remarks to the demon. As for the rest, I have noticed that the noise is louder and the attacks more numerous when some great sinner is to visit me the following day.'"

It was a great discovery and a wonderful consolation to know that sinners from every corner of the diocese, even from every part of France and sometimes from abroad, were coming to him, a humble curé, to make their confession.

"I used to be afraid," he said later to a faithful friend who gave evidence at the process. "At first I used to be afraid: I did not know what it was all about, but now I am happy. It is a good sign: next day the catch is always good."

On another occasion: "The Devil has caused me a lot of trouble tonight: we shall have a lot of people tomorrow ... the *Grappin* is an idiot: he tells me about the great sinners who are coming.... He is in a rage ... so much the better!"

A MEMORABLE INCIDENT

One of the most remarkable examples of these demonic infestations took place on the occasion of the Jubilee Festival at Saint-Trivier-sur-Moignans in December 1826. This little town is about ten miles from Ars. All the priests in the locality had arranged to be there for the Jubilee celebrations, which, they hoped, would attract many visitors and produce a considerable number of conversions.

The Abbé Vianney had left home well before dawn. As he walked, he recited the rosary. It was his favorite weapon against Satan. Something inexplicable in this winter month was happening around him. The air itself seemed on fire and the hedges by the roadside seemed aflame. He supposed that Satan, foreseeing the harvest of souls the Jubilee would produce, was trying to frighten him away. But he continued his journey.

When he reached the presbytery of Saint-Trivier, he embarked at once on his allotted tasks. When evening came, and everything in the house seemed at rest, peculiar noises were heard, which seemed to come from the room assigned to the Curé d'Ars. His colleagues, disturbed by the unaccustomed sounds, came and complained. "It's only the *Grappin*," he replied, simply, "he's annoyed about the good work being done here!"

But his colleagues only made fun of his assurances: "You don't eat, you don't sleep, you've got noises in the head, it's the rats running about inside it."

He was the constant butt of similar remarks in the course of the next few days. But one evening, when the remarks became more pointed, he said nothing. Scarcely had everyone gone to bed than a noise was heard like the passage of a heavily laden cart. Everyone got up in alarm.

While they were still asking themselves what could have caused the disturbance, such an uproar arose in the Curé's room that the local priest, M. Benoît, cried out: "They're murdering the Curé d'Ars!" Whereupon they all rushed upstairs into his room. The Abbé Vianney was sleeping peacefully in his bed, which unknown hands had pushed into the center of the room. He woke up and remarked calmly: "It's the *Grappin* who has been pulling me about and making all this noise. I am sorry I forgot to warn you. It's nothing to worry about. It's a good sign: tomorrow we shall catch a big fish."

Nobody grasped what was meant by a "big fish."

His colleagues still made fun of him, being not a little alarmed by what they called his "hallucinations." But he was not mistaken, as was proved when a well-known local figure, the Chevalier des Murs, who had long abandoned all practice of his religion, walked into the church and went straight up to the confessional of the Curé d'Ars. From that time onwards one of his most aggressive critics began to look on him as a "great saint."

FURTHER MANIFESTATIONS

These infestations continued for many years longer. Sometimes the saintly Curé was the only one to suffer. At other times the Devil tried to distress the souls of those around him. On certain nights the orphans and supervisors of the Providence, an invaluable institution founded by the Curé, heard strange noises. Or the Devil would play tricks on the community.

"One day," according to the evidence given later by Marie Filliat, "after I had washed out my saucepan, I put some water in it to start making soup. I noticed little pieces of meat in the water. It was a fast day. I emptied the saucepan, washed it out and filled it with fresh water. When the soup was ready to serve, I saw that some pieces of meat had got into it. When I told the Curé, he replied: 'It is the Devil who has done it. Serve the soup all the same.'"

As one can see, the Curé d'Ars did not allow himself to be disturbed. His good sense was unshaken and his trust in God put him beyond the reach of attack. When someone asked him one day if he was never afraid, he replied simply: "One gets used to everything ... The *Grappin* and I have got used to each other."

Not that this implies that they made common cause. On December 4 he confided to the ladies at the Providence: "Listen to this: last night the Devil entered my room whilst I was reciting the breviary. He was breathing heavily and seemed to vomit something up, something like wheat or corn, on the floor. I said to him: 'I'm going across the way, [to the orphanage] to tell them what you are doing, so that they will despise you.' And he immediately became quiet."

On another occasion, when the Abbé Vianney was trying to get some of the sleep he so desperately needed, the Devil, trying to exhaust his energy as much as possible, began to cry out: "Vianney, Vianney, I shall get you! You watch out, I shall get you!"

"I am not afraid of you," answered the holy man.

At the presbytery of Ars one is shown a bed belonging to him, which was burnt through some unknown cause when he had already left for the church. When he was told that his house was on fire, he merely gave someone his key so that he could go and put the fire out. But he added unemotionally: "That *Grappin!* He couldn't catch the bird, so he burnt down the cage!"

More often than not the Devil would insult him, hurling threats at him, making animal noises. His epithets were coarse: "Vianney! Vianney! Truffle-eater [the local word for potatoes]! What, not dead yet? ... I shall get you!"

All in all, it was more grotesque and puerile than dangerous. For the Devil, fortunately, is not allowed unrestricted license. The Abbé had been allotted a task by God. If the Devil made it more difficult, by robbing him of sleep, assailing him on every side, he thereby made its performance more meritorious and efficacious. The infestations were, in fact, turned back upon their author. We shall see the same thing happen in certain cases of possession.

At the present time there are victims of possession who have accepted their ordeal in order to be associated with the Cross of the Redeemer, that Cross which was to have been Satan's triumph and which proved his worst defeat. But this will become clearer later. We are convinced it was the same for the Curé d'Ars. He accepted all the affronts of Satan, for the salvation of souls. He learnt early, from daily experience, that his conflicts with the Devil were bound up with the conversion of great sinners who were led to him by the hand of God, from every part of France and even from abroad.

But we should like to mention some of Satan's most remarkable interventions in the life of the man who was justly entitled "the model of all Catholic priests."

THE SERPENT

From St. John the Evangelist onwards, the Dragon or serpent which tempted Eve has been identified with Satan. It is therefore not surprising that the Devil should appear occasionally in the form of a serpent. We shall find an example of this in the demonic possession of Claire-Germaine Cèle, the South African girl, whose case will be discussed later. In the case of the Curé d'Ars, we have the evidence of Catherine Lassagne, known for her devotion to the Curé, as recorded by his first biographer, the Abbé Monnin:

"One evening (it is Catherine talking), M. le Curé had come to our house to see a sick person. When I returned from church, he said to me: 'You're always on the look-out for news: well, here's something you haven't heard yet: listen to what happened this morning. I had something on my table; you know what it is?'"

It should be explained that he was speaking of his scourge. He had never spoken of it to Catherine, but she had more than once found that terrible instrument under his bed. She knew it was no idle ornament, for it was common knowledge that the saint used it frequently, if not every day. But she had never mentioned it, and neither had he. It was curious therefore that on this occasion he said to her: "You know what it is?" Then he went on:

"'It began to move about on the table like a serpent! I felt rather frightened. You know there is a cord at one end: I caught hold of it and it was as stiff as a bit of wood: I put it back on the table: three times it started to move again.' 'Perhaps you shook the table?' objected one of the teachers who was standing near.

'No,' said M. le Curé, 'I wasn't touching it.'"

APPARITIONS

The Abbé Monnin was also interested in discovering whether the Devil had ever appeared to the Curé d'Ars. We know that on many occasions the Devil had "breathed in the saint's face," or that the Curé had felt something like a rat or a mole creeping over his face. But in reply to the question whether he had ever seen Satan, and in what guise, the Abbé Monnin quotes two facts.

One day, at 3 o'clock in the morning, the Abbé Vianney saw a great black dog, with hackles up and flaming eyes, scratching in the ground where the body of a man who had died unconfessed had been buried a few weeks earlier. The sight of such a dog in such a place alarmed him considerably. He had no doubt as to its identity. He was convinced it was the Devil and fled for refuge to his confessional. Something very similar, adds the Abbé Monnin, occurred in the life of St. Stanislas of Kotska, to whom the Devil appeared once during an illness in the form of an angry dog which seemed about to jump at him and had to be driven off three times with the sign of the Cross. The Abbé Vianney also said that the Devil had appeared to him in the form of bats which haunted his room and fluttered around his bed. There were so many that the walls were black with them.

It is important to enquire, as the Abbé Monnin did, whether the saint was the only one to hear, feel or see so many strange things.

EVIDENCE

The reply is ready to hand. When the infestations began the Curé was not aware of their significance. He had asked for and obtained the help of some of his parishioners, of whom Verchère had been one. All heard the same sounds that he did. All were afraid, even more than he was. And all reached the same conclusion, that it was impossible to attribute these sounds to natural causes. But the Abbé Monnin mentions other witnesses, from whom we shall quote, since they confirm the fact of demonic infestations at Ars around the person of St. Jean-Marie Vianney.

When these "devilments" had already lasted about five years, that is in 1829, there arrived at Ars a young priest from the Diocese of Lyons, the son of a pious widow Bibot, who had been of great service to the Abbé Vianney at the time of his induction in 1818.

The Abbé Bibot, who shared his mother's confidence in the Abbé Vianney, had come to stay with him for the purpose of making a retreat. He was naturally received with the greatest affection by the Curé d'Ars, who cherished a grateful remembrance of his mother. The young man was put up in the presbytery.

The Abbé Bibot has left us an account of what took place, which has been passed on by a friend of his, the Abbé Renard, who questioned him on the matter:

"You slept in the house? So what have you to say about the Devil? Is it true that there were strange noises? Did you hear him?"

"Yes," replied Bibot, "I heard him every night. He had a wild, shrill voice, and imitated the cry of a wild beast. He clung to the bedcurtains and shook them violently. He called M. le Curé by name: I clearly heard the words: 'Vianney! Vianney! What are you doing here? Get out! Get out!'

"These noises and cries must have frightened you?"

"Not particularly. I am not timid and, incidentally, the presence of M. Vianney was reassuring. I commended myself to my guardian angel and I managed to get to sleep. But I was heartily sorry for the poor Curé: I would not have liked to have to live there. Since I was only there for a short while, I managed as best I could, with God's help."

"Did you question M. le Curé about it?"

"No. I did think of doing so, but I was afraid of distressing him, so I kept quiet. Poor Curé! Poor good man! How could he live in all that uproar?"

This is the first confirmation, and a weighty one. The Abbé Bibot heard it. He pitied the Abbé Vianney. He considered that it would be beyond his own capacity to endure such constantly repeated onslaughts. The continual resistance that was required was something very real and very exacting.

But there is something else to note in this story, and it is the words the Abbé Bibot heard: "Vianney! Vianney! What are you doing here? Get out! Get out!"

We shall revert to these words later, but for the moment it is enough to point out that they were one of the forms taken by this persecution or infestation of the saintly life of that tireless confessor and fisher of souls, Jean-Marie Vianney.

FURTHER EVIDENCE

But there is further evidence to be drawn from Monnin's biography.

In 1842 — thirteen years after the Abbé Bibot's visit — there arrived at Ars a penitent who was still vacillating in his intention to confess to the saint of Ars. This penitent was an old soldier turned gendarme, from the department of Ain. As was usual, he had risen in the middle of the night to wait at the door of the church for the arrival of the famous and deeply venerated confessor. Since he was a long time coming, the gendarme began to walk around the church, which was quite close to the presbytery. He had recently experienced some deep personal troubles and was suffering from a confused aftermath of sadness, anxiety, and religious terrors. At the bottom of his heart the Christian message both attracted and alarmed him. He wanted to make a confession, but was still in great conflict about his intended conversion.

It was during this inner conflict, so familiar to many, whether at Ars or elsewhere, that he suddenly heard a strange noise which appeared to come from the window of the presbytery.

"He listened," writes the Abbé Monnin, "a loud, shrill strident voice, like the voice of a damned soul, repeating, again and again the same words, which he heard quite distinctly: 'Vianney! Vianney! Come here! Come here!' This terrible sound froze his blood. He went away, deeply agitated. At that moment one o'clock struck from the great clock in the church steeple. Soon M. le Curé appeared, a light in his hand. He found the man, still very much upset, reassured him and accompanied him to the church. Before questioning him, or hearing anything of his life story, he astonished the man by remarking: 'My friend, you have had great trouble: you have just lost your wife in childbirth. But have confidence: the good Lord will help you.... But first you must put your conscience in order. Then it will be easier for you to put your affairs in order.'

"'I did not even try to resist,' said the gendarme. 'I fell on my knees like a child, and began my confession. I was so troubled that I could hardly put two sentences together, but the good Curé helped me. He had soon penetrated to the bottom of my heart: he spoke of things he could not have known about, and which astonished me beyond words. I would never have believed it possible to read anyone's heart in such a way.'"

In this connection we should perhaps point out that one of the typical indications of demonic possession is, as we shall show, the knowledge of hidden facts. In later chapters there will be several instances of satanic awareness of what is passing in a human mind.

This, it is hardly necessary to add, does not imply that the saint of Ars had acquired his gift of reading souls from the Devil. Whatever capacity Satan may have in this direction, he has it in virtue of his angelic nature, although fallen from this estate. In the case of the Abbé Vianney, his ability to see into the inmost heart of man was a gift of grace, which he used for the better conversion of sinners. The gendarme's statement is only one example amongst many others we could quote.

THE DOCTOR'S EVIDENCE

We are now able to exclude the rather summary interpretation of these demonic manifestations as being due to the excessive fasting practiced by the Abbé Vianney, or to his tendency to seek for a supernatural explanation of everything that occurred. His colleagues had at first adopted this explanation but had been compelled to abandon it. All had finally paid tribute to his robust and healthy calm, the tranquil realism of his accounts of these events. He was, in fact, quite willing to talk and even sometimes to make jokes about them. Catherine Lassagne made many notes of his remarks to other people. One of his retorts to the Devil was even: "I shall tell them what you are doing, so that they can laugh at you."

But there is no harm in listening to what his physicians said on the subject. Every doctor who had to deal with him agreed on this point, that from both the physical and moral point of view he was perfectly well-balanced.

When his usual doctor, M. J.-B. Saunier, was being interrogated on the subject of these infestations, someone ventured to pronounce the word "hallucination." The doctor replied categorically: "We have only one thing to say about the so-called physiological explanation of such phenomena, for although such explanations may be acceptable when dealing with facts accompanied by pathological symptoms such as apathy, convulsions, signs of mania, such as are usually present, and which reveal their true nature, it is impossible to accept them when the phenomena are combined, as in the case of M. Vianney, with the regular functioning of the physical organism, a serenity of thought, a delicacy of perception, a sureness of judgment and opinion, perfect self-possession and, above all, astonishing good health, which practically never failed, in spite of all the arduous tasks imposed on him by his profession."

The doctor was right. The supernatural gifts with which God had endowed the Curé d'Ars were grafted on to the natural qualities which were a matter of common knowledge. He was more gifted than any other priest of the diocese, or perhaps of his time, in the function of exorcism. His Bishop, Mgr. Devie, who had once silenced the Curé's critics by saying: "I don't know whether the Curé d'Ars is educated, but I do know that he is enlightened," was so persuaded of this gift that he gave him unconditional permission to use his powers as exorcist whenever occasion required. We shall see him at work in a later chapter.

But before passing on to this subject, we should study the way the Devil endeavored to undermine this modern saint.

THE GREATEST TEMPTATION

In his great panegyric of St. Jean-Marie Vianney, which Mgr. Fourrey, Bishop of Belley, pronounced in Nôtre-Dame in Paris on April 12, 1959, the year of his centenary, the demonic infestations were described as follows:

"I will not dwell on the strange affliction which covered a period of thirty-five years, and which would have paralyzed the ministry of any other priest. As soon as he discovered its demonic origin, he was reassured; the Master whom he served was stronger than the Adversary. He was even able to rejoice when these nocturnal phenomena became most terrifying: to him it was a sign that on the following day great sinners—the big fish, as he used to say—would, at his confessional, become the prisoners of grace."

The bishop went on to comment on what was, to him, the most important feature of the demonic persecution of this great saint.

> I must draw your attention to the subtlest of the Evil One's maneuvers, when he tried to overwhelm him with despair and then, under the cloak of the most saintly motives, to get him to withdraw from the task allotted to him by the Church.
>
> The very passion for the salvation of souls which filled the heart of the Curé d'Ars was to be,

paradoxically, the chief weapon the enemy would employ in an attempt to blind him as to his true purpose. He was to involve this man of God in the most heartrending inner conflict known to man. In trying to save souls, did he not, ignorant and incapable as he believed himself to be, risk drawing them down to damnation with himself? Perhaps his true duty lay in giving place to a priest of higher caliber, and in hiding his immense misery in retreat, penitence and prayer. But he was torn in pieces by the dilemma: the head of his diocese ordered him to remain at his post and to continue to carry out his duties, which he felt to be beyond his strength, and to fulfil the functions which he felt he was betraying.

Such an inner conflict is moving indeed. The Devil had laid hold on him by what one might call his "weak point" if it had not, in reality, been his "strong point." He was the faithful priest, loving, and wishing to serve. But he knew the abyss within and humbled himself before Christ. The Devil, however, continued to lay hold of this humility in order to carry it to excess, and was on the verge of converting a very great virtue into a peril for the soul. So adroit a maneuver could not fail to endanger the person against whom it was employed. The saintly Curé was strengthened in his purpose to withdraw by the belief, common to many great priests of his time and before him, that it would be fitting to spend a little time between the exercise of the ministry and death, in endeavoring to repair, by penitence, any inadequacy of action in the course of his life.

"The Evil One," continued Mgr. Fourrey, tried to lure the Curé d'Ars into the sole pitfall by which he might be caught. He drove him along a path other than that laid down by God, by working on the agonizing spiritual conflict in which he found himself.

Let us hear what Brother Athanasius had to say: "The Servant of God endured much inner suffering. In particular, he was tormented by a longing for solitude: he often spoke of it. It was, as it were, a temptation which obsessed him by day and more particularly by night. 'When I cannot sleep, my mind goes off on its travels: I am at La Trappe, or La Chartreuse: I am looking for a quiet corner where I can weep over my miserable life and do penance for my sins.' He would often say that he could not understand why he did not fall into despair at the thought of his spiritual poverty. He was greatly afraid of the judgment of God and trembled whenever he spoke of it; he would weep and say that his greatest fear was of falling into despair at the moment of death. He was overwhelmed by his pastoral duty, which he carried out in fear and trembling. He did not want to die a Curé. It was this fear, he admitted, which led to the second temptation to take flight. 'I wanted,' he said, 'to pin God down, to make him realize that if I die a Curé, it is in spite of myself, and because he wishes it.'"

Perhaps, on the contrary, God wished him to be an example to a later generation, when vocations would be less frequent, to show that a priest can, and should, die in harness. In his day there was not such an acute shortage of priests, which explains the following dialogue:

"I shall leave!"

"The bishop won't like it!"

"The bishop doesn't need me: he has enough priests. I must have a little time to weep over my past life and prepare by penitence for death."

This conversation, on the same lines as one he had with Brother Athanasius, was with Catherine Lassagne, who concluded her report with the words: "This was why he tried to go away."

Yet if we are to trust the Abbé Monnin, who was conversant with every detail of his life, the saint knew, himself, that his longing for retreat was intemperate, and that the Devil was taking advantage of it to tempt him. We know the wild cry: "Vianney! Vianney! What are you doing here? Get out! Get out!" which had been ringing in his ears ever since he began his ministry, or at least from 1829 onwards, according to the testimony of the Abbé Bibot. So we might well say that it was the dominant temptation of his life, that he resisted it courageously, although twice almost giving way, and that finally he obeyed the will of God and the order of his bishop, dying at his post, as Christ wished.

His "flights," added Mgr. Fourrey, were in no sense acts of rebellion. On leaving, he wrote to the head of his diocese: "You know that I will return when you wish it." But this method of attracting episcopal attention to his spiritual dilemma seemed to him the best way of achieving the final liberation he so much desired. "He believed that, by running away, he was obeying the will of God," remarked Catherine Lassagne.

"It was only after the failure of the 1853 attempt that he recognized the trickery of the Evil One, in his obsessional desire for solitude and penitence, far from Ars."

Such was the nature of the fiercest battle the Curé d'Ars had to wage with the *Grappin*. If the Devil sometimes played grotesque, even childish tricks on him, he could also show himself a master of singularly adroit and almost overpowering temptations.

THE CURÉ D'ARS AND SPIRITUALISM

Our study of the Curé d'Ars and the Devil would not be complete without some reference to his very clear-cut views on spiritualism, which he always regarded as an invention of Satan.

Count Jules de Maubou, proprietor of estates not far from Villefranche in the Beaujolais, liked to visit the saint, who was both his confessor and his friend, whenever he visited the district. It so happened that he had been at a fashionable party where the guests had been "amusing themselves" by table-turning and such like, and the count had taken part in the game, simply in order not to give offence.

Two days later he went to Ars, and seeing the Abbé Vianney, went up to him as usual, smiling and holding out his hand. He was dumbfounded when the good Curé stopped him with a single gesture, before he had spoken a word, and reproached him, sadly and sternly:

"Jules, the day before yesterday you had truck with the Devil. Come to confession!"

Now it would have been impossible for the Abbé Vianney to know by ordinary means what had taken place on the evening in question. Astonished but docile, the young Count fell on his knees in the confessional and promised that he would never again take part in a game which the man of God declared to be of diabolic inspiration.

Shortly afterwards, when he had returned to Paris, he found himself once more in a house where a session of table-turning was about to take place. He was invited to take part, but he refused. Although his hosts pressed him to join in, he remained firm, so the others started without him. Hands were linked in a chain around a little table. The Count de Maubou remained at a distance, and from his corner registered an inward protest against the game which had now started. Contrary to all expectations the table did not move. The medium, that is to say, the ringleader, was astonished, and finally remarked: "I can't make it out! There must be a stronger force present which is paralyzing us."[7]

There is also another, very similar story.

A young officer, M. Charles de Montluisant, having heard of the marvelous happenings at Ars, desired, out of motives of pure curiosity, to pay it a visit with some friends. On their way the officers agreed that each of them should ask the Curé d'Ars one question. M. de Montluisant alone declared that "having nothing to say to him, he would say nothing."

They reached Ars, and one of the party, wishing to have a joke at his friend's expense, turned to the Curé and said:

"Monsieur le Curé, here is M. de Montluisant, a promising young officer, who would like to ask you something."

The captain, caught in a trap, decided to enter into the spirit of the game, and not knowing what to say, asked a simple question:

"Look here, Monsieur le Curé, all these stories about the Devil and you which everyone is talking about, they're not really true, are they? Isn't it just imagination?"

The Curé gave the officer one penetrating look and replied, briefly and categorically:

---

[7] Mgr. Trochu adds a footnote (*Le Curé d'Ars, 304*), "This story is based on notes written on May 16, 1922, by M. de Fréminville, great-nephew of M. de Maubon, who has authorized the writer to mention both his name and his great-uncle's."

"My friend, you should know something about it. Without doing what you did, you would never have been able to get rid of *it*."

An enigmatic, yet confident reply. The officers looked at one another in silence. To the astonishment of his friends the young captain did not reply. But when they were alone again, his companions insisted on an explanation. Either the Curé had answered at random, in vague terms, or he had something definite in mind. If so, what was it?

De Montluisant replied that when he was studying in Paris he had joined a small circle of supposedly philanthropic nature, which turned out to be a spiritualist circle.

"One day," he said, "when I got back to my room, I got the impression that I was not alone. Rather disturbed by this strange feeling, I looked around everywhere, but found nothing. The next day it was the same.... And then it seemed as if an invisible hand was taking me by the throat. I was a believer. I obtained some holy water from St. Germain l'Auxerrois, my parish church, and with it I sprinkled every nook and cranny of my room. From that moment the sense of a supernatural presence disappeared. And I have never set foot again amongst the spiritualists. I have no doubt that it was to this rather remote incident that the Curé d'Ars was alluding."

These facts should be classified under the heading of spiritualism, to which we shall refer later. But when one thinks of the divine inspiration by which the Curé d'Ars was guided throughout his life, and of the experience he gained through countless confessions, one cannot fail to be impressed by his unshakeable conviction that the majority of the activities of spiritualism proper are of demonic inspiration.

The Curé d'Ars saw things we do not see and knew things we do not know. His views on such subjects are by no means negligible, which is our reason for dwelling on them, without thereby purporting to resolve problems as complex as those raised by psychic phenomena as such.

Assessment and Comparison

To conclude this chapter, which has dealt with such very special and, to our modern minds, such very strange occurrences, it would be right to make some final assessment and establish some comparisons. The assessment can best be made by the Devil himself, who provides a satisfactory explanation for the furious obstinacy of his attacks. The comparison we can make, with the aid of the Abbé Monnin, will help us to locate the saint in the tradition of the great servants of God of former ages.

If the Devil was so preoccupied with Jean-Marie Vianney that he employed every means at his disposal to divert him from his task, either by exhausting his energy by insomnia, or by bringing him into such anguish of mind that he wanted to escape into the wilderness, it is because he knew the efficacy of the saint's prayers, of his scourgings, of his ministry to sinners. A woman who showed many signs of possession, and who seemed to be almost a mouthpiece of Satan, reproached him one day in front of witnesses:

"How you make me suffer.... If there were three more like you on earth, my kingdom would be destroyed.... You have stolen more than 80,000 souls from me."

At the time these words were spoken, the Curé d'Ars had in his parish a missionary whom he had asked to preach to his flock. Turning to him the Curé remarked, reducing by three-quarters the figure which all had heard mentioned: "Did you hear that, my friend? The Devil claims that between us we are destroying his empire, and that we have stolen 20,000 souls from him?"

The Devil had, of course, said quite clearly 80,000, without mentioning the missionary. The modification was only another example of the saint's humility.

The number mentioned by the possessed woman was by no means the final figure. As the Curé d'Ars himself said one day, pointing to his confessional: "God alone knows all the good that is done there." Although his penitents were by no means all converted, it is undeniable that for many of them, perhaps for the majority, it meant a return to the faith, or at any rate, to the practice of their religion.

To come now to a comparative assessment. When one studies Vianney's spirituality more closely, it becomes clear that his immense desire for penitence was inspired by the example of the great saints of former days, and more particularly of the saints of the Thebaïd and the Egyptian desert. We know for a fact that the Curé had studied the lives of the hermits and cenobites of Egypt, and that he was fond of quoting episodes from their lives in his famous catechisms and his sermons.

He had been taught by his tutor, the Abbé Bailey, to respect these saints, and he had one further trait in common with them, in that he too suffered from demonic infestations. We cannot, for instance, think of St. Anthony the Great, the father of all hermits, without recalling the demonic infestations from which he suffered. The visitors who sought him out on the barren hillsides of Kolsim seldom went away without having heard a confused and terrifying medley of sounds, like the noise of horses and weapons breaking the silence of those bleak spaces. It sounded, they said, like a city besieged by hostile armies. All this uproar was caused by invisible spirits, as troublesome as the *Grappin* was to be many centuries later.

Another famous solitary, St. Hilarion, could not begin his prayers without hearing all around him the barking of dogs, the bellowing of bulls, the hissing of serpents, and other noises no less strange and terrifying.

The devils made such an uproar around the cell of St. Pacomius, the first cenobite, that it sounded as if they were bent on its total destruction. And around the cabin of St. Abraham there would be devils, axe in hand, as if about to demolish it. At other times they would set fire to his matting, as they did to the Curé d'Ars bed.

As the Abbé Monnin has pointed out, we can read through the lives of the saints and almost everywhere we find them in open and sometimes memorable and violent conflict with Satan. We need only mention St. Benedict, St. Francis of Assisi, St. John of God, St. Vincent Ferrer, St. Peter of Alcantara, and amongst the women saints, Marguerite of Cortona, Angela of Foligno, Rita of Cascia, Rose of Lima, amongst so many others.

It is not surprising, therefore, that we find many instances of Satan's presence at Lourdes, in connection with the humble Bernadette, as we shall see in the following chapter.

$\backsim 2 \backsim$

SATAN AT LOURDES

A LITTLE TOWN

IF THE OBSCURE village of Ars owes its reputation solely to its saintly Curé, in the sense that it was totally unknown before his time, the same is not true of Lourdes. Abel Hugo, the elder brother of Victor Hugo, described it thus in his *France pittoresque,* published in 1835: "This capital of the former Lavedan-en-Bigorre used to be called *Miranbel,* which means, in the local patois, "the beautiful view."

Lourdes had an old castle, mainly used since the fourteenth century as a state prison. The castle, writes Abel Hugo, had just been restored. And he adds: "The town clusters round a rock on the opposite side of the Gave, and extends into a ravine through which runs a swift stream. Solidly built, but irregular, it has no particular buildings of note; but it is well placed at the junction of four valleys, through which pass the roads to Pau, Tarbes, Barèges and Bagnères."

But it was not for the beautiful view that millions of pilgrims flocked to Lourdes in 1958, the year that marked the centenary of the "Appearances." We know well what these appearances were. On February 11, 1858, Bernadette Soubirous, a young girl, simple, poor, ignorant, but very pious, suddenly became aware of a "young girl in white" in the entry to the Grotto of Massabieille, in the hollow of a rock.

The vision was repeated eighteen times between February 11 and July 16. But we do not need to repeat the rest of the story which is already well known throughout the world. What is relevant here is the Devil's intervention in this extraordinary episode. Silence or absence on his part would be astonishing, since he had been remarkably active at Ars in troubling a saint. He would therefore hardly be absent when miracles were occurring in the Grotto at Lourdes. All the many authors who have written about Lourdes have stressed the element of demonic intervention. This took the form of what is known in theology as "infestation" and, in the case under consideration, it had a truly satanic grotesqueness.

THE FIRST ALERT

According to J.B. Estrade, one of the first reporters of these appearances or visions, there may well have been a first alert on February 11, during the first vision.

As Bernadette was returning to the town from the Grotto, she is supposed to have declared that the vision had been disturbed by strange and unaccustomed noises. These sounds seemed to rise from the River Gave. There were many sounds seeming to echo and reply to each other. There were voices, questioning, contradicting, shouting, like the voices of a crowd in tumult. Amidst all these confusing voices, one more distinct than the rest could be heard uttering the furious, menacing cry: "Flee! Flee!"

Bernadette understood immediately that this injunction was addressed less to her, too insignificant to be dangerous, than to "the young girl in white," who had appeared to her ecstatic gaze, and whose name she did not yet know. But, according to J.B. Estrade the Vision of Light had only to turn her eyes for a moment toward the point whence the voices appeared to come, and her one look was so effective, so endowed with sovereign authority, that the voices immediately fell silent.

J. B. Estrade declared that the story of this first alert was related directly by Bernadette to him and his sister. The Abbé Nogaro, vicar of the cathedral of Tarbes, was also informed of it by the ecstatic herself.

We consider therefore, as does Mgr. Trochu, that the facts are incontrovertible, but the actual date seems less certain. As a matter of fact, Fr. Cros, S.J., who has made such a detailed study of the visions, does not mention it, either on February 11 or later. Since Fr. Cros has more than once had occasion to question the accuracy of the worthy M. Estrade's memory, one is inclined to believe that he has misdated this episode too, by antedating it considerably. We do not consider the episode spurious, but merely that it should be placed much later.

We come now to instances of demonic activity which are better dated and more reliable. Since we propose only to deal with well-attested facts, we shall follow very closely the account given by Fr. Cros.[8]

First to the facts, and then to the interpretation.

MANY VISIONARIES

On Thursday, April 15, the mayor of Lourdes, M. Lacadé, made a preliminary report to the sub-prefect of Argelès on visionaries other than Bernadette Soubirous. We must note the date. According

---

[8]   L. J. M. Cros, S.J., *Histoire de Notre-Dame de Lourdes* (Beauchesne: 1927), particularly Vol. 2, 47 *et seq.* and *passim*.

to Fr. Cros's calculation there had already been eighteen appearances, from February 11 to April 7.[9] The series was therefore completed. Bernadette remained aloof from all that followed. Here is the mayor's report:

"Last Saturday, 10th April," he wrote, "three girls from Lourdes were praying in the Grotto, at two in the afternoon, when, according to them, the Blessed Virgin appeared to them. One of them has made a written deposition which is in the hands of the Cure, who has forwarded it to the Bishop.

"A certain Pauline Labantès, who went to the Grotto yesterday morning, 14th April, at ten o'clock, in order to pray, declares that she saw the Blessed Virgin."

This was only the beginning.

Then the highly conscientious police superintendent, M. Jacomet, made his report, as in duty bound, first to the sub-prefect, then to the prefect.

The visionaries waxed and multiplied. Bernadette, one might almost say, was put in the shade. She could no longer compete with so many others who were seeing marvels. The superintendent was precise in his details, which are invaluable in helping us to assess the worth of these new visions. They never occurred in the exact place where Bernadette had seen the Blessed Virgin and heard her name from her own mouth. Some invisible protection seemed to encircle the spot and also the person of Bernadette herself. Whereas she always remained completely "natural," that is, just what she was, very simple, very modest, very ignorant, but totally sincere and upright, other characteristics are to be found among these new visionaries.

---

[9]   We know that Bernadette had one further vision on July 16, but Fr. Cros does not include it. For him, the series ended on April 7.

On April 10 there were five of them, and not three, as stated in the mayor's first report. The police superintendent wrote:

> One of them is Claire-Marie Cazenave, twenty-two years old, a virtuous girl, very religious and with a powerful imagination. "I saw," she says, "a white stone and, at almost the same time, the shape of a woman, of normal height, supporting a child on her left arm: her face was smiling, her curly hair fell to her shoulders, on her head was something white, held in place by a sort of comb: then a white dress. As for the child, I did not see him very clearly the first time, and I did not see him at all later."
>
> The second, Madeleine Cazaux, forty-five years old, married, of bad reputation and addicted to drink, describes her vision thus: "I saw something on the white stone, about the size of a ten-year-old girl: over her head she had a white veil, which fell to her shoulders, her hair was long and covered her breast. Every time the candle was moved the figure disappeared."
>
> The third, Honorine Lacroix, over forty years old, a prostitute with a bad reputation, says that she was the first to see the Blessed Virgin. "The Virgin," she says, "looked like a little girl of four, covered by a white veil, her hair fell to her shoulders and was swept back over her forehead. Her eyes were blue, her hair blonde, the lower half of her face very white and her cheeks pink."
>
> As for the two foreign women, one of whom is also said to have seen the vision, no one has heard any more of them: no one knows where they are.

All this, even at first glance, is more than a little suspicious! But the site of these alleged visions is no less suspect.

THE SITE

We are indebted to the same superintendent of police for a careful description of the site.

After Bernadette's visions, the Grotto had become a popular resort for pilgrims, and a rough altar had been set up, on which visitors laid offerings of wild or garden flowers. The shape of the Grotto was roughly that of an oven, about thirteen feet deep, with a domed roof about eight or nine feet high. At a height of about eight feet in the roof of the Grotto, that is to say, at a point which could only be reached with the help of a small ladder, a narrow corridor led out of the Grotto and turned sharply up into the interior of the rock. This corridor was about thirteen feet long and led into an oval opening about eight feet in diameter. Beyond this the corridor narrowed again. At a further thirteen or fourteen feet along, the way was blocked, but by the light of candles it was possible to see some whitish rock surfaces.

It is clear that in order to get into this hollow in the rocks it would be necessary to crawl along on one's stomach, a very awkward business and, for a woman, somewhat grotesque. In addition, the "clairvoyants" had not brought a ladder, as was later done. They had climbed sacrilegiously on to the altar at the back of the Grotto, in order to be able to climb into the mysterious corridor. Their illumination was provided by candles and, no doubt, their fitful light cast shadows which, with a little imagination, could be variously interpreted as a woman of normal size, a girl of ten, or even of four.

The superintendent expressed his disapproval very clearly: "The first time these women ventured to visit the spot I have described was on Saturday, 10th April. Neither decency nor respect for the altar they had to trample on held them back. There were five of them, a curious group, in view of the differences of age, habits and way of living."

This first visit did not attract much attention. Marie Cazenave, the most honorable of the three "visionaries" seems, according to the superintendent, to have been "ashamed of what her rather disreputable companions claimed to have seen." But the story got about, all the same. Curiosity proved sharper than natural respect. Other women climbed into the hollow in the rock. Many of them saw nothing and returned somewhat abashed. But on April 14, Suzette Lavantès, a servant aged fifty, climbed into the gallery and returned transported. She was surrounded by eager questioners. She had seen. She was still shaking all over. What had she seen? "A white form, about my own size, a sort of vapor, like a veil, and beneath it a long trailing gown, but I could not see any human form, neither head nor shoulders, nor legs nor any part of the body. In any case," she added, "what I saw was so vague and confused that I can't make out what it was."

These few happenings were enough to fan the flames. From then onwards pilgrimages to this most inaccessible gallery were multiplied. On April 17 both men and women joined in this questionable exploration. A young girl, Joséphine Albario, aged fifteen, began to cry and show signs of agitation. She was comforted and brought down from the gallery. It was necessary to take her home and put her to bed. She declared that she had seen "the Immaculate Conception, carrying a child in her arms, and standing beside her a man with a long beard." And this same vision seemed to haunt her even at her bedside.

Public opinion was in a turmoil. Two currents of opinion began to form. Some were full of admiration, believing in every apparition, whether to Bernadette or to her emulators. Others, shocked by many details in the accounts of these new visions, no longer believed even in those vouchsafed to Bernadette. The confusion was extreme. On April 18 the mayor's own servant was seized with convulsions because she too had seen something. But she had not needed even to climb into the rocky corridor, for the convulsions occurred as she was telling her beads in front of the altar in the Grotto. The mayor had complete confidence in his servant. He determined to investigate whether some trick of light might not have occasioned the visions which were turning the heads of so many women. On April 19 a small investigating committee climbed into the upper Grotto, in order to clear the matter up and to see whether the visions, particularly the visions seen by Joséphine Albario, which had led to an ecstasy of three-quarters of an hour, might have some natural explanation. But the results of the investigation were purely negative.

We should note, however, that the appearances to Bernadette had occurred in quite different circumstances from those we have just described. But it is clear that the public tended to confuse the two. Serious-minded people, such as Superintendent Jacomet, thereby felt justified in dismissing both without further ado, as attributable to regrettable delusions. On April 18 the Procureur, M. Dutour, wrote to the Procureur Général to complain of the attitude of the clergy:

"Nothing is being done to restrain religious sentiment from becoming ever more deeply committed to the path it is already pursuing, misled either by folly or deliberate deceit. Visions abound: miracles are too frequent to relate: the clergy and the Mayor seem to be content merely to record them." And he repeats, like Jacomet, the story of all the new visions.

It is now obvious that toward the end of April 1858 public confusion with regard to the appearances was at its height.

First Fears

There was, however, one voice to be heard amidst all this confusion, which we should note as providing some principle of clarification. There were, as we said, two trends of opinion, either to accept and wonder at everything, or to discredit and discard everything. The first quiet suggestion of what would afterwards be recognized as the truth came from a priest.

At about this time the "visionaries" included a certain Marie Bernard, of Carrère-basse. "She claimed," said the Abbé Pène,

> that she had seen a group of three persons in the Grotto: a man with a white beard, a fairly young woman, and a child. The old man had a bunch of keys in one hand, and with the other was twisting his moustache. It was at first said in the town that it might be the Holy Family. The same vision reappeared later, with the addition that the same persons had indulged in indecent gestures. Neither I nor my sister were able to establish whether these gestures had been observed by the same visionary or by others who had had the same vision. The girl, however, was my penitent, and often told me the same story, to which I paid little attention, considering that *it was nothing but a trick of the Devil, designed to cast a shadow on the earlier appearances.*

The italics are ours. They seem, in fact, to suggest the most reasonable explanation for all the phenomena quoted.

Whether or not one attributes the visions which followed on the appearances to Bernadette to exaltation, imagination, or mental confusion, it is clear that the advantage derived from them was in favor of the powers of evil, and that in all these episodes, of which we have described only a few, we can begin to see the first outline of a purpose: that the authentic visions and well-established appearances of the Blessed Virgin should be smothered under a flood of odd or grotesque imitations, which would later be absorbed enthusiastically by some of the population of Lourdes, whilst the more circumspect would merely shrug their shoulders. To drown truth in falsehood is a truly diabolical activity. Later events were to confirm this first interpretation of events.

It should be noted in passing that all the later opposition to belief in the authentic appearances to Bernadette had at least one good effect in that it restrained or repressed the more extreme forms of demonic manifestation. With the passage of time it became clearer that it was not a question of either accepting or rejecting everything, but simply of making a distinction.

The most fully accredited of all these "visionaries" was the young Joséphine Albario. But in her case, there was rather too much excitement and agitation and too many tears. M. Estrade, whom we have often quoted and whose judgment is more reliable than his memory, at first placed her, in his own mind, on the same level as Bernadette, but later he wrote:

"My admiration, however, was disturbed by an obscure feeling which seemed to warn me that the truth did not lie here. I compared the two, and remembered that I felt uplifted at the story of Bernadette, whereas at the story of Joséphine … I was only surprised. On looking more closely into the first appearances, I was able to grasp the sense of truly divine action: on looking at the other manifestations, I could only see in them the agitation of an over-excited organism."

In thinking thus M. Estrade, like other persons of good sense, was practicing that necessary act described by St. Ignatius Loyola as "the discernment of spirits" And Loyola himself was only repeating in other words St. Paul's great precept: "Extinguish not the spirit. Despise not prophecies. But prove all things; hold fast that which is good" (1 Thess. 5:19-21).

REASONABLE JUDGMENTS

The truth, therefore, was becoming more evident. Gradually people's minds were becoming clearer although, as we shall see, there was still a long way to go.

But before dealing with another series of disturbances and agitation, in which the element of demonic infestation became more and more apparent, we should give some further examples of contemporary evaluation of the far too numerous "visionaries" competing with the humble Bernadette. We have just mentioned Joséphine Albario, a young girl, incidentally, of excellent character. There was another, Marie Courrech, the mayor's servant. It would take too long to give her own statements, which can be found in Fr. Cros's book (Vol. 2, p. 96 *et seq.*).

What is, however, striking, is a contemporary opinion expressed by a local woman, Antoinette Garros:

"I had no faith," she said,

> in Marie Courrech's visions. She had neither the face nor the gestures of Bernadette. She suffered from sudden twitchings and convulsive movements. Often, when she saw her visions on the other side of the Gave, she would rush forward, explaining afterwards that the Vision had been calling her to the Grotto. If we had not restrained her with great difficulty, she would have thrown

herself into the river. One day as I was struggling to hold her back, some people who were looking on began to shout: "Let her go: if she can cross the Gave, there will be another miracle." But I did not heed them; I preferred to stop her from getting drowned, and I said to myself: "If the Blessed Virgin wants her to cross the Gave, she will certainly give her enough strength to get out of my grasp."

The point of the examples and comments is that there is always a way of distinguishing the authentic gift, the true charism, from its demonic counterfeit.

A CROWD OF VISIONARIES

These disorders, to call them by their right name, were not for long confined to a few women or young girls. The visionaries of both sexes grew in number and their generally grotesque and occasionally ridiculous posturings, were to continue up to the beginning of 1859.

Fr. Cros, some twenty years later, made an enquiry into the subject. "In June 1878," he writes, "we were able to unearth, at Lourdes, the names and histories of more than thirty of these visionaries, of both sexes and all ages: and the ones we discovered were only *the best-known,* since no one was any longer proud of having been a visionary."

Thus Fr. Cros was able to prove that Superintendent Jacomet, who had often been reproached for prejudice, excessive harshness, and hostility toward anything of divine origin, had in no way exaggerated. The superintendent, in fact, was not informed of every case:

he had only reported some, and either ignored or was unaware of the others. The manifestations reached such a pitch of exaggeration that they became a public scandal, and the Curé of Lourdes himself was obliged to preach a solemn sermon, exhorting parents to put a stop to it by preventing their children from indulging in such unending eccentricities.

When we read the evidence accumulated by Fr. Cros, we feel as if we were dealing with an epidemic. Here are some typical depositions:

> *Brother Léobard, in charge of the Lourdes schools:*
> The Devil prompted the appearance of a host of visionaries, who indulged in the wildest extravagances. Did they really see anything? Yes, there is every reason to believe that many of them did see something, the Evil One, in various guises. Many of my pupils claimed to have seen visions. They often played truant ... These extravagances occurred not only in the Grotto and by a stream which runs close to the Basilica, but also in their own homes, where they improvised little chapels.
>
> *Brother Cérase:* A *crowd* of small boys and girls claimed to have seen the Blessed Virgin. I sometimes met them on their way to the Grotto. They would be holding candles in their hands, or kneeling down by the side of a small pond. On one of these occasions a man said to me: "My little daughter also sees the Blessed Virgin at the Grotto; so many of them do!" I treated it simply as a joke, and *I began seriously to doubt the value of Bernadette's visions, at which I had never been present.*

The italics, again, are ours. Bernadette's mission was seriously endangered by this outbreak of demonic manifestations. There will be further proofs of this danger.

But to continue with examples drawn from the patient investigations of Fr. Cros.

> *Dominique Vignes, Marie Portau, Dominiquelle Cazenave, Ursule Nicolau,* all excellent witnesses, have often seen visionaries at the Grotto. They would snatch the bouquets of flowers that people were taking to the Grotto, and pluck out any lilies or roses they contained and throw them into the Gave, saying: "The Virgin wants neither lilies nor roses."
>
> I heard a girl of ten or eleven moaning, shouting and screaming in front of the rocky hollow where the custodian's house now stands: There, she said, was the Vision. This child was as much honored as the others. People would embrace them in pious devotion.
>
> Each of them held a rosary — but all the rosaries were new and unconsecrated — they did not want any others. They would hold the rosary loosely, with the crucifix on a level with their eyes, and the beads swinging in front of their faces: they used to run about in every direction, bent almost double, making strange faces and noises like young dogs baying at their prey.
>
> I once saw a procession of them coming from the fountain of Merlasse, as far as the post — the post which had the notice telling you not to go

into the Grotto. When they got there, one of them shouted: "Come with me, you will see the Blessed Virgin!" Some women joined the procession and followed them.

One evening, when night had already fallen, one of the visionaries, crowned with a laurel wreath, cried out: "All of you are to recite a Rosary: the Lord is going to recite the Rosary." It was no use pointing out that to suggest that God was going to pray to the Virgin Mary was turning the world upside down: they were carried away. A little later the visionary called out: "Kiss the ground forty times, forty times." All present kissed the ground. As for myself, I laughed, but I was secretly furious at seeing all these devilments.

Mlle. Tardhivail: One has no idea, nowadays, of the credulity that prevailed in Lourdes at that time: people's minds were aflame; a stranger, coming from Saint-Pé, declared on entering the town, "I looked at the Grotto as I passed: there I saw the Blessed Virgin who was walking about; everyone saw her." A crowd of people thereupon rushed to the Grotto: my sister and I were among them.

Jean Domingieux: One day, from the Ribère, I saw a visionary standing in front of the Grotto, and he shouted to the dense crowd which had collected between the canal and the Gave, and which had even spread over beyond the Gave into the field where I was: "Bring out your rosaries! I shall bless them for you!" Everyone produced a rosary and the visionary blessed them with water from the Grotto.

The most revealing feature in the antics performed by these unfortunate children was their habit of making the most horrible grimaces. On this subject there is further evidence, again collected by Fr. Cros.

> *Gamekeeper Callet:* One day I followed the visionary Barraôu, as far as the mill. He went into a bedroom and started climbing up the curtains of the bed, with hideous grimaces: he was grinding or gnashing his teeth, and his eyes had a wild look.
> *Mme. Prat:* Once I was present when Minino was having a vision: he was braying, and his face was so terrible that I could not bear to look at it.

Other witnesses have mentioned the ridiculous antics of these impromptu visionaries: they had once seen Bernadette eating grass. Or, at least, she was said to have done so, so they wanted to copy her, and thus obviously brought discredit on her without intending to, for the majority behaved without any clear consciousness of the significance of their actions.

But they also had activities of their own invention.

> *Pauline Bonrdeu:* I have seen a dozen of them coming down our street from the Grotto, with garlands of flowers round their heads.
> *Basile Casterot:* S., the visionary, was walking through the town, wearing round his head a ribbon he had taken from a girl's hair: "The Blessed Virgin," he said, "told me to do it." A lot of people

were following him. Some said he was mad, but the majority maintained he had had a vision.

Mme. Baup: One day, on the road to Bois, I met the visionary M. in a kind of ecstasy, but with his face all awry. I shook him, but he said nothing. Finally, he came out of his ecstasy and began to move off abruptly. I asked him: "What did you see?" He would not reply and moved away. I insisted: "What did you see?" Finally, he said, just as he moved off: "The Blessed Virgin in a white robe, with a crown." Just at that moment my niece came to fetch me to see three or four other visionaries on the same road. "Come and see," she said: "there's a little girl in the most beautiful ecstasy!" I saw the little girl, who was about ten or eleven, on her knees, her face transfigured. Another little visionary was passing by at the time, a candle in her hand. I took the candle and moved it backwards and forwards in front of the ecstatic's face. She never blinked an eyelid. Little by little the ecstasy died away, and the child told us: "I saw the Blessed Virgin, in a white gown with a blue sash, and a crown on her head." "What did she say to you?" "She said: 'Go away! I must go to the watering-pot.'"

Nothing very sinister in all this, one must agree, but the real danger lay in the shadow cast on the genuine appearances to Bernadette, which had now ceased.

And, as a fact, people were dubious, questioning and self-questioning. Even the clearest minds were confused by this plurality of visions, some obviously spurious, and by all these alleged miracles, some of which were more than doubtful.

There is a striking example of the effect of this confusion. Among those who were numbered at the outset amongst the doubters was a director of the Grand Seminary of Tarbes, Canon Ribes, who, in all good faith, was skeptical about all the happenings at Lourdes. He has himself related how he visited Lourdes in August 1858, accompanied by a foreign priest. Both came in quest of information. They wished first of all to see Bernadette. She was, after all, still the most important person at that time in Lourdes, since it was she to whom the first appearances had been vouchsafed.

The two visitors went to Bernadette's parents and asked to see her. She was not there. So they promised to return to the mill then owned by her father. The following scene then took place:

"From the mill," said Canon Ribes,

> we went to the Grotto, down a little path alongside the castle. We descended a steep and barren slope, now planted with trees, and made more accessible by the zig-zag path so well known to pilgrims. We reached the miraculous Grotto: the entry was closed by a barricade of planks. Behind it, kneeling, was a boy of about twelve or fourteen, fingering his rosary and bowing to a mysterious being and moving slowly forward toward the foot of the rock. The ground rose toward the rock in a kind of small amphitheater in which the successive flood waters of the Gave had cut a series of shallow steps. We studied the visionary for a few moments: His features were contracted and repellent. My companion shouted to him:

"Get out of there! You are doing the Devil's work!" The child, pretending not to hear, continued to move forward: "Get out of there!" he thundered at him, "Go, or the hand of God will strike you!" Immediately the visionary extinguished his little candle, climbed over the barricade, and disappeared.

This was only the first episode in their investigations. The two priests were searching, doubting, but they knew they could not be at fault if they prayed. The story goes on:

> We prayed, we drank some water from the fountain, and we went to see the Curé. Bernadette was waiting for us. She related, with her usual candor, what she had seen and heard at the Grotto. I made some remarks about the "three secrets," which, it seemed to me, might be an imitation of La Salette. She replied without hesitation that the secrets had been entrusted to her alone: she was not to disclose them to anyone, not even to the pope, and she was convinced of her ability to keep them to herself.
>
> My companion declared that he believed. For myself, I was not yet convinced. I said to him: "I am inclined to believe, but I would like further proof."

This hesitation was badly received by the Curé of Lourdes, who was by now entirely and justifiably convinced of the authenticity of Bernadette's visions. He wrote to the bishop a few days later, saying:

"How can you expect strangers to believe in the visions, when the directors of the Grand Seminary are not convinced?"

The next year, however, Canon Ribes returned to Lourdes, to celebrate a thanksgiving Mass for a cure obtained through the use of water from Lourdes. M. le Curé remarked to him: "You owe this reparation to the Blessed Virgin, for opposing her work." But he had been right in waiting for definite proofs. And in the month of August 1858 such proofs were still debatable. The Devil had, as we pointed out, "drowned" the truth in falsehoods. With all these fantastic apparitions and alleged miracles, it is understandable that Superintendent Jacomet should have written to the prefect about the suggestion that an episcopal commission should be designated to examine the facts: "Sensible and truly religious persons are wondering who has had the audacity to suggest involving the higher clergy in matters redolent of charlatanry."

The prefect, however, agreed to the commission, being persuaded that it would categorically denounce all stories of visions, including those of Bernadette, which had first started the avalanche.

"A commission has been nominated to verify the miracles of Lourdes," wrote M. Massy, the Prefect of Tarbes. "It is hoped that by performing its task conscientiously and without prejudice, the commission may put an end to the whole wretched business. I am willing to provide all the information necessary to present these allegedly supernatural incidents in their true perspective."

MINISTERIAL INTERVENTION

If, as many of the more enlightened maintained, these wholesale imitations, which distorted the impression created by the appearances to Bernadette, were inspired by the Devil, it must be admitted that they were, at least, adroitly inspired. The facts we have related were, at any rate in part, known to the civil authorities. This was not astonishing, since it was the duty of the authorities to maintain public order, an order frequently and transparently endangered by the disturbances at the Grotto and in neighboring villages. On July 30, 1858, Ministre des Cultes M. Rouland wrote a very necessary letter to the Bishop of Tarbes, Mgr. Laurence. This letter is so revealing that it is worth quoting in full:

> Monseigneur, recent reports on the Lourdes affair seem to me liable to cause profound distress amongst sincerely religious people.
>
> The blessing of rosaries by children, the manifestations so frequently associated with women of loose character, the crowning of visionaries, the grotesque ceremonies, which are nothing but parodies of religious rites, all this would have stimulated a flood of attacks from Protestant and other papers, if the central authority had not intervened to restrain their ardor.
>
> But these scandalous scenes are none the less calculated to discredit religion in the eyes of the people, and I conceive it to be my duty, Monseigneur, once more to invite your most serious attention to these facts.
>
> Your Grace will understand that the Government had no objection in principle to the setting up of a new center of pilgrimage. If I insisted firmly that there should be no sequel to the first manifestations at the Grotto of Lourdes, it was because detailed reports from various sources had convinced me that there was nothing serious or

reputable either in the origin, the development, or in the fruits of this popular movement.

Events have confirmed my conviction: the multiplication of visionaries and ecstatics, which recall the unfortunate scenes of the eighteenth century, and the wild demonstrations which are now taking place on the banks of the Gave, would alone be sufficient to justify the measures taken by authority.

These regrettable manifestations seem to me to warrant the clergy departing from the strict reserve they have hitherto maintained.

For the rest, I can only make an urgent appeal to your Grace's prudence and strength of mind, by enquiring whether you would not see fit to utter a public condemnation of such profanations.

This letter is clearly a courteous but categorical demand for action. What the Minister wished, expected, and requested, as made clear by his allusions to the historic disorders in the cemetery of Saint-Médard in the eighteenth century, was no less than episcopal intervention, which should take the form of a general reproof and condemnation of *all* stories of visions, including Bernadette's, which had certainly stimulated all the others. If the Bishop had yielded to this request and intervened without regard to the Pauline precept: "Hold fast that which is good," it would indeed have been a victory for the powers of evil.

VILLAGE JEALOUSIES

This danger was in fact by no means illusory since, in the month of July 1858, the bishop had just been informed by one of his Curés of a new epidemic of collective exaltation in the vicinity of Lourdes.

There was a new wave of competition in supernatural visions, occurring in neighboring villages, and not only in Lourdes where so many of the inhabitants had already felt able to improve on the record of poor little Bernadette, so unqualified, they felt, to be chosen by the Blessed Virgin in preference to others.

On July 9 the Abbé Pierre Junca, Curé of Ossen, had written to Mgr. Laurence to inform him of what was taking place in his parish.

A young boy, Laurent Lacaze, aged ten, had asked to be allowed to go to the Grotto one morning after school. It was July 2. He was so insistent that his parents gave way. At about noon Laurent, with his brother aged eight, was in front of the Grotto. He was reciting a Rosary when he raised his eyes and saw "a woman dressed in white, carrying a very small child on her left arm. This child had a bouquet of three red roses in his right hand. On his head was a red cap, decorated with three white roses, held in place by a red ribbon. The woman had three red roses in her right hand. From her right arm was hanging a broad red scalloped ribbon. Hanging from the same arm was a beautiful rosary. On her head was a white bonnet, with a white ribbon round it. Two men were standing one on each side of the woman, both clad in black and wearing blue berets. The man on the right had a long white beard. Both the woman and the men were wearing black shoes."

Such is the description in the Curé's letter of July 9. So the young Lacaze had had plenty of time in which to elaborate his miraculous vision. The woman had told him to come again that afternoon, so he obeyed. And he had again seen the same personages as in the morning. Then they had all set off together, leading the boy and his mother, who had accompanied him; along the path which led to their own village of Ossen. On the way the woman shared in Laurent's childish jokes.... On the days which followed Laurent returned to the Grotto and had more visions. But he was now accompanied.

Processions formed up behind him. The Curé, having been informed, felt it advisable to sprinkle the child with holy water, and also the place where he said he had seen the woman—without, it appears, any perceptible result.

The stories themselves are banal enough. But the inhabitants of Ossen were in a turmoil. They reproached their Curé for betraying signs of doubt. As for him, he consulted his bishop as to his line of action. Meanwhile other visionaries had appeared: Jean-Marie Pomiès, thirteen, and Jean-Marie Sarthe, ten. The latter was from Ségus, another village in the vicinity. But his visions did not last long. The Curé and others ordered him to stop at home. He did so, and there were no more visions.

The two children from Ossen, however, continued their activities, which have been described as follows: "For some considerable time they were, so to say, pursued and obsessed by the Vision. They ran after her in the streets and into houses as if they were on a hunt. Their cries were often more like howls and their movements awkward and ungainly: more often than not people were shocked by their disorderly and unseemly conduct. The parents, taking an innocent pride in the belief that their sons were seeing the Blessed Virgin, were partly responsible for failing to terminate these regrettable scenes." We are quoting from the report sent in by the Curé of Ségus.

The mayor of Ossen, Jean Vergez, was also taking note of what was happening. Fr. Cros quotes extensively from his report, which follows the same lines. It seems clear that young Lacaze really saw visions. Those who were present could not fail to believe that they were visions of the Blessed Virgin, and this was not astonishing. Why should Bernadette have a monopoly? Laurent Lacaze's parents certainly did not see why. The mayor, who questioned them, reported: "The Lacazes did not go to work: both parents, and particularly the father, rejoiced at what was happening to their son. One evening

I met the father, who was going haymaking. I said, 'You have lost a day's work.' He replied: 'Yes, but at least we have been in good company, the company of the Blessed Virgin.'"

But this was not all. According to the mayor's deposition, astonishing things were happening to the children of the village. For instance, Laurence Lacaze, who previously only knew the patois, now began to speak in French. There was more to come. According to the mayor's report:

"One day Jean-Pierre Pomiès, a boy of thirteen, was in the Lacaze house, standing about six feet from an attic window overlooking the courtyard. This window was two feet high by eighteen inches broad, and more than three feet from the floor. Suddenly the boy looked into the courtyard, saw a vision there, and disappeared like a flash of lighting through the window without touching the sides, landed on his feet in the yard and ran after the vision. This so upset me that I immediately withdrew, and when I got home, I said to my wife: 'There's something queer about this business: I can't get over it.'"

Fr. Cros quotes other witnesses to the event. He states that he has himself examined the place where it happened and finds it "humanly inexplicable." He adds that the young visionaries displayed another anomaly, which was common to all of them: they had a horror of rosaries which had been blessed and wanted only new and unblessed rosaries. No object that had been blessed was returned by them if put into their hands.

Mgr. Laurence had received accurate and detailed reports of all these events. On July 12, 1858, he replied to the Curé of Ossen:

"I consider the boys Lacaze and Pomiès, the visionaries, to be suffering from an affliction of the nerves. They must be treated as such. As far as I can judge, there is nothing supernatural in their experiences. Celestial beings do not make futile remarks. They are not frivolous or familiar. If these children say or do unseemly things they must be scolded and treated with severity."

But the bishop had to repeat his recommendations before they were accepted and respected by ordinary people. So the Ossen visionaries were to continue their bizarre activities for some little time longer. There is abundant evidence as to how these young prophets were followed, admired, and obeyed. When passing the Lacaze house, people would kneel in the street and utter a prayer to the Blessed Virgin. Some spent the night in the room where the visionary slept. The Curé, from his pulpit, spoke of the bishop's letter, forbidding children under fifteen to go to the Grotto, and prohibiting the others from communicating with the visionaries. His parishioners refused to believe him until he showed them the actual letter. The Curé's sister, Francoise Junca, adds: "The neighboring villages were jealous of Ossen: for us it was a heavy responsibility: my brother spent many a sleepless night over it."

We have already drawn attention to this jealousy of Ossen in the neighboring villages. There was a similar outburst against Lourdes.

"One day," relates an inhabitant of Omex, another nearby village,

> I was at the Grotto, and the young visionaries from Ossen, with many others from Lourdes, were in the hollow of the rock, when the Devil appeared to them. Suddenly a voice could be heard coming from the cleft in the rock, a very light voice, like that of a rather spoilt and affected child. The voice was saying: "In the valley of Batsurguère, and especially at Ossen, there are a lot of good people: at Lourdes they are only riff-raff." So I stood up in front of everybody and said: "Whoever it is, he's more devilish than the Devil himself. The Blessed Virgin doesn't despise anyone, and still less those who are badly in need of conversion.'"

But those who were present were none the less disturbed and agitated. One woman from Ossen was so flattered by what she had heard that she would have built a chapel to the Virgin in her room if her husband had not stopped her. This unfortunate woman, incidentally, went mad and died within a year.

But we have said enough to show the extent of the disturbances provoked by these "devilments" at Lourdes and in the immediate neighborhood, and to make it abundantly clear that the bishop had need of all his prudence to steer a path through all these more or less fantastic manifestations. If the Devil had wished to discredit the appearances of the Blessed Virgin to Bernadette by confusing them in a medley of grotesque imitations and exaggerations, he was, one must admit, not far from achieving his aim. Fortunately, Mgr. Laurence did not allow himself to be imposed on. On July 28, 1858, he signed the order convoking a commission of enquiry into the Lourdes visions. What was remarkable however was that, from the beginning, the only name specifically mentioned as the object of the enquiry was that of Bernadette Soubirous. There was no mention, for instance, of all the numerous other manifestations we have described. In the eyes of sensible persons, they were nothing but imagination, exaggeration, oddities, perhaps even the work of the Devil. The reader who has had the opportunity of studying this collection of phenomena may well be astonished at their number, intensity, and peculiarity, and may even have formed a rather unfortunate impression, in retrospect, of the appearances to Bernadette. Yet, if he reflects a moment, he will note that still more astonishing is the way all the heavy clouds of doubt and suspicion disappeared quite naturally and simply in the light of truth.

The bishop's commission set to work without delay. The simplicity, uprightness, perseverance, and evident sincerity of Bernadette, on the one hand, and on the other the miracles, the authentic miracles which had meanwhile occurred at the Grotto, were sufficient to convince the commission, and when, at the end of three years' work, it completed its task, Mgr. Laurence was able to set the seal of his solemn approval on the events at Lourdes, such as we know them from the life of Bernadette.

But it is natural to wonder what happened to the host of impromptu visionaries whose exploits had been a household word in the district of Lourdes for so many months.

THE OSSEN VISIONARIES

When, in 1878, Fr. Cros made his historic investigation with such scrupulous exactitude, he came to know the Ossen visionaries. Naturally, by 1878 they had grown up. How much of their earlier experiences remained in their minds?

Nothing, or almost nothing. They had both become excellent Christians. Both Laurent Lacaze and Jean-Pierre Pomiès were amongst those serving as chief acolytes in the parochial procession of the Holy Sacrament. Fr. Cros questioned them. Laurent Lacaze, the first, said that he had hardly any recollection of what he had seen and done in 1858.

"I remember," he said, "that I used to go to the Grotto with other children: that I saw a *kind of shadow*, but I have no idea whether *it* had any outline, or whether it was a man or a woman. I don't remember what I was doing on the road from Lourdes to Ossen."

To the majority of those who remembered a little better, this "kind of shadow" that Laurent had seen could only have been the Devil!

Jean-Pierre Pomiès, when questioned by Fr. Cros, declared:

> I used often to go to the Grotto, attracted by all
> the stories of what was going on there. During
> these visits I twice had a vision, the first time I saw
> a dazzling light in the hollow of the rock, and in
> the middle of it, a *rather thick shadow*. The light

was neither red nor white, and stood about three feet high. I could not distinguish any face. This lasted about a quarter of an hour. The second time I saw the same thing, but I was very surprised at what happened to a little girl who also had visions. I was kneeling, between her and a boy: we all three saw the same light. Then the little girl stretched out her hand toward the place where we saw the light, and the candle she was holding in her hand suddenly disappeared and we could not make out where it had gone to. We were all very surprised.

Thus Jean-Pierre Pomiès, too, had only seen "a rather thick shadow" with a light which was neither red nor white but very bright. This was the same boy who, in the presence of witnesses, had so light-heartedly and with such preternatural dexterity jumped through a very narrow window. Yet in 1878 it could be said of him, together with his fellow visionary Laurent Lacaze: "They are living as honest and Christian men; the spirit of evil took advantage of their innocence; but neither of them was the deliberate accomplice of Satan."

Such is the tribute paid by Fr. Cros, after having seen and spoken to them.

THE VISIONARIES OF LOURDES

The same faculty of oblivion was to be found amongst the numerous visionaries of Lourdes.

Fr. Cros naturally questioned them as well and observed that the majority only retained the vaguest recollections of their so-called visions from 1858 to 1859. Indeed, shortly after the epidemic of apparitions, the Abbé Serres, priest at Lourdes, and in constant touch with the catechism class, had already noted that the greater number, on reaching the age of their First Communion—assuming that this occurred at Lourdes, as in many other French dioceses, between twelve and fourteen—had only a confused memory of the sights which had appeared to them at the Grotto or elsewhere.

But Fr. Cros questioned some of them, twenty years later. Here is the reply made by one, Alexandre-Francois L.:

> I didn't like wandering about, and my parents kept me close to their side, so I should not have gone to the Grotto unless some of my school-friends had persuaded me. So I climbed with them into the upper cavity and knelt down to pray. Then I saw a vision, white as a sheet of paper, emerging from the back of the cave; it did seem to have human shape, but I could not make out either face or hands or feet. As soon as the other children began to speak I could not see it. I told them to be quiet and the vision reappeared. I saw it come back like this at least five times. Believe it or not, I did see it, and it was beautiful.

Another, whom Fr. Cros calls "the most famous of the former visionaries," who had now become the father of four children, replied:

> I was present once or twice when the visions appeared to Bernadette, and at the time I was impressed, like the others, but I didn't think much about it afterwards, until one day, coming back with a boy of my own age from a walk in the forest, we went to the Grotto together. As I was

there, praying, something passed in front of my eyes, something which had the face of a man. I began to laugh, and then to cry, and everyone said I had had a vision. I told my friend what I had seen.

Some women came to my house and took me to La Ribère. Sometimes I saw nothing at all; at other times I saw the same thing, and I would cry: "To your knees! To your knees! Kiss the ground!" because I was frightened. Sometimes I also saw this apparition moving from one tree to another in the field.

I used to ask people for their rosaries and bathe them in the Gave, because I felt like it.

One day, when I was alone in the Grotto, seeing the vision, the priest who had the cross put up on the top of the Ger, came to the Grotto and seeing me, said "Get out of there! What you see is the enemy of the True Vision," and I went away.

The other children would make faces, just as I did, and they would shout, but I don't know what they were shouting: I was afraid. I never went to the Grotto alone except by day. I would not have dared to go there at night if the women hadn't come and fetched me. They believed I used to see the Blessed Virgin. Sometimes it was ten, or half-past ten, when we got back. The women used to ask me: "What did you see?" I used to answer: "The Blessed Virgin," *but it was really a man that I saw.* The face wasn't always the same. There was sometimes a beard. Once I saw this being dressed in white, but I don't remember noticing any feet or hands.

It's all very mixed up now. I couldn't say exactly what it was.

This was the closest Fr. Cros could get to any precise recollection of all these visions, twenty years later. However, the former visionaries were all positive on two points: firstly, that no one had ever induced them to simulate visions, but that they came from within — or from the Devil, shall we say, as many others have done — and secondly, that their activities were always frowned on by the police, and other persons in authority.

CONCLUSION

Our conclusion could hardly be very different from that reached by Fr. Cros, who studied the phenomena very closely, and to whom we are indebted for many facts. He was convinced that Satan was truly the mainspring of all these manifestations because there was a similarity, a sequence and, one might even say, a strategy behind them all, which could hardly have been the work of any of the protagonists. They resembled the chorus of a Greek tragedy, whose voices we hear, but whose leader could only have been the Devil. If we see Satan as the orchestrator of the phenomena, it will explain the bizarre character of these events. For Satan cannot fail to sign his own handiwork. By God's grace, there was such a difference between the visionaries, whether women, young girls, or boys and little girls, and the composed and tranquil Bernadette, that no one could be mistaken, and the distinction between good and evil, the true and the false, became self-evident.

We should mention Fr. Cros's final appreciation of the situation, in which we concur:

> We have shown elsewhere how the proof of what is divine arises from the impotence of the most powerful contradictions: whether the opponents be official or self-appointed; neither the one nor the other can stop what is happening or slow it down; what was happening, in their eyes, was nothing but Bernadette, and Bernadette herself was nothing. The cloud of visionaries was dissipated, and soon they were no more spoken of: the light of the true visionary pierced the cloud, and the cloud itself served only as a foil to the purity of her light.
>
> Thus the opposition of the Devil was overcome, like the opposition of men. For a time Satan could count on the support of religious people led astray by his devices, and this was the greatest danger of all. Yet even this dark shadow was illuminated by the divine work: the most powerful patronage was of no avail to the visionaries, who disappeared with their grimaces leaving only the luminous figure of Bernadette, bathed in sincerity and peace.[10]

The success of the centenary celebration which ended at Lourdes at the beginning of 1959 is a proof of the radiance which now encircles the name of the humble Bernadette Soubirous, who saw

[10] Cros, *Histoire*, Vol. 3, 272.

the Blessed Virgin in 1858. We should not forget, however, that Bernadette, of simple peasant stock like the Curé d'Ars, ended her days in the convent of Nevers, and that in her last hours she had to struggle against the Devil as the Curé d'Ars had had to do throughout his life.

As she lay dying, in fact, she displayed for a moment a great fear, and one of the nuns who was tending her heard her say very clearly: "Leave me, Satan!" But soon afterwards the little saint recovered her tranquility and died in an atmosphere of victorious peace.

$\backsim 3 \backsim$

POSSESSION, ITS NATURE, CAUSES, AND TREATMENT

IT SEEMS ADVISABLE to explain the Catholic doctrine as to cases of *possession*, which are quite different from the cases of *infestation* which we have just described.

AN EXTRAORDINARY FACT

There can hardly be anything more extraordinary than a case of *demonic possession*. Many authentic examples have demonstrated that this does, in fact, occur. No doubt there were cases of possession long before the birth of Christ. Cases occurred during Christ's ministry, for which we have the evidence of the Gospels. There are numerous cases in the history of the early Church, as is shown by the creation of the order of exorcists from amongst the ranks of the clergy. In the following chapters we shall give some striking examples which have occurred, selecting, as far as possible, the more recent cases. Catholic theology has, of course, dealt with the problem and can provide a documented theory of demonic possession; whilst the Roman ritual, the official basis of each ecclesiastical action, indicates the symptoms by which true possession can be recognized and the way in which it is to be treated. The treatment is purely and simply *exorcism*, which we shall deal with later.

Regarding the nature of possession and its causes, we cannot find a better or more accurate guide than Mgr. Saudreau: *The Mystic State and the Extraordinary Facts of Spiritual Life.*[11]

If demonic possession has sometimes been compared with the Incarnation, it is solely by way of analogy. Possession is an imitation or, as one might say, an "apeing" of the divine by Satan—a caricature of the Incarnation. Mgr. Saudreau hastens to add: "Possession never goes as far as animation." This means that the Devil does not take the place of the soul of the possessed person, he does not give life to the body but, *without our knowing how* he gets control of the body, takes up residence in it, either in the cerebellum or the bowels and, in every case, in the nervous system. Thus he deprives the soul of its normal mastery over limbs and body, he distorts the face into a strange, demonic cast which expresses his fury and frustration, his pride, his purposes, and—when under the hammer of exorcism—his *suffering*. The Devil seems to look out of the eyes of the possessed, to speak through his mouth, to the extent that he often uses language of an extreme coarseness, even if his victim should happen to be a gentle, well-bred person to whom such language would be totally foreign. And since devils are numerous and each has his own personality, they leave their own mark on the possessed person, so that one may distinguish which particular devil is operating, in cases of multiple possession.

We should, however, note that this demonic action is conditioned by the nature and character of the possessed person. The Devil, in fact, can, if he wishes, imitate a normal way of speaking and acting.

---

[11] Auguste Sandreau, *L'Etat mystique ... et les faits extraordinaires de la Vie spirituelle, 2nd ed.* (Paris: Amat, 1921), Ch. 22, "Faits préternaturels diaboliques."

The Devil is not always present in the possessed person. He enters at will. He provokes crises. A possessed person may even be temporarily liberated by exorcism and then repossessed. In the normal state the victim is like everyone else. He gives no sign of being subject to the very peculiar manifestations that are provoked by crises. These crises, however, are not always of equal violence. Sometimes the possessed person retains consciousness throughout. But he cannot control the completely alien contortions, gesticulations, and words produced by something within him. On other occasions he is, as it were, stupefied, and knows nothing of what has occurred within him, and thus cannot recall it later. Quite frequently the possessing spirit moves up and down the victim's body, transferring itself from head to feet, making one limb as rigid as an iron bar without affecting the others.

These spirits, incidentally, do not all behave in the same way, for they are far from resembling each other. This fact was observed as far back as the fourth century by the biographer of St. Martin, that redoubtable hammer of the Evil One.

He believed, not without cause, that the old pagan gods were devils, but he made a wide distinction between Mercury, for instance, an agile demon, malicious and persistent, and Jupiter, whom he considered brutal and sluggish: *Jovem brutum atque hebetum esse dicebat (He said Jove is brutish and dull)*. Similarly, in John Cassianus, the Abbé Serenus declares: "Not all devils show the same cruelty or fury, just as they are not all endowed with the same strength and malice." We shall see later that there is a devil of pride, Satan, a devil of avarice, Beelzebub, and a devil of impurity, which took the name Isacaron in a case of possession which we shall study later. But there are also devils of sloth, of intemperance, blasphemy, etc. This does not mean that because a devil has, as it were "specialized" in one form of evil, he cannot therefore practice the other forms as well.

Neither are devils always of equal strength. Some are driven out with little trouble by exorcism, never to return again. Others resist a long time, refusing to depart, or returning again and again. As Mgr. Saudreau remarks: "When the trouble is caused by the first kind of devil, a few prayers or pious observances, or a few adjurations, are usually enough to put an end to the matter."

In the most celebrated cases of possession, however, the exorcists have had to wage a long and bitter struggle with what seem to have been veritable princes of darkness.

In a later chapter we shall describe a special case which, in spite of six years' work and many vicissitudes, is still not cured, in 1959.

Causes of Possession

Natural good sense would tend to suggest that the first responsibility for a case of possession lies in *the faults of the possessed person*. This is not so. Cases of possession are, in fact, very varied and relatively few in number. If we agree with Professor Lhermitte, to whom we shall refer later, that they are "more numerous than is believed," this does not necessarily imply that they occur in a high percentage of sinners. If the Devil was allowed to attack as and when he wished, mankind would be thrown totally off balance, we should no longer be masters of our destiny, and God's work amongst us would be diverted from its purpose. This is inconceivable, and however powerful the spirits of evil may be, it is still true that "the dogs are chained." Whether it be a case of infestation, as with the Curé d'Ars, or cases of obsessions or possession, nothing happens except by God's permission. The evil spirits can only act on us to the extent, as is said in the Book of Job, that they obtain the permission of God, the Lord of all. The case of Job himself, afflicted by satanic infestations, is a proof that the faults of the victim have nothing to do with his ordeal. In the case of the Curé d'Ars we have, if possible, even stronger proof. The assaults of the Devil have a meaning, and we suggest that it is possible to know what this meaning is.

Possession in general, and the more spectacular cases of "bedevilment" which we have already quoted or shall describe later, are proofs of the existence of a supernatural world in which so many persons no longer believe. God gives a free hand, in certain cases, to the pride or homicidal envy of a particular devil, in order to outwit a more general strategy. To use Baudelaire's well-known phrase: "The Devil's deepest wile is to persuade us that he does not exist."

It is interesting to recall that Baudelaire, born in 1821, died young in 1867. It was just at the time that he was formulating this explanation that, as an exception to this general strategy, there occurred demonic manifestations at Ars, at Lourdes, at Lyons, in Alsace and other places, which destroyed any possibility of believing that the Devil "does not exist."

But if infestations, or even the much more serious possessions, are not always attributable to the faults of the victims, it does happen that such faults may be the precipitating factor in such misfortunes. The Abbé Saudreau quotes numerous cases in the past. Then he adds, referring to a recent case: "We know of a recent case—which may still not be cured—of a woman to whom this happened, after saying a prayer to Mercury, on the advice of an old woman who claimed to be a healer."

SORTILEGES

In many of the cases we shall mention it seems that the original cause of the possession was a *malefice*, or what the general public usually calls a "spell." The Abbé Saudreau is quite definite on this point. "One of the most frequent causes of demonic persecution is a malefice." And he adds that "these malefices are the Devil's sacraments."

The Devil acts through "sortileges," the secret of which he has entrusted to his adherents. Amongst pagan people it is still normal for the *sorcerer* to enjoy some form of authority and pre-eminence. Everyone hates him, but also fears him and seeks his aid. He has powers which are believed to be supernatural. He is expected to exercise a certain control over illness, natural forces, and even over meteorology. The sorcerer has not entirely disappeared even from countries with a long Christian tradition. In country districts you can still find persons credited with considerable and mysterious powers. These powers operate through what are called "charms" or "spells." It is true and regrettable that a great deal of this belief in their efficacy is derived from superstition, but it remains to be shown whether this belief is entirely unfounded. The ritual, in any case, recognizes the existence of charms and enjoins that they should be combatted. There are prayers against charms in the ritual. It would seem that the Devil, having established his own ritual for the casting of spells, is obliged to act if the sorcerer observes the formulae he has prescribed. We have been informed that copies of these demonic rites are still in circulation in the French countryside. Books such as *The Red Dragon* and *Albertus Magnus* give the magical formulae which must be employed to injure the objects of one's dislike or jealousy. A sorcerer "casts a spell" and these spells are not always harmless. This has been suggested as a possible explanation of the ups and downs which can occur during exorcism. The Devil flees before the beneficent power of the exorcists, but later returns to the attack. One might almost say that he has gone to complain of his sufferings to the sorcerer who set him to work, and that the sorcerer has ordered him to return to his post. This has been clearly stated by the Abbé Saudreau: "A devil who, after pious exhortation and prayer, may appear to have lost almost all his strength, will sometimes show signs of renewed vigor, and when questioned by the exorcist will be obliged to admit that he owes his renewed strength to magic practices."

Spells, therefore, are effective, and they owe their efficacy to demonic forces. The Abbé Saudreau makes this clear when he says: "Nearly all well-known cases of possession were due to malefice; for instance, the case of Madeleine de la Palud, or Louise Capel of Marseilles, the Ursuline nuns of Loudun, and the Soeurs hospitalières of Louviers."

But the spells themselves are not always of the same strength, and they are the more effective the more sinister the forms in which they are perpetrated. From time immemorial—and even today—there have been forms of sortilege which were deliberately sacrilegious, such as the profanation of the Host, or the impious celebration of the black mass. A celebrated trial in the seventeenth century revealed that the malefices were based on infanticide, crimes against nature, and sacrilegious masses.

In these cases, quoted by the Abbé Saudreau, "the authors of the malefices were outcast priests, and the consecrated Host was hideously desecrated in order to make spells." Finally, there is reason to believe that there is some terrible hierarchy amongst these sorcerers or casters of spells, which reserves to the most perverted and malevolent amongst them the power to "recruit," as one might say, Lucifer's most formidable lieutenants or even Lucifer himself.

Some aspects of this demonic action are still open to conjecture, but that there have been, and still are, pacts with the Devil, seems to be well established. This question, however, will be dealt with later, under the special heading of Satanism.

UNCLARIFIED MYSTERIES

Having dealt with the first two causes of possession, the faults of the victim or, as is more frequently the case, the malefices used against him, the list of possible explanations is still, according to the Abbé Saudreau, not exhausted. There remain cases which do not fall into either category.

Possession can be, and surely sometimes is, an ordeal allowed by God, as in the case of Job, or the Curé d'Ars, without either infestation or possession being attributable to malefice or the faults of the victim. The Devil receives, or obtains at his own request, permission to act. It is a test like any other, and worse than many, but which ends in the confusion of Satan and his pride. The *Grappin*, who finally became an "old friend" of the Curé d'Ars, had no success to boast of, although he had vented on him the full force of his raging spleen. The Curé d'Ars was stealing souls from him. He harassed him unceasingly, without being able to overcome him.

We shall later describe, in the case of Antoine Gay, a devil who was "authorized" to possess a man and then was never allowed to leave him. This case deserves our special attention. But the Abbé Saudreau mentions another very similar case, that of Nicole Aubry of Vervins, the story of whose possession excited the whole of France (1565). She had not been put under any spell. During the exorcisms, the devils declared, most unwillingly, that this possession had occurred by the will of God, to bear witness to the power of Catholic exorcism, and thus to induce the Calvinists of the district to seek conversion. These devils added that they suffered greatly through thus testifying against themselves, and through possessing the woman in question. We shall find exactly the same situation in the case of Antoine Gay. In the case of Nicole Aubry a considerable number of Calvinists were, in fact, converted.

It has been proved true in certain cases of possession that, as St. Augustine says, God prefers to extract good from evil rather than to suppress evil entirely. There have been historical records of souls which have used the suffering of possession in order to attain a high degree of sanctity. "If Marie des Vallées, whose possession was due to malefice," writes the Abbé Saudreau, "had not had the courage to undergo this ordeal, which became a long and terrible martyrdom, she would not have attained that pitch of heroism which earned her the title of the Saint of Coutances" (1590–1656). There is also, as everyone knows, the celebrated case of Fr. Surin, whose ordeal of possession lasted for thirty years, and was the undeniable source of his very great merit.

We know of cases which are impervious to exorcism, to such an extent that the devils themselves are obliged to admit that they would willingly depart, to avoid the pain inflicted on them by exorcism, but *that they cannot leave*, because God does not permit it.

In the historic case of Madeleine de la Palud of Marseilles, which we have already mentioned, exorcism led, in 1611, to the departure of Asmodeus and two other anonymous devils, but by divine permission there remained one, Beelzebub, who would indeed have left had he not been compelled to remain captive in her body.

In similar cases, one of the most striking of which occurred fairly recently, the exorcist may succeed in loosening the fetters of possession. One woman, for instance, prevented from going to Confession and Communion, succeeded in doing so from time to time, as the result of exorcism, but the devil would either not be completely expelled, or would return. In this case the victim was aware of her state and accepted it, knowing the spiritual strength she could draw from it. She knew that she was possessed of a devil, raging like a beast in her heart, but unable to do her any lasting harm.

"The victim of possession," writes the Abbé Saudreau, "continues to suffer, but these sufferings are invaluable to the Church, since the Devil can now only act upon a soul he all unwillingly renders more saintly, and countless weaker souls thereby escape his attentions."

Fr. Boulay, a recent biographer of St. Jean Eudes, declared that there were in his day (1907) more than thirty persons who had thus willingly accepted the role of victim for the salvation of souls. Referring to this, the Abbé Saudreau adds: "we know of several others, in other dioceses, who were unknown to him, and therefore not included in this total." A modern and very active exorcist has also told us that there are such "victims" who offer up their suffering for the clergy of today, who are in such need of it.

However, we should not believe there is no compensation for such dedicated souls. Most of the time it is quite the contrary.

"When devils take possession of a truly religious person," continues the Abbé Saudreau, "God often grants the faithful soul special help from Heaven, which is a counterweight to the extraordinary ordeal imposed from below. If there are demonic visions there are also, frequently, celestial visions: if the devils strike, the guardian angel brings comfort. The saints to whom one has prayed, the angels one has invoked, sometimes ward off the malice of the devils, and aid in the performance of acts of merit which weaken the enemy and speed the soul toward perfection."

To sum up, cases of possession are only the extreme limit of a field which embraces the whole spiritual world, the field of conflict between good and evil, between the City of God and the City of Satan.

Seen in its proper context, possession is only a rather startling episode in this battle for souls. Its justification lies in this very element of visibility. If it is true that "the Devil's deepest wile is to persuade us that he does not exist," here he is guilty of the most flagrant self-contradiction, revealing himself most openly in the illogicality of possession.

Far more terrible than these extreme cases are the cases of invisible possession, cases where Satan has no need to reveal himself, although he is more than ever present, and whispers his diabolic suggestions into the ears of those who are already his own. This was surely the case with that apostle whose name is hardly ever mentioned in the Gospels without the epithet "the Betrayer." No doubt he had not literally invoked Satan, but in the Gospel according to St. John, it is expressly said that after he was given the piece of bread at the Last Supper the Devil entered into him.

St. Augustine, commenting on this verse, remarked: "He entered in order to possess more completely one who had already abandoned himself to him."

TREATMENT

It is clear that there must be a remedy for demonic possession. There is no predestination to evil and damnation, and God therefore would not abandon his creatures to the power of the Devil without providing them with sufficient means to escape his domination.

The remedy provided by God is what we call, by a word taken from the Greek, *exorcism*, which signifies *adjuration*. But there are very precise rules governing the use of exorcism. The first thing to be done is to make sure that it is really a case of possession and not an illness of a natural kind. Reason alone would suffice to suggest the method to be employed; if the subject manifests the presence of an indwelling intelligence other than his own, it is possession and not illness. Later we shall give the exact rules laid down on this essential point by the Roman ritual. But every author is agreed that the onset of possession is usually most insidious. The Devil has long known that exorcism is of general usage in the Church, that it has tremendous power over him, making him suffer physically and morally, that is to say, in his pride. In order to avoid exorcism he tries for weeks and even months to conceal the fact of possession. In one case which we shall mention later, regular exorcisms did not start until three years later. Satan's purpose seems to have been, in this particular case as in many others, to make the possessed woman appear to be mad, so that she would be confined in a psychiatric clinic and deprived of any spiritual intervention. This diabolic strategy had already been exposed by Fr. Surin in the seventeenth century. And the ritual, which embodies the secular experience of the Church, says clearly: "The devils are in the habit of giving mendacious answers, and are with difficulty constrained to manifest themselves, in order to make the exorcist desist, or to persuade him that the patient is not possessed."

These tactics of silence and anonymity are all the easier in that nowadays many doctors, even if they are believers, do not admit the possibility of possession and treat these patients by natural methods, which leave the devils unperturbed. It is therefore a question of striking a very delicate balance, not to assume too hastily it is possession before all possibilities of natural causes have been ruled out, and not to delay too long the use of the treatment laid down by the Church when the facts of possession have been established.

The first symptoms to suggest the possibility of possession are by no means conclusive, but merely indicate a need to keep the suspected person under close observation. According to Saudreau, quoting a specialist of his day, Dr. Helot (*Neurosis and Possession: Diagnosis*), these symptoms are as follows: (1) Convulsions, displaying an intelligence foreign to that of the patient, and frequent alternations of normal and abnormal states; (2) extraordinary movements which could not be produced without long practice, such as jumping, dancing, balancing feats, complicated creeping movements, blows, wounds, falls without apparent cause, twisting of the neck, etc.; (3) distortions, intolerable pain immediately relieved by the application of holy water, the sign of the Cross, a blessed wafer, etc.; (4) sudden loss of senses and feelings, immediately restored by conjuration; (5) animal cries, strange howlings of which the patient is unconscious in the sense that he does not remember them afterwards; (6) strange and demonic visions in an otherwise normal person; (7)

sudden and violent rages caused by the sight of sacred objects or of a priest, or on passing a church when a companion wishes to enter it; (8) inability to swallow or retain blessed food or drinks.

All these symptoms, whether isolated or together, are only indications. They sound a note of warning. When they are observed, all one's courage is needed. The exorcisms will be a battlefield, and the battle may be long and hard. There must be no weakening in face of the difficulties which may arise. The ritual pronounces, with every reason: "The devils erect all possible forms of obstacle, in order to prevent the patient being exorcised."

It is, of course, essential to consult one or more medical men, to obtain their opinion of the case, provided that they are both competent and prudent, that is to say, that they are not unreasonably prejudiced against the possibility of possession, which would lead to a deadlock. Dr. Helot remarked of some of his colleagues: "They have ears but do not hear."

It is obvious that it would be regrettable to start on a process of exorcism that was not justified, as this would cast discredit on the Church. But it would be equally unwise to postpone exorcism indefinitely when it is the only means available of bringing relief to the unfortunate sufferer. For if help is not available at the right moment, it is not only nor even principally the body which is endangered, but also the soul. Once it has been agreed that exorcism is necessary, it should be undertaken without delay, and, the exorcist having prepared for his task by prayer and fasting, all the resources of the Church should be brought to bear. Such intervention is *not* optional. Just as secular law considers it an offence not to go to the assistance of a man in danger, so theology considers it a sin in those who have the cure of souls not to go to the assistance of someone undergoing a demonic assault. Such is Saudreau's opinion: "Moreover, theologians who have written *ex professo* on the subject, declare that there is *mortal sin* in anyone who has a cure of souls if he does not proceed to exercise the possessed. It is therefore clear that there is mortal sin in opposing an exorcism and in preventing help from reaching the unfortunate souls who have to suffer such a terrible spiritual and physical ordeal."

ESTABLISHED CASES

We come now to the evidence required by the ritual to constitute indubitable proof of possession. This evidence consists, in the main, of indications in the patient of an obviously alien intelligence. Such indications are, according to the ritual, as follows: (1) speaking an unknown language, or understanding someone who speaks it; (2) revealing distant or hidden events; (3) the exercise of strength beyond the normal capacity of the patient, allowing for his age and constitution: such as being suspended in the air without any point of support, walking head downwards, with the feet against the ceiling or an arch, remaining motionless in spite of the combined efforts of several strong men, etc.

The examples given are not actually in the ritual, but form part of an authorized commentary on it.

In addition, during the exorcism the priest, armed with authority from his bishop in the case of a public or semi-public exorcism — for private exorcism is permitted to all Christians — will soon find that he is faced with an intelligent adversary, whose repartees will often be unexpected and quite different from those which the subject would have made in a normal state. Thus a devil in possession of a woman, and speaking through her mouth, will always speak of himself in masculine terms, will vaunt himself outrageously — as we shall see later — will reveal hidden things, and will reply with more or less good grace when summoned in the name of God, in the name of Christ, and more particularly, in the name of the Virgin Mary, to give an account of himself. As soon as the devil has been constrained to reveal his quality, "it is as easy," says the Abbé Saudreau, "to establish the fact of possession as it is easy to ascertain any other fact of normal life."

The exorcist must never draw back, never lose patience or courage, but it is most important for him to be prepared, by prayer and mortification, for the very violent battle in which he will be engaged. The struggle against Satan is no small affair. On the contrary, it is deadly earnest and very moving. The exorcist may be assured that the devil will try to be revenged on him for the suffering he will endure. But to console the exorcist is the knowledge that he is the champion of God and Christ against the powers of evil. He has the sure knowledge that by his action he may gain pre-eminent grace, so that he is entitled "to regard the task that falls to him as one of the most powerful means of sanctification which Providence can grant him" (Saudreau).

Incidentally, one of the most urgent tasks of the exorcist is not only to "cure" the possessed person, but also to lead him toward sanctity. There is nothing which can so surely diminish the power and dominion of Satan as the conversion of the victim, if conversion be necessary, or his progress in virtue, if it be not. The vices or failings of the patient were the Devil's departure point in his persecution, and therefore any acts of piety carried out by the patient with the aid of the exorcist are the strongest pledge of the Devil's eventual defeat.

CANON LAW

To conclude this chapter on the doctrine of possession, it is indispensable to mention the provisions of Canon Law regarding exorcism. The articles or canons of the *Codex juris ecclesiastici* are three in number: 1151 to 1153.

Canon 1151: "No one, even though qualified to act as an exorcist, may proceed to the exorcism of obsessed persons without the special and explicit permission of his Ordinary, that is to say, of his Bishop.

"The Bishop will not grant this permission except to a priest known to be pious, prudent, and of irreproachable conduct: and the priest will not undertake the exorcism until it has been adequately established, after cautious and careful examination, that the subject to be exorcised is really possessed by the Devil."

Canon 1152: "Exorcisms practiced by authorized ministers may be undertaken not only for the faithful and for catechumens, but also for non-Catholics and the excommunicated."

Canon 1153: "Those who are authorized to employ the exorcisms used in baptism, consecrations, and benedictions are the legitimate ministers of these sacred rites."

This last canon means that although anyone may, in an emergency, perform a baptism, it is only the minister of solemn baptism, that is, baptism accompanied by the full rites laid down by the Church, and the ministers authorized to perform ritual consecrations and benedictions, who may with episcopal permission practice public and official exorcisms. As a matter of fact, the bishop only gives this permission to hold a solemn exorcism to a priest carefully chosen for his known competence and approved way of living.

$\backsim 4 \backsim$

THE PARTICULAR CASE OF
ANTOINE GAY [1790-1871]

SOURCES

IN VIEW OF the extraordinary events which are to be related in this chapter, it seems particularly advisable to state the sources from which they are drawn.

Under the rather enigmatic title *Le Possédé qui glorifia l'Immaculée*, J. H. Gruninger, a writer from Lyons, has recently (1952) recorded the life and sufferings of Antoine Gay. His documentation was drawn from a booklet written by one Victor de Stenay and published by Delhomme and Briguet in 1896. The name, incidentally, was a pseudonym adopted by M. Blanc, the local president of the Association of Saint-Francois-de-Sales. As a basis for his booklet M. Blanc relied on a notebook compiled by M. Houzelot, an engraver from Paris, who frequently visited Lyons on business. Further, he had a large number of letters, certificates, and reports on Gay's possession, which he had himself collected, and the life of Fr. Chiron—who had taken a deep interest in Gay—written by the Abbé Zéphyrin Gandon and, in addition, the recollections and evidence of many persons who had actually known Antoine Gay.

This case gave rise, it must be said, to the most heated discussion. Many who knew the man considered that the fact of possession was undeniable, and that he could only be relieved by exorcism. But there were doubts and opposition, and the exorcism never in fact took place. There is good reason to believe that this was due to a special dispensation. The author of the book we are about to discuss is convinced that the trials endured by Antoine Gay had a divine purpose, or, as we should call it, a *finality*, similar to that shown in the case of Hélène Poirier.

As in the case of Bernadette Soubirous, this purpose might be seen as the intention of proving the existence of the supernatural in a world increasingly given to doubt and incredulity. In other words, the answer to the often quoted saying of Baudelaire: "The Devil's deepest wile is to persuade us that he does not exist."

The trick could lead us into mortal danger. The Devil desires nothing better than to be free to act without being recognized. But God does not permit this. He is obliged, willy-nilly, to reveal himself. The facts we are about to repeat are a case in point.

EARLY HISTORY

Antoine Gay was born at Lantenay, in the department of Ain, on May 31, 1790. He was baptized the next day and we have his certificate of baptism which records that his father was *notaire royal,* or public notary, at Lantenay, a little village in the canton of Brénod in the district of Nantua. The boy received a very sketchy elementary education but became an excellent carpenter, and after doing his military service under the First Empire, settled in Lyons. As a man he was reasonably good-looking, tall, dark, and with regular features expressive of gentleness and calm. The anti-clerical outbursts of the French Revolution had no effect on his religious development. He was very pious and even, in early youth, had cherished the desire to become a monk. For unknown reasons his entry into a monastery had to be postponed, and it was only in 1836, when he was forty-six, that he applied for admission to the Abbey of La Trappe d'Aiguebelle, to which he was admitted as a lay brother. He was obliged to leave as the result of a nervous disorder, whose true character was not yet apparent. Those who came to know him later are convinced that this nervous disorder was none other than possession. The demon that possessed him was to admit later that he had been there for fifteen years, without anyone, and least of all Gay, knowing anything about it.

When he left La Trappe, however, the signs of possession became increasingly clear. By 1837 Antoine Gay was prey to terrible sufferings. The Devil had laid hold of him.

PROOFS

It is reasonable to require some proof of such a statement. Let us consider what documentary evidence exists.

We have, first of all, in Gruninger's book, a copy of the certificate issued by Fr. Burnoud, former Superior of the Missionaries of La Salette, and addressed to Mgr. Ginoulhiac, at that time Bishop of Grenoble, as follows:

> We have examined Master Gay of Lyons three
> times, each session lasting from one to two hours.
> We consider it very probable that this man is pos-
> sessed by a devil. Our opinion is based on the
> following grounds: (1) he has disclosed several se-
> cret things which he had no means of knowing;
> (2) there were visible signs of discontent when we

pronounced various formulae and prayers of the
ritual in Latin. As it is undeniable that Gay does
not know Latin, we can only attribute these contortions which, in view of the circumstances, had
something preternatural about them, to the presence of a higher intelligence; (3) we questioned
him several times in Latin and since the replies
were made in French through the mouth of Master Gay, this seems to indicate a knowledge of
Latin on the part of that higher intelligence; (4)
the good faith, virtue, and sincerity of Master Gay
are vouched for in numerous testimonials delivered to him by worthy and reliable persons. If
these testimonies are true, Gay is not playing
tricks: in that case, he must be possessed.

However, the conclusion reached by M. Burnoud in this document
is only that of "great probability." Nevertheless, he continued to follow
the case with interest. In a letter written by M. Houzelot to M. Blanc
we find, in fact, the following lines: "I saw Fr. Burnoud, when he was
priest-in-charge of Vinay: he told me that after having examined M.
Gay very carefully, *he was convinced that he was truly possessed.*"

A MEDICAL CERTIFICATE

The following is a medical certificate signed by Dr. Pictet on November 12, 1843:

We, the undersigned, doctors of medicine, resid-
ing at the Croix Rousse, certify that Master Gay
was presented to us for examination by the Abbé

Collet and by M. Nicod, vicar of the town, in accordance with the instructions of Mgr. the Cardinal Archbishop of Lyons, that he should be put under medical observation. Having therefore observed M. Gay scrupulously every day for four months, at all times and in all situations, such as at church, at Mass, accompanying him whilst he made the Stations of the Cross, in public and personal conversation, at table, on walks, etc., we have not been able to discover the least sign of moral or physical weakness. On the contrary, he enjoys perfect health of body and mind, an uncommon strength of judgment and reasoning, which never shows the least deterioration, not even in the extraordinary crises which occur so frequently and so unexpectedly under the influence of some occult power, which we are naturally unable to detect by medical means, and which activates his body and speaks through his mouth, independently of his will.

We certify further that having by prayer and by a total abnegation of ourselves, our science, and our own reason made common cause with M. Gay to implore the assistance of the Holy Spirit, we remain convinced that his extraordinary state can only be attributed to possession. This conviction is reinforced by the fact that during our first interview with M. Gay, that *extraordinary thing* which speaks through his mouth revealed the inmost secrets of our heart, told us the story of our life from the age of twelve

onwards, giving details that are known only to
God, our confessor, and ourselves. And we have
seen the same thing happen with other persons,
many of whom have been converted.

WHY NO EXORCISM?

After such a certificate it seems more than astonishing that the
archbishop did not see fit to authorize an exorcism. In fact, in
spite of all the evidence, this was never done. Taking everything
into consideration, one can only conclude that this was the will
of God. We should, in fact, accept the repeated assertions of the
principal devil that possessed Gay. He never tired of proclaiming,
not perhaps without an element of boastfulness, common to all
devils, "*This case of possession is the most extraordinary that has
ever happened.*"

The extraordinary thing about it was that the devil was there, so
to speak, *on duty*. He was obeying God's orders, and God did not
allow him to be driven out, for that very reason.

In the letter from M. Houzelot to M. Blanc, mentioned above,
we find the following lines:

"I have seen priests ask the devil very difficult questions. He
resolved them immediately, as they themselves have admitted.... *I
have seen the devil weeping as he was forced to admit the truths of the
Christian religion, or to give good advice, or proofs of possession.* 'The
greatest suffering that God can inflict on me,' he would say, 'is to
be obliged to destroy my own work.'"

It is therefore understandable, we think, that God should never
have allowed exorcism in this particular case. It would almost, if
one might presume to say so, have been unjust of God to inflict

the torment of exorcism on a devil who was there, although involuntarily, in obedience to divine omnipotence.

At any rate, whatever the reason, Gay was certainly never exorcised, in spite of the fact that all who met him were convinced he was possessed.

UPS AND DOWNS

It should not be assumed that the authorities who witnessed these strange spiritual adventures cherished any feeling of aversion or distrust toward the unhappy Antoine Gay. On the contrary, as Dr. Pictet's certificate shows, they were convinced of his great merits. In the autumn of 1843, that is to say, after Dr. Pictet's long observations, Gay's friends tried to have him readmitted to the Trappe d'Aiguebelle, where he had been seven years earlier. First of all, the abbot was asked to perform the exorcism. But he raised objections, on the grounds that he was in the Diocese of Valence, whereas the subject was from the Diocese of Lyons. The abbot was, nevertheless, convinced of the fact of possession and sent Gay to his friend, the almoner of the Friars of Privas, in the neighboring Diocese of Viviers. Gay remained there twenty-two days, during which he gave many indications of possession, but he finally returned to Lyons, no exorcism having taken place.

From 1844 to 1847 he was to be found in Lyons, at 72 rue des Macchabées, not far from the church of St. Irénée. He could sometimes be seen wandering about the town, gesticulating and uttering strange words. One day he was arrested as a lunatic and taken to the Antiquaille, where he remained three months, to be released thanks to the kindly intervention of the celebrated Bossan, the future architect of Fourvière. But there was still no exorcism. In 1845 two worthy priests had indeed presented Gay to the Archbishop Mgr. de Bonald, who had received him kindly and promised to make the matter his personal concern. But, for no known reason, there it remained.

FR. CHIRON

A new development occurred when Gay found a fresh protector in the person of a very saintly man, Fr. Marie-Joseph Chiron. Fr. Chiron, whose memory is venerated throughout the Diocese of Viviers, was particularly suited to the task. He had, in fact, founded a community — one of whose aims was to look after the mentally disturbed. He never believed that Gay was mad, but considered that he was possessed and resolved to devote himself to helping him, in so far as God would permit.

Meanwhile Gay had become a tertiary of the Franciscans, under the name of Brother Joseph-Marie.

In 1850, Fr. Chiron left with him for the monastery of Vernetles-Bains, in the Diocese of Perpignan, in order to present him to the bishop and obtain permission to exorcise him. Again, this did not take place, and no one knows why, unless we accept the hypothesis that the Devil was actually there "on duty." During this journey there occurred an episode which sheds some light on a mysterious world.

THE DISPUTE AT PERPIGNAN

In Perpignan Fr. Chiron was taking an interest in a woman with three children who had been possessed for twenty years. A whole parish had seen her running at great speed at a level of about two feet from the ground — a performance which we find repeated by another possessed woman.

Whilst Fr. Chiron was in this woman's house, he was shown another unfortunate woman, nicknamed Chiquette, but whose real name was the Catalan for Francoise. Chiquette, who was thirty-six, was dumb, but she was possessed by a devil called Madeste, who was far from dumb. A dispute of extreme violence immediately arose between Madeste and Isacaron, the devil who inhabited Gay. Fr. Chiron has related the story himself:

> No sooner had he encountered the presence of Isacaron than a remarkably violent dialogue arose between the two fallen angels. The two devils sounded like mad dogs. They spoke a totally unknown language, very softly and we understood nothing. I was later informed by Isacaron, who translated the dispute for me, that it was on a question of precedence, as to which was the greater of the two. They insulted and poured scorn on each other. I was often obliged to stand between them to prevent their coming to blows.
>
> The two possessed, it is needless to say, had never met each other, but the devils in possession knew each other well. Six times during the following days there occurred the same violent disputes, in the same unknown language, and in the presence of several witnesses.
>
> These events created a profound impression on Fr. Chiron. In a letter he wrote a few days later to the Bishop of Clermont-Ferrand, he recounted them in detail, concluding very reasonably: "Such facts are inexplicable except as cases of possession."

After these events Antoine Gay and his protector returned to Lyons to wait until the end of summer before going to La Salette.

A VISIT TO ARS

The reputation of the Curé d'Ars was so great, and Ars so close to Lyons, that it was natural that Gay should be presented to the Abbé Vianney. The Archbishop of Lyons, Mgr. de Bonald himself, issued instructions to M. Goussard, one of Gay's intimate friends: "You will take him to the Curé d'Ars and stay with him several days." So, in 1853, they went to Ars, the pilgrimage lasting fifteen days. M. Houzelot, always deeply interested in the case, went with them. This was at the end of November. The following Sunday, December 8, the little parish of Ars was to celebrate the feast of the Immaculate Conception.

It is relevant to note here that the dogma of the Immaculate Conception had not yet been proclaimed and was not, in fact, promulgated until December 8, 1854.

Then an entirely unexpected event occurred. Antoine Gay was found kneeling at the foot of a statue of the Virgin, his arms extended in the form of a cross, and his eyes filled with tears. From his lips there streamed forth a solemn declaration which could only have come from the infernal spirit that possessed him, since Antoine Gay himself had not the theological background to pronounce such an impressive discourse:

HOMAGE TO MARY FROM A DEVIL

O Mary, Mary, masterpiece of God's handiwork: God has made nothing greater than thee!

Incomparable creation, admiration of all the heavenly host! All honor thee, all obey thee and acknowledge thee as Mother of the Creator. Thou art raised above the angels and above all the court of Heaven: thou art seated near to God, thou art the Temple of Deity, thou hast carried in thy womb all that is strongest and greatest and most powerful and most loving!

Mary, thou hast received in thy virginal womb Him who created thee, thou art Virgin and Mother, there is none to be compared with thee. After God, thou art the greatest; thou art the Strong Woman, there is more glory to God in thee than in the heavenly host.

In thee there has been no stain, Anathema be they that deny that thou art Virgin and Mother; thou wast conceived without sin, thou art *immaculate*!

I praise thee, O Mary, *but all my praises of thee ascend unto God, the author of all good.* After the Sacred Heart of Jesus there is no heart to be compared with thine. O loving heart! O tender heart! Thou wilt not abandon even the most thankless or the most guilty of mortals. Thy heart is overflowing with kindness, even to the unfortunate who merit chastisement alone, yet thou obtain for them grace and compassion: the worst of sinners is converted by thee!

O, if all the inhabitants of the earth should know thee! If they could understand thy tenderness, thy power, thy goodness, not one of them should perish! All that turn to thee in trust and hope and pray to thee continually, whatever their state may be, thou wilt save them, thou wilt bless them eternally.... *I am compelled to*

humble myself at thy feet and implore thy pardon
for all the outrages I inflict on the one I possess!
I confess today, one of the most solemn feasts of
the whole year, that thy divine Son compels me to
say that it is the most solemn of all the feasts.

Thus spoke Isacaron, the devil of impurity, through the mouth of Antoine Gay, and the words were noted by M. Houzelot, who has handed them down. After this enforced confession, we understand more clearly why Mary, five years later, should have answered Bernadette's plea to reveal her name, by saying: "I am the Immaculate Conception!"

The Abbé Toccanier, assistant to the saintly Curé d'Ars, was present when this memorable panegyric to the Blessed Virgin was pronounced by Isacaron.

It occurred to M. Houzelot to ask Isacaron to dictate more slowly all that he had said, so that he could write it down, and the devil complied. The Abbé Toccanier could not conceal his emotion. "There has been nothing like it since the Fathers of the Church," he declared to the onlookers. Incidentally, on another occasion, he undertook a theological discussion with the devil, and was amazed at his capacity for close and accurate reasoning, in the most orthodox terms.

STILL NO EXORCISM

The possessed man had, however, come to Ars with the hope of being delivered of his troubles. It was hoped that the saint would be able to exercise the same power over Antoine Gay as he had done over so many others.

Although at this time the Abbé Vianney was much in request and difficult to approach, Antoine Gay was brought to him several times and the Curé took him into his house. One evening in particular, the good Curé was astonished to see Antoine Gay fall down suddenly at his feet, as if he had been brutally struck down by some unknown force. But at the same time the possessed man shook his fist at him and shouted at him in threatening tones: "Vianney, you are a thief! You are stealing from us the souls we have had such difficulty in winning!"

On hearing this the saint was content to make the sign of the Cross over Gay's head. The devil was heard to utter a cry of horror.

However, it was decided that exorcism should take place. The Curé was totally convinced that he was really dealing with a case of possession. At his request, the Abbé Goussard therefore went back to ask Cardinal de Bonald for permission to employ exorcism.

"The Curé d'Ars," replied the archbishop, "has no need of my permission; he knows very well that I grant it: or he should perhaps approach Mgr. de Belley."

Without delay the Abbé Toccanier wrote to Mgr. Chalandon, then bishop of Belley, and immediately received the required permission. And yet exorcism was once again postponed and finally omitted. Why? The Curé d'Ars felt it would be better to perform the ceremony with great solemnity at Fourvière, in the sanctuary of the Blessed Virgin.

But time passed and no decision to this effect was made. Antoine Gay was taken back to Lyons without having been delivered from his intolerable companion. Here again it is difficult not to believe that God did not wish for any termination: firstly, Antoine Gay was steadily gaining in spirituality by means of his ordeal, and secondly, the devil within him had to complete the task he had been assigned. Let us consider this latter point first:

A PAGE FROM ST. GRIGNION DE MONTFORT

It may at first seem astonishing to find a devil, such as the one that possessed Antoine Gay, accepting so humbly the role of pronouncing a solemn eulogy of the Blessed Virgin, both at Ars and on several other occasions during the forty years he tormented the unfortunate man. But it is sufficient to recall the remarks of St. Louis Grignion de Montfort in his celebrated treatise *Concerning True Devotion to the Blessed Virgin.* Speaking of the hostility between Mary and Satan, the saint writes:

> God has only fashioned and shaped one enmity, and that an irreconcilable one, which will endure and even increase, until the end: it is that between the Virgin Mary and the Devil, between the children and servants of the Blessed Virgin and the children and accomplices of Satan; so that the most terrible of the enemies of Satan created by God is Mary, his Blessed Mother. Even from the days of the Earthly Paradise, when she was still only a thought in the mind of God, he endowed her with so much hatred of this accursed enemy of God, so much concern to expose the malice of this old serpent, so much strength to overcome, cast down, and trample on his impious pride, that the Devil fears her more, not only than men and angels but, in a certain sense, than God himself. It is not that the wrath, the power, and the hatred of God are not infinitely greater than those of the Blessed Virgin, since Mary's perfections are limited: it is because, in the first place, Satan, being proud, suffers infinitely more from being overcome and punished by the little, humble servant of God, her humility humiliating him more than the divine power;

and secondly, because God has given Mary such great power over devils that, *as they have often been obliged to admit, in spite of themselves, through the mouths of possessed persons,* they are more afraid of one of her sighs of grief over some poor soul, than of the prayers of the saints, and more daunted by a single threat from her than by all their other torments.

And this is precisely what we have heard confirmed by the words of Antoine Gay, the mouthpiece of the Devil Isacaron.

We shall now hear further evidence from the same personage in the role imposed on him by Providence.

A PATHETIC STRUGGLE

Those who heard Antoine Gay, and they were many, have all confirmed that he gave evidence of a strange duality. This duality was not only between him and the devil who possessed him, but also between the various modes of speech used by that devil himself.

It was easy to distinguish the natural tones of the true Antoine Gay. He always expressed himself in a gentle voice, slowly, and with obvious goodness, and always in terms of the utmost courtesy.

When the principal of the three devils who had taken up their abode in him spoke — that is, Isacaron — his voice became curt, imperious, and passionate; he adopted a tone of authority, addressing everyone as "tu," without compromise or discrimination, even if he were addressing the highest dignitaries of the Church.

In the words he used, however, one could distinguish two quite different scales of value. Sometimes he spoke, as one might say, in his capacity as devil — which was indeed necessary, so that his nature might be known — and then he would display his rage by grinding his teeth and blaspheming horribly. His hideousness was reflected in the features of the possessed man, and all who saw him in this state affirmed that he was hateful both to hear and to look at. This was the first scale, the infernal scale, to call it by its right name.

But when he was acquitting himself of the task laid upon him, when he was expressing himself as the slave of God, and *playing his allotted role*, he was not only orthodox in his remarks, but would speak in an unctuous, eloquent, sometimes even sublime tone.

In the course of a single dialogue both possessor and possessed would take it in turns to speak, and it was possible to see the heart-rending conflict which was taking place in the heart and mind of Antoine Gay. For instance, he would be speaking, deploring his state, and giving proof of his very genuine piety. Suddenly, and without transition, Isacaron would intervene through his mouth. His voice would change, becoming raucous and producing an outburst of shouting, laden with insults and abuse. The man who had previously been all gentleness and humility suddenly became bitter, sarcastic, and foul-mouthed.

CONFESSIONS OF A DEVIL

But what is astonishing, and almost unparalleled in previous records, is the admission of the devil himself that he had been given a mission, which he must fulfil whether he liked it or not. This was no single assertion, but one made ten times a day: "I am compelled to praise Thee, O sovereign Lord," he cried. "All creatures are compelled to acknowledge Thee, to acknowledge Thy power, Thy goodness, and also Thy terrible justice!"

"I, Isacaron, prince of the devils of impurity, am compelled by Him Who is everything, to see that all these many things are written down."

At this time, in fact, the persons present, and particularly M. Houzelot, were constantly making notes of all that he said. And the voice continued:

> Must I then serve as an instrument for man's instruction, when my chief delight is in their destruction?
>
> I am constrained to speak of things which seem to astonish even the wisest: I speak to the glory of the Almighty, to the shame and confusion of infernal spirits.
>
> It is Heaven's will, which all must obey, that I, the devil Isacaron, possessing the body of Gay, should speak through his mouth, and through his limbs, make horrible grimaces, utter terrifying cries. I, who am forced by God to give daily proof of my presence in this man.
>
> O great Master, how Thou dost make me suffer. I am compelled to dismantle my ramparts, my strongholds. Cursed be the day when I entered this body. I should never have thought it possible that I should be thus forced to labor for the glory of the All-Highest, to labor for the conversion of souls!

There is abundant proof that Isacaron wished to be relieved of his task, that he would have liked the exorcism to take place so that he could depart. One day, when someone was talking about Fr. de Ravignan, who had been appointed to succeed Lacordaire in charge of the *Conférences de Notre-Dame,* the devil called out through Gay's mouth: "That is a man! That is a priest! You shall tell him to say a

Mass for the deliverance of the possessed, and to have my power over his body removed before his deliverance."

A SERMON

The following scene was recorded by Brother Prime, of the Christian schools at Feurs (Loire).

Fr. Chiron, on his way from Lyons to Clermont-Ferrand with Antoine Gay, wrote to Prime that he would stop en route at Feurs, with a possessed man. When they arrived Brother Prime and the whole community stared at Fr. Chiron's travelling companion. What they saw was a very composed, obviously respectable, and even affable man. The brother could not believe his eyes. He whispered in Fr. Chiron's ear: "Didn't you say you had a possessed man with you?"

But scarcely had the remark passed his lips when the expression of this obviously respectable man underwent a sudden change. "Foaming at the mouth, his eyes bloodshot, his tone of voice made me blench," wrote Brother Prime. "Don't you see me?" he asked. "I believe," added the friar, "that if Fr. Chiron had not supported me, I should have collapsed in terror."

And it was always the same. Just when it was least expected, poor Gay was suddenly involved in incredible contortions, throwing himself to the ground, or twirling on his heels without ever losing his balance. But although constitutionally a heavy man, he became endowed with extraordinary agility and suppleness. One day he aimed a kick with his left leg at the head of a very tall questioner and recovered his stance as easily as an acrobat. Yet when scenes of fury were expected there was often another very sudden change. His eyes would fill with tears. The devil's voice became softer. From the same lips that had uttered such outrageous comments, there would issue a sermon, such as follows:

The evildoer is not happy. If one is full of oneself, one is full of a devilish spirit. We destroy men's souls through their senses.

God makes use of men to test them. If you suffer affliction, receive it as an act of grace. The Cross is preferable to all things. God carried the Cross for the salvation of men, and He makes those whom He loves carry it too.

The world believes that humility is weakness and incapacity: and I say that humility is power and grandeur.

If you knew the misery of the reprobate, you would all be saints!

There is no language to describe the torments of the damned; there is no human mind able to comprehend them.

He who loves men more than God will not be loved by God.

God allows misfortunes for the spiritual betterment of men; in order to bring them to Himself and make them return to Him.

Never forget that crosses are better than honors.

We must understand that life is short and that we must endure our troubles in a spirit of penitence, as they came from God.

One cannot love God without loving one's neighbor. Happy are they who can leave all for God.

Ah, if only men could see how beautiful is a soul in a state of grace.

Happiness is not here below: he who possesses God possesses everything.

The rich should be the banker of the poor. God has put these riches into his hand to help his fellow men: he is God's businessman.

The rich man should despise himself and follow the teaching of our Savior, Who said: "It is easier for a camel to pass through the eye of a needle, than for a rich man to enter into the kingdom of God" (Mark 10:25).

But, strange to relate, Isacaron had no sooner pronounced these edifying remarks than he fell into a rage and began to blaspheme God, insult God's creatures, even insult himself. "Woe to the proud," he cried, "Woe to me, Isacaron. It was pride, ingratitude, and disobedience that led to my rebellion and damnation."

ISACARON'S REFLECTIONS

Here are some further reflections by Isacaron on various subjects:

On Pilate: Pilate, as a judge, knew that he was condemning an innocent Man, and yet the Devil drove him to condemn the sovereign Judge, the Judge of judges. Pilate, by washing his hands, soiled them.

On Mary Magdalene (from whom, according to the Gospels, Our Lord drove out seven devils): Mary Magdalene is a very great saint, in whom one can put one's utmost trust. As soon as she had the good fortune to know God, her contrition was so great, her tears so abundant, that no devil could make her sin again. She is a model for all true penitents, who should make her their special advocate with God, for God grants great favor to those who invoke her aid.

On meditation: If you meditate truly on the life of our Savior and of His Blessed Mother, I defy you to commit the slightest sin against God.

Hunger, thirst, death, are nothing: only sin is to be feared.

On Christian perfection, replying to a lady who asked Isacaron to tell her the nature of Christian perfection, and the way to attain it, he said:

To hold mortal sin in horror; not to commit even venial sins voluntarily; not to lose sight of the presence of God; to know how to humble oneself all the days of one's life, for pride is the worst of all vices; to set a good example and give good advice; to do penance, as the Forerunner demanded. And let him who is holy become still more holy.

Prayer to Mary: To conclude these aphorisms from so strange a source, here is a prayer to Mary, composed and dictated by the devil Isacaron:

PRAYER

O divine Mary,
I turn toward you
In total trust,
For you abandon no one.
You who have at heart
The salvation of man,

To whom God refuses nothing
That you ask Him.
Take me under your powerful wing.
If you deign to grant
My humble prayers
All hell is harmless against me.
You who are, in some way,
The mistress of my fate,
My fate is in your hands.
If you abandon me
I am lost without help!
No, you are too good
To neglect those who hope in you.
Pray to the Holy Trinity for me
And I am sure of my salvation!
Ah, if I could make you known
To all dwellers on earth,
If I could proclaim
Your power everywhere!
That which I cannot do myself
I beg the Heavenly Hosts to do.
Let even devils be obliged
To proclaim that you
Are the masterpiece of God's works,
That the power of God lies in your hands,
That you are terrible to devils,
And that all is subject to you.
You are the incomparable,
You alone are Virgin and Mother,
You gave the world its Redeemer.
You stand apart with St. Joseph.

Thus you are more to be revered
Than all the angels and all the saints:
You are truly divine.
I trust in you, in the firm belief
That the infernal powers
Cannot triumph over me.
So be it!
All the angels, all the saints
Bless you forever!
So be it!

Having made this prayer, we are told that the devil suddenly became jovial and, alluding to the fact that Antoine Gay had been shut up for three months as a madman at the Antiquaille in Lyons, remarked: "They can go and look in all the asylums before they find a madman who can dictate a prayer like that!"[12]

THE END OF ANTOINE GAY

It is clear that the life of Antoine Gay was something quite exceptional. There had been a remarkable case in the seventeenth century where possession had led to the sanctification of the possessed man, after the most terrifying ordeals. It was the case of Fr. Surin, a Jesuit, who suffered from demonic possession for twenty years, after taking part in the exorcisms of the Ursuline Sisters at Loudun. Antoine Gay's case is a little different, but both have one undeniable trait in common: their sanctification. Gay's later years were marked by a general neglect, even more terrible perhaps than possession itself.

[12] For further details on Antoine Gay, see J.H. Gruninger, *Le Possédé qui glorifia l'Immaculée* (Lyons: Editions & imprimeries du Sud-est, 1953).

Fr. Chiron, who had taken so much care of him, died in 1852. The Curé d'Ars, who had also taken an interest in him, departed this world in 1859. Antoine Gay lived another twelve years, but there was no longer anyone to come to his aid, at least in any lasting way. Yet he accepted everything with a marvelous resignation. His family was ashamed of him. Two of his sisters were antagonistic. The younger of the two prevented her two children from going to see their uncle. Yet when she was ill, Antoine Gay, out of the simple goodness of his heart, gave her 200 francs—in those days a considerable sum—for medical treatment. The devil was always there. Antoine Gay struggled tenaciously against his cruel enemy by a life of prayer and strict penitence. He lived like one of the Desert Fathers: fasting on bread and water, sleeping on a bare plank, wearing a hair shirt, and scourging himself.

For the last six years of his life, he was looked after in his humble lodging, 72 rue des Macchabées, by pious and charitable Lyonnais, particularly by one compassionate lady who remained at his side for many hours at a time. These visits were a great consolation to him, for the devil tormented him less in the presence of certain persons.

But he had one more ordeal to undergo, a trial which we find repeated in more recent cases: Isacaron, the master of his body, did not want him to go to Confession, as he would have wished to do. Isacaron was adamant. He declared that Gay should not go to Confession before he had been exorcised. One can only understand this insistence if we suppose that the devil was himself under some fortunate restraint. He was there, we have seen, "on duty," and he was acting a role that was a peculiar torture for him. He would therefore have preferred to have been liberated by exorcism. And since this exorcism did not take place, he hoped at least to destroy the soul of the unfortunate being from whom he could not escape, by keeping him away from the Sacraments.

He was very precise on this point:

"You shall not go to confession until I am free!" And he added: "There has never been a possession like mine, and there will never be another." Which we may well believe.

The devil, in fact, once prevented Antoine Gay from going to Mass for a period of three weeks. One day Fr. Perrier came to see him, in company with M. Blanc. Fr. Perrier had formerly been at the Jesuit house at Lalouvesc, where he had met Antoine Gay. He had just been sent to Lyons and visited the possessed man with a view to making his confession easier. But Isacaron once again insisted that Gay should make no confession until he had been exorcised and Isacaron liberated. The two visitors waited, but in vain. As long as they were there, Gay was unable to speak a word.

In 1869 Gay, then seventy-nine, returned for a few weeks to Lantenay, his birthplace, to settle some matter of a legacy which was causing a dispute between him and his family. In a letter to the lady in Lyons who used to come and see him, he wrote these pathetic lines: "The devil is causing me more suffering than at Lyons. I want people to say many prayers for me, for my end is approaching. I don't know when I shall be able to get back to Lyons; obstacles keep cropping up, everybody takes the devil's side. My affliction is increasing. I beg you to present my humble regards to the Rev. Fr. Perrier. Kindly tell him that I commend myself to his prayers, and beg that he should not forget me when he celebrates the Sacrament of the Mass."

And as postscript, these words: "The infamous Isacaron says to me: 'Reply quickly.'"

After this letter Antoine Gay returned to Lyons, where he soon fell into a pitiable state. People shook their heads with compassion as he passed. He could be heard to say: "I cannot stay any longer in my miserable tenement." His inner enemy allowed him no respite. He would weep continuously. Yet his faith remained. "All that I can say or do," he would say, "is to appeal to the Blessed Virgin and to St. Joseph, to help me." During the war of 1870–1871, which the devil had foretold through his mouth, he was more afflicted than ever. Isacaron obliged him to remain for hours on end with his arms outstretched in the form of a cross. He knew that his end was near at hand. On June 4, 1871, Mme. T., the kindly woman who used to visit him from time to time, found him very ill, and stayed with him for an hour and a half. He kept repeating that his end was near, but that he would not be delivered from his enemy. For two months his state of weakness had prevented him from going to Mass. The vicar of St. Irénée, who lived nearby, was warned of his condition by Mme T. Once again, he tried to hear his confession. It was the June 13, the feast of St. Anthony of Padua. The priest's every effort was unsuccessful. "Not before exorcism," said Isacaron. And after these astonishing words, Antoine Gay, under demonic pressure, became dumb. The priest nevertheless gave absolution and Extreme Unction to the dying man, which he received with every sign of the deepest piety. A quarter of an hour later he died, in the presence of the priest, who rendered every assistance possible. For more than half a century this valiant Christian had lived in bonds of close and painful proximity to a prince of darkness.

The registration of Antoine Gay's death is to be found in the parish church of St. Irénée, as follows:

"On June 14 in the year 1871, I gave Christian burial to Antoine-Louis Gay, deceased on the 13th of this month, at the age of eighty-one," signed: Chazelle, assistant priest.

In addition to those who knew him well and had shown him sympathy, mention should be made of such persons as Père Chiron, the Curé d'Ars, Père Perrier, l'Abbé Toccanier, and such eminent people as R. P. Collin, founder of the Manst Fathers, l'Abbé Chevrier, founder of the Prado, and many others.

⌒ 5 ⌒

CASES OF POSSESSION IN THE NINETEENTH AND TWENTIETH CENTURIES

IN THIS CHAPTER we propose to group together certain cases of possession spread over the latter half of the nineteenth century and the first half of the twentieth. We shall start, once again, at Ars. But now we shall consider its saintly Curé, not as the subject of demonic infestations, but as casting out devils by the power of his exorcisms.

First, there is an incident witnessed by the village farrier, who gave evidence at the process of canonization.

A possessed woman had been brought to Ars by her husband. She was in a rage, uttering inarticulate cries, so that no one could understand what she was saying. The Curé d'Ars, having examined her, realized that she was a victim of demonic activity, and said that she should be taken back and presented to the bishop of her diocese. Suddenly the woman recovered the power of speech and began to curse:

"What's that? The *creature* shall go back? ... Ah, if I only had Christ's power, I would swallow you up in Hell!"

"So you know of Christ?" the Abbé Vianney rejoined immediately. "Well, then, take her to the foot of the high altar."

Four men took hold of her, and in spite of her resistance, placed her at the foot of the altar. Then the Abbé Vianney took out the great reliquary which he always carried with him and placed it on the woman's head. She collapsed as if she were dead. After a moment, however, she stood up of her own accord and left the church with rapid steps. An hour later she came back, very calm, took some holy water, crossed herself, and fell to her knees. She was completely delivered. She stayed three days more at Ars with her husband, amazing all the pilgrims by her great composure and piety.

The Curé's action was equally efficacious in the next case, that of a woman who came with her son from the region of Clermont-Ferrand. This woman had been afflicted for forty years, and it was considered that she was possessed of a devil. At Ars she gave evident signs of possession. She was observed singing and dancing a large part of the day, close to the church. This, of itself, might have been simple mania. But what was significant was that when someone caused her to drink a few drops of holy water, she became suddenly furious and began to bite the walls of the church.

A passing priest took pity on her and led her down a path between the presbytery and the church, to a place where the Abbé Vianney would see her as he passed. The saint, in fact, soon arrived and gave the woman, whose mouth was bleeding, his blessing. Immediately the unfortunate woman became quite calm, and the terrible crises she had endured for so many years never reappeared.

A third case came from the Diocese of Avignon. A young woman teacher who gave signs of possession was brought to the Curé d'Ars on the order of the bishop, who had personally studied her case. She was accompanied by a priest from the parish of St. Pierre d'Avignon, and by the Mother Superior of the Franciscan nuns of Orange. They reached Ars on the evening of December 27, 1857. On the following morning she was brought to the sacristy at the moment when the saint was vesting himself for the celebration of the Mass. The possessed woman immediately began to cry out and try to leave the room.

"There are too many people here," she protested.

"There are too many people?" answered the Curé. "Very well, they can leave."

And at a sign from him he was left alone, face to face with Satan. From within the church, they could at first hear nothing but a confused and violent noise. Then voices were raised. The priest from Avignon, stationed near the door, overheard the following dialogue:

"You are determined to go out?" asked the Abbé Vianney.

"Yes."

"And why?"

"Because I am with a man I don't like."

"So you don't like me?" enquired the Curé, ironically.

"*No*," shouted the infernal spirit, and this "no" was shrill and furious.

But soon afterwards the sacristy door opened, and all could see the young teacher, weeping for joy, and now modest and collected, with an expression of gratitude on her face. But then suddenly she was seized with panic and turned to the Curé:

"I am terrified lest *he* should come back."

"He will not, my child," replied the saint, "or at any rate, not immediately."

The girl was able to return to her home and start work again as a teacher in Orange. And *he* did not come back.

Another memorable example of the Abbé Vianney's encounters with Satan occurred on the afternoon of January 23, 1840. A woman from the neighborhood of Puy in the Haute Loire had just knelt down in the confessional of the saintly Curé. As he was urging the woman to start her confession, he suddenly heard a loud, bitter voice crying:

"I've only committed one sin, and anyone who likes can have *that*! Raise your hand and give me absolution! You've given me absolution before, you know, because I am often beside you in the confessional."

The Abbé Vianney realized that he was dealing with a devil, but to confirm it, asked him in Latin the ritual question:

"*Tu quis es?*" (Who are you?).

"*Magister caput*" (the chief master) replied the other, and then continued in French:

"Black toad, you make me suffer too much. You are always saying you want to leave. Well, why don't you? Other black toads wouldn't hurt me so much."

"I shall write to Monseigneur," replied the Curé, "to get you to leave."

"Yes, but I shall make your hand shake so much that you won't be able to write.... I shall get you! I've got stronger people than you!... And you, you're not dead yet! If it hadn't been for that ... [a coarse epithet for the Virgin Mary] up there we should have got you long ago: but she protects you, with that great dragon [St. Michael, presumably] which is on the door of your church.... Say, why do you get up so early in the morning? Your *purple gown* [your bishop] told you not to. Why do you preach so simply? It makes you look ignorant. Why don't you preach in a big way, as they do in towns?"

The tirade continued for a long time, with fulminations against various bishops and categories of priests. But Satan had to admit, in spite of himself, that he had met his match in that stout servant of God, the Curé d'Ars. Mgr. Trochu, from whom the story comes, does not say how the battle ended, but we may suppose that it ended as satisfactorily as others had done.

In this case, we may note, there was both possession of the woman, and infestation of the Curé.

To conclude, there was the case of a possessed woman treated by the Abbé Vianney toward the very end of his life, on July 25, 1859. The following day he was to take to his bed, never to rise again. At about 8 o'clock that evening, a woman, "said to be possessed," was brought with some difficulty to the Curé. Her husband was with her and they came to the presbytery together, where the Abbé received them. It is not exactly clear what happened, except that the woman was liberated. The little group of people waiting at the presbytery door saw her suddenly emerge, free and happy. One of them reported that "we could hear a sound like a violent breaking of branches inside the courtyard. There was such a noise that everyone there was alarmed." "Yet," added M. Oriol, in his deposition, "when I went in after the evening service, none of the elder trees was damaged."

Once again it was a case both of possession and infestation.

POSSESSIONS AT ILLFURTH

From Ars, scene of so many cases of possession brought thither from all parts of France, we pass to Alsace. The Curé d'Ars had died on August 4, 1859. The facts of possession we are now reporting occurred at Illfurth between 1864 and 1869. Illfurth, a large village with, at that time, about 1,200 inhabitants, is situated about five miles from Altkirch on the junction of the Ill and the Largue, and on the Rhine-Rhone canal, in the region of Mulhouse.

The victims were two brothers, Thiébaud Burner, aged nine, and Joseph, who was only seven. Toward the end of 1864 they began to produce symptoms which puzzled all the doctors. In September 1865 the phenomena produced were quite abnormal. For instance, if the boys were sleeping on their backs, they could turn over and over, like living tops, at an incredible speed. But this was not all: they were sometimes overcome by an insatiable hunger. Their stomachs swelled to an alarming degree. They would explain this by saying they had something like a ball in their stomachs and that a live animal was running up and down inside them.

Neither was this all: sometimes when they were sitting on a chair, the chair, with them in it, was lifted up and held suspended in the air by an invisible hand. As we have already seen, M. Saudreau quotes such phenomena as precursors of possession. There were many witnesses to these facts in Illfurth, sober, well-balanced, educated persons, not liable to give credit to such extraordinary events without sufficient evidence. M. J. H. Gruninger states that his own father was among the witnesses to these events at Illfurth, and used often to recount what had happened, which was a topic of discussion throughout the neighborhood.

Naturally enough, in an enlightened diocese like Strasbourg, it soon occurred to both priests and laymen that it might well be a case of possession. Investigations were undertaken on this basis, and there were attempts at exorcism, during which the devils were called on to state their names.

We have already heard the Curé d'Ars pronouncing, on a similar occasion, the sacramental words: *Tu quis es?* But when these particular spirits were summoned to declare themselves, they demurred for a long time, no doubt finding themselves confronted by a lesser spiritual authority than that of the saint of Ars. Finally, however, it was discovered that there were at least two evil spirits in each child. The elder, Thiébaud, was being tormented by two devils who claimed to be called Ypés and Oripas. The younger brother was possessed by one devil called Zolalethiel and by another whose name was never discovered.

The indications of possession required by the Roman ritual were fulfilled in this case by the fact that they spoke many languages, or at least replied to questions put to them in Latin, English, French,

German, or in the local dialect. This knowledge of languages which they had never learnt was in itself significant. Another indication was their insurmountable aversion to holy water, or to any blessed object. A third was their prediction of forthcoming events. A careful watch over the two boys revealed nothing. They evinced a knowledge quite out of keeping with their age or education, in that they could always answer any question put to them, even on difficult or embarrassing subjects. Since this knowledge was obviously unnatural, it could only be supernatural, and in view of the circumstances, everything went to show that it was of diabolic and not angelic inspiration.

The facts of the case were soon known throughout Alsace, and the story spread to Paris. The Bishop of Strasbourg, as in duty bound, ordered an enquiry. Similarly, the sub-prefect of Mulhouse, at the request of the Prefecture of the Haut-Rhin, ordered the head of the local gendarmerie, M. Werner, to present a report on the case.

Werner thereupon visited Illfurth. If in any sense he was prejudiced, it was against a belief in such phenomena. He was convinced that any belief in the Devil, in the middle of the nineteenth century, was unpardonably childish. But he was soon undeceived. It was clear that something beyond his understanding was happening at Illfurth.

The ecclesiastical authorities, on the other hand, had long since come to the inevitable conclusion that exorcism should be used. It was now 1869 and the boys were fourteen and twelve, respectively. Their "bedevilment" had lasted five years.

Their deliverance was to be secured in two stages: one brother after the other.

DELIVERANCE OF THIÉBAUD

We owe our account of the exorcism, which took place in the orphanage of St. Charles at Schiltigheim, to a recent book by M.

Suter, the Curé of Eichofen in Alsace, and Francois Gaquère, *docteur-ès-lettres,* doctor of theology, and Canon of Arras.[13]

The first thing to note about this exorcism is that the boy, although brought up in a Christian family, had a horror of sacred objects.

"For him," says this book, "a church was a pigsty; holy water was dirt; priests, just sky-pilots in black skirts; nursing sisters, old hags; Catholics, dirty twisters; children, noisy brats."

This is obviously the Devil speaking through his mouth. When the Devil was present the child fell into a sort of trance, lying prostrate like a corpse. Although normally a good-looking boy, if somewhat pale and melancholic, at such times he looked like a neglected waif.

When he was taken to the orphanage, he appeared calm and did nothing except play or walk about in the courtyard. Although he had never spoken French, he spoke it faultlessly in reply to questions, even answering in Latin if he was questioned in Latin, although he never took the initiative in using this language, which he had never learnt. He moved about freely except to the chapel. As soon as he approached this consecrated spot, even if he was blindfolded so that he should not know where he was going, he would stiffen, baying like a hound, and refusing to move. His expression became terrible. If sprinkled with holy water he would squirm like a crushed worm, and only became calm if he was allowed to go away. The day chosen for the exorcism was Sunday, October 3, 1869. The boy had to be carried into the chapel by three men, M. Schrantzer, M. Hausser, and the gardener, André. They strapped him into a chair, which was put on a carpet in front of the Communion table and firmly held

---

[13]   Paul Sutter and Francois Gaquère, *Aux Prises avec Satan: Les Possédés d'Illfurth* (Genval, Belgium: Editions Marie-Médiatrice, 1957).

in place by the three men. The boy's face was toward the tabernacle. His cheeks were flushed, and the foam from his lips trickled down to the floor. He was turning and twisting in every direction, as if on a grille, and kept looking for the door.

The exorcist was Fr. Souquat, delegated to this task by Mgr. Raess, Bishop of Strasbourg. He was for a moment dumbfounded when, from the lips of this child whom he scarcely knew, he heard a brutal adjuration, in a harsh violent voice:

"Get the hell out of here, you bastard!"

Only temporarily at a loss, the exorcist, surrounded by many church dignitaries, pulled himself together and began the litany of the saints. At the words: "Holy Mary, pray for us!" the Devil uttered a terrible cry: "Get out, you swine! I don't want it!" At each invocation he repeated the same words. He cried out even louder at the words: "Holy angels and archangels, pray for us!" A little later, as the exorcist pronounced the words: "Deliver us, O Lord, from the wiles of the Devil!" the boy shivered and his whole body began to tremble. He began to howl savagely, and his struggles became so violent that the three men had difficulty in holding him down.

After the litanies the father went and stood in front of the boy and continued the prayers of the ritual.

The boy was still shouting "Get out, you swine!" But when the exorcist came to the Latin words *Gloria Patri et Filio,* the Devil, through the mouth of the unfortunate boy, who knew no Latin, protested: "I don't want to!" which was interpreted as meaning "I do not want to glorify the Father, the Son, and the Holy Ghost." Before reading the Gospel according to St. John over the boy, as is laid down in the ritual, the father made the Sign of the Cross over him, over his forehead, his mouth, and his heart, and this led to further howls. The possessed boy even tried to bite his hand. Then there began a dialogue, in German, between Fr. Souquat and the demon.

"Spirit of darkness, vanquished serpent, I, priest of God, order you in His Name to tell me who you are."

"It's none of your business, you dirty beast. I will tell you when I want to."

"That is your pride; those are the haughty words you used to the Almighty when He cast you out from Heaven. But I repeat, leave us, Satan, leave this church. You do not belong in the House of God, but in the House of Shadows!"

"No," cried Satan, "I don't want to: my time has not yet come."

The exorcism lasted three hours. The priest was worn out and dripping with sweat. He had to suspend the ceremony. As soon as the boy was taken out of the chapel he quietened down.

That evening he made an odd remark to the Abbé Schrantzer, who had brought the exorcist in a carriage.

"You were quite right to slip him a medallion."

"Slip who a medallion?"

"Why, the coachman, of course."

The Abbé had, in fact, given the coachman a medallion of St. Benedict, but he was sure the boy had not seen him do so. So he questioned him again:

"How do you know? And what would you have done if I hadn't?"

"I should have upset the whole carriage, all the people and the horses too. I was galloping along beside you."

"Well, you must admit we gave you a lot of trouble. Do you know who gave you the blessing?"

"Of course I do. He has already driven out one of our strongest."

Fr. Souquat had, in fact, exorcised a house of its devil many years previously. But how could the boy know that? These little details merely confirmed Fr. Souquat in his belief that Thiébaud was truly possessed. He prepared therefore for a second session.

THE SUPREME MOMENT

The following day, Monday, October 4, 1869, at 2 o'clock in the afternoon, in the presence of many witnesses, the exorcism began again.

The boy was put in a straight-jacket and firmly strapped down in his red armchair. The Devil was not thereby prevented from displaying his powers. The armchair was suddenly seen to rise in the air, in spite of the efforts of three strong men who were clinging to it desperately in an effort to keep it on the ground. They were thrown violently from side to side, whilst the possessed boy yelled horribly, jets of foam streaming from his mouth.

However, the chair settled down and the exorcism began. After two hours, having recited the litanies and said the preliminary prayers of the ritual, the priest rose from his knees and began to question the Devil again.

"Now, spirit of evil, your time has come. In the name of the Catholic Church, in the name of God, in my name, as priest of God, I command you to tell me who you are."

"It's none of your business, you dirty beast!"

"Those are words of pride: words that are spoken in Hell. You belong to the Abyss, and not to the Light! Return there, foul spirit!"

"I don't want to return: I want to go somewhere else."

"Well, then, Satan, I command you to tell me how many there are of you!"

"We are only two."

"What is your name?"

"Oripas."

"And the other?"

"Ypès."

"Then, foul spirits, I command you, leave this house of God; here there is nothing for you. Fallen spirits, leave us! I command you in the name of the Blessed Sacrament!"

"I don't want to! You can't make me, you swine, my time has not yet come."

Once more the exorcist was bathed in sweat and shaking all over. The onlookers were no less moved, and some frankly terrified. However, Fr. Souquat took up the struggle again. Taking up a crucifix, he held it in front of the possessed boy.

"Wretched fiend, you do not even dare to look this image in the face, you turn your head away in order not to see it, and you defy the priest. I command you, leave us, and go back to your place in Hell."

"I don't want to," stormed the demon, "it's not good there!"

"You should have been obedient to God, but you chose the path of misfortune. You preferred to be a spirit of darkness. Withdraw from the light and go back to the shadows prepared for you."

"My time has not yet come. I will not go."

Then taking a candle blessed by the Holy Father, the exorcist continued:

"Presumptuous Satan, I am placing this candle on your head to light you the way to Hell. This is the light of the Holy Catholic Church, and you are a spirit of darkness. Now go back to Hell and rejoin your true companions."

"I am staying here, because it's good here. In Hell it's not good."

Finally, the priest took up a little statue of the Virgin Mary:

"Do you see the Blessed Virgin Mary? Once again she shall bruise your head. She will brand you with the names of Jesus and of Mary, so that they burn you forever.... You will not give in? I have commanded you in the name of Jesus. I have commanded you in the name of the Holy Catholic Church, in the name of our Holy Father the pope, in the name of the Blessed Sacrament. You are deaf to the voice of the priest! Well then, Satan! Now it is the Mother of God who commands you! She commands you to be gone. Foul fiend, flee from the sight of the Immaculate Conception! She commands you to leave!"

At this moment the onlookers began to intone the *Memorare* in Latin.

Suddenly, in a deep, powerful voice, the Devil called out: "Well then, *I am going.*"

Then the poor boy was seen to writhe like a worm. A crashing sound was heard. The boy relaxed, leant forward and fell into a faint. The Devil had left!

A terrified silence fell on the spectators. A minute before they had seen Thiébaud's flushed face, threatening and furious, and heard, coming from his mouth, the arrogant responses of Satan.

Now the boy was resting. He slept for an hour after his deliverance. When he was shown the crucifix, or sprinkled with holy water, there was no reaction. He quietly allowed himself to be carried to his room. After a time, he woke up of his own accord, rubbed his eyes, and seemed amazed to find himself surrounded by a lot of persons whom he did not know.

"Don't you know me?" asked M. Schrantzer, who had talked to him the evening before.

"No," said the boy, "I don't know you."

His mother was there and could not contain her joy. Her son, who had been afflicted with deafness by the Devil, now enjoyed normal hearing, and was free. All present gave thanks to God for having endowed His Church with such great power. Mother and son returned to Illfurth, hoping that the younger boy would soon be delivered in his turn.

The Deliverance of Joseph

Curiously enough, when Thiébaud returned to his home he remembered nothing. The four years he had passed in a state of possession had been obliterated from his memory. He no longer recognized his parish priest, the very pious Abbé Brey, who has been compared with the saintly Curé d'Ars, and who suffered like him from demonic infestations. He could not remember having seen the new town hall. He had brought with him from Strasbourg some blessed medallions, which he offered to his brother. Joseph threw them to the ground, saying:

"Keep that sort of thing for yourself. I don't want it."

"Has he gone mad?" Thiébaud asked his mother, who was careful not to let him know that he himself had been in the same state, for he remembered nothing of it.

On Wednesday, October 6, 1869, the younger boy suddenly exclaimed:

"My two companions," — it was understood that he meant Oripas and Ypès, the devils cast out of Thiébaud — "are weaklings. Now I am the master: I am the strongest. I shall stay here for another six years. I'm not afraid of any old priest."

"Are you so strong?" asked the mayor, a M. Tresch, an excellent Christian.

"Of course," he replied. "I like it here, and I'm very comfortable. I've settled down in a quiet spot, and I shan't leave it till I want to."

The Abbé Brey, however, had immediately requested the bishop's permission to undertake the exorcism. Whereas Thiébaud had reverted to the satisfactory behavior of former years, going to church, school, and confession, with no recollection of his four years of possession, Joseph's state became steadily worse. The bishop's authorization arrived at last, and the Curé fixed the date of exorcism for October 27. This date was, however, kept secret, to prevent crowds assembling. It was a Sunday. Only a few witnesses had been invited and the ceremony took place in the chapel of the cemetery of Burnkirch, a quarter of an hour from the village. Together with the mayor, M. Tresch, there were the boys' parents, the schoolmaster, the stationmaster, the headmistress of the girls' school, Professor Lachemann, and two gentlemen of the name of Spies and Martinot.

At six in the morning, when the Mass began, the possessed boy began to kick and twist in every direction. His arms and legs had to be tied, but before the prayers at the foot of the altar were finished, the boy had managed to struggle free and kick the celebrant. M. Martinot then picked him up and held him on his knee. The boy began to utter inarticulate cries, yapping like a puppy, grunting like a young pig. To the surprise of the onlookers, however, he remained calm from the *Sanctus* to the conclusion of the Mass.

Having been unvested of his liturgical vestments, the Curé put on surplice and stole and began the exorcism. When he came to the ritual dialogue with the Devil, the Abbé Brey summoned him to declare how many demons there were in the boy.

"There's no need for you to know," was the curt answer. When the priest returned to the attack the Devil tossed him the name of Ypès, one of the devils who had possessed the brother.

During the reading of St. John's Gospel, the possessed boy cried out:

"I will not go!"

There followed a torrent of insults. This continued for three hours. The onlookers began to feel tired and discouraged. But the good priest, himself exhausted and sweating, exhorted them to stand firm. All the while M. Tresch, the mayor, had been holding the boy. Quite worn out, he passed him over to Professor Lachemann, at which the Devil remarked:

"So you're here, too, Flatnose!"

Meanwhile the priest, on his knees before the altar, had been praying for a moment or two, vowing to perform a *novena* if the exorcism were successful.

Descending the altar steps, he said to the boy:

"I adjure you, in the name of the Immaculate Virgin Mary, to leave this child."

Satan raged: "Why does he come after me with his Great Lady? *Now I am obliged to go!*"

At these words a wave of emotion swept over the onlookers. All of them understood that deliverance was at hand, and that the Virgin Mary was to be its cause. The Curé repeated his summons.

"I am leaving!" screamed the Devil. "I am going into a herd of swine!"

"To Hell!" commanded the priest.

"I want to go into a flock of geese," begged the Devil.

"To Hell!" repeated the priest, adding, each time, the ritual adjuration.

"I don't know the way," said Satan, "I'm going into a flock of sheep."

"To Hell."

"Now I am obliged to go," wailed the demon.

At these words the boy turned right and left, stretched himself, blew out his cheeks, had one last convulsive spasm, and then fell back, suddenly inert and silent. He was released from his bonds and his arms fell limply to his sides and his head lolled backwards. This only lasted a few moments. Then he was observed to stretch like a man waking from sleep, and to open his eyes, which he had kept shut throughout the exorcism. He seemed surprised to find himself in the chapel with people all around him.

From the beginning the Devil had announced: "If I am obliged to go, I will mark my departure by breaking something." In fact, the rosary and the little pectoral cross which had been hung round the boy's neck, were found to be broken to pieces. Since he had been tied hand and foot, he could not have broken them himself. The scene had profoundly shaken all the onlookers. They sang a *Te Deum,* the litanies to the Blessed Virgin, and the *Salve Regina.* Their voices were half strangled by sobs. More than once the Abbé Brey was almost overwhelmed by his emotion.

It was certainly a unique testimony. Near the village square at Illfurth, in a garden on the site of the boys' home, there is a beautiful monument erected to perpetuate the memory of these events. It is a tall column, decorated with stars, and surmounted by a statue of Mary Immaculate. On the pedestal there is a Latin inscription, which runs as follows:

"In perpetual memory of the deliverance of two boys possessed by devils, Théobald and Joseph Burner, granted by the intercession of the Blessed Mary Immaculate. A.D. 1869."

It was erected by subscription in 1872 and is still scrupulously maintained.

THE CASE OF HÉLÈNE POIRIER

Before going on to the remarkable case of the bewitched woman of Piacenza, we shall deal briefly with some other cases, particularly with that of Hélène Poirier. She was a woman of excellent character, who endured the most terrifying ordeals, and who died in 1914 at the age of eighty. Her misfortunes are related in detail by Canon Champault in his book *Une Possédée contemporaine* (1834–1914) (Paris, Téqui). The author of this work had detailed and voluminous documentation at his disposal. He was at the time director of an establishment at Gien (Loiret) and had himself been eyewitness of many of the events which he relates. In addition, he had an ample supply of material collected by the two priests who succeeded him in the parish of Coulions, where the possessed woman lived. Further, the woman herself was for many years in Canon Champault's service, and he remained in touch with her until her death.

Hélène Poirier was an honest country girl who worked as a laundress. No one can say why this simple woman was subjected, with God's permission, to an unending series of demonic persecutions. She was first obsessed, then possessed, the two words indicating different intensities of demonic manifestation. Since God would not permit such things to happen if they were devoid of all purposive quality, it is probable that they are intended to demonstrate the terrible dangers to which we should be exposed if the Devil had a free hand. We know that, fortunately for us poor humans, he is not permitted to do all that he would like.

But to return to Hélène Poirier. Her life is, so to speak, a tissue of demonic activities, tricks, rough jokes, horseplay, beatings, levitations, and the like.

She was literally possessed, at least twice, over a period of six years, and in each case she was exorcised. In the interval between these crises she was the victim of more or less violent obsessions. For the greater part of her life she was a martyr to the Devil's activities and his incessant cruelty. Yet, on the other hand, she gave proof of the Abbé Saudreau's statement, that the courage and patience of the possessed person may be a source of great spiritual power.

In the second part of her life, Hélène Poirier was granted marvelous compensations for this demonic persecution by the intervention of her guardian angel and visions of the Blessed Virgin and Our Lord Himself.

We can only give a brief summary of some of the innumerable instances of the violence of this diabolic persecution.

Whilst she was still living in acute poverty with her mother, Hélène would often receive, from an *invisible* enemy, kicks and slaps, even attempts at strangulation, all of which her mother had to witness without being able to help her. These were no fantasies of the imagination, for her face, her arms, and her legs would all bear for weeks the marks of the treatment they had received.

The Devil would appear to her in the most hideous shapes. He would overpower her by his weight, throwing her to the ground—this happened frequently—and would breathe in her face.

There were numerous instances of levitation: in each case Hélène was seized by the hair, *always by some invisible power,* pulled around the room, lifted from the ground, and finally thrown, in a half-strangled state, upon her bed. Once she was suddenly seized by the head and transported over the neighboring houses, a distance of some forty-five yards.

At night she often had the same experience as the Curé d'Ars, of some infernal spirit shaking the curtains of her bed and running the curtain rings noisily backwards and forwards for hours on end. Once Hélène shouted for help and when help arrived there were more than twenty witnesses to this agitation of the curtains. Their names are given, so there can be no doubt as to the reality of the facts quoted.

Although Hélène Poirier was able to work through all these afflictions to a high degree of saintliness, most of us would be content to pray that we might not be led to sanctity along such a terrifying path.

Two Other Cases of Possession

In his book on the possessions at Illfurth,[14] Canon Francois Gaquère has also included, though with less detail, two other more recent cases of possession.

[14] Francois Gaquère, *Les possédés d'Illfurth, de Natal et de Phat-Diem (1956)*

There is first the case of a young Bantu girl, Claire-Germaine Cèle of Natal, who was twice possessed and twice delivered by exorcism, once on September 10, 1906, and again on April 24, 1907. This young African girl, who had been baptized in her cradle, was brought up by nuns of the mission. Her family background was one of conflict and frequent quarrels. As a girl her health was delicate, and she was also very temperamental. Soon after her First Communion she ceased to partake of the Sacraments. Her eyes shone with a somber gleam. At night she was very agitated, and she could be heard to cry like a madwoman, "I am lost! My Confession was sacrilegious! My Communion was sacrilegious! I shall hang myself!" One day she passed a note to the missionary, Fr. Erasme, in which she said she had sold herself to the Devil. On August 20, 1906, she appeared more tormented than ever. She was gnashing her teeth, barking like a dog, and calling for help.

"Sister," she cried, "send for Fr. Erasme. I want to confess everything. Quickly, quickly, the Devil wants to kill me! He's my master. I've nothing blessed any more, and I have lost all your medallions."

Up to that moment it had been possible to believe that it was a simple case of mania. But several very definite symptoms emerged to show that it was a case of genuine possession. Germaine had a horror of all blessed objects and pushed them aside saying that they burned her. She knew of remote, hidden events. She understood all the languages used in speaking to her and could repeat in Latin the long formulae of the ritual even correcting any errors made by those who recited it. Her devil was talkative and enjoyed revealing the most intimate secrets and hidden sins of those who were present, which made most of them retreat hastily. Any invocation of Jesus or Mary enraged him. He displayed the most cruel ingenuity in his persecution of the poor girl. Sometimes he would lift her into the air, in spite of all efforts to hold her down. Sometimes he would inflate her chest or stomach, sometimes her head became monstrous, her cheeks inflated like balloons, her neck would lengthen, and a hideous goiter would make its appearance. A lump would form under her skin and travel over every part of her body. At other times she would writhe on the ground, darting out her tongue like a serpent. Yet if she was sprinkled with holy water, or blessed by a priest, all these symptoms would disappear.

On the whole the spectacle of the effects of possession had a very great effect on the onlookers. Many were converted and there was a great increase in religious observance. The exorcisms, which twice delivered the unfortunate girl, demonstrated the power of the prayers of the Church. The final exorcism was conducted by the bishop himself, Mgr. Henri Delalle, Oblate of Mary Immaculate. During the ceremony, an incident occurred which would be unbelievable if it had not been witnessed by so many persons. After two and a half hours of prayer the possessed girl was suddenly levitated six feet from the ground, and from this height called out to the dumbfounded bishop: "What's the matter, bishop? Why do you have to stand there gaping at me? Do as I do!" This accompanied by a shrill cackle that made the spectators' blood run cold. Yet, finally, she was set free. Her life afterwards was a model of piety, until she died, six years later, on March 14, 1913, of a chest complaint. The devil never reappeared. Her ordeals, therefore, resembled that of the Illfurth boys, whose afflictions were not repeated, but who also died young, Thiébaud, the elder, at the age of sixteen, and the younger, Joseph, in 1882, at the age of twenty-five.

POSSESSION AT PHAT-DIEM

The second case of possession related by Canon Gaquère was a collective one. The facts are recorded in the admirable *Bulletin de la*

Société des Missions étrangères de Paris, published in Hong Kong in the year 1949-1950. The writer of the articles was Mgr. de Cooman, now Vicar Apostolic of Thanhoa. The possessions occurred in 1924 and 1925 at Phat-Diem, in the province of Ninh-Binh, Tonkin.

The first victim was a young novice of the convent of the Amantes de la Croix, an indigenous congregation. It began with violent noises, blows directed at the novice by an unknown hand, volleys of sticks and stones flung, not only at Marie Dien, the novice in question, but at all who came to her assistance.

In cases of possession, it is not always possible to locate the source of persecution. Later we shall give cases in which the origin of the possession can be clearly traced to the intervention of sorcerers who have made a pact with the Devil. In the case of Germaine Cèle the origin lay in sacrilegious Communions. In the case of the two Illfurth boys, it was suggested that the cause could be attributed to a woman suspected of sorcery, who had made the boys eat an apple. In the case of Marie Dien, there was a young man of twenty, called Minh, who had made a pilgrimage to a well-known pagan pagoda to entreat the spirits for the girl's hand. On September 22 the Devil, striking Marie Dien about the face and mouth, declared:

"This is the fourth time they've been to the pagoda to ask for your hand. I shall end up by getting you!" The strangest forms of persecution continued for more than two years, spreading terror amongst the novices: alarming sounds, flying missiles coming from no one knew where, stones, bits of wood, potatoes, and empty bottles, or bird cries, the whinnying of horses, hooting of car horns, doors banging, and sarcastic laughter, or heartrending sobs — in a word, all the phenomena we have already encountered in the infestations at Ars.

But the most alarming thing was that the other novices began to be affected by some fantastic contagion. They began to climb the areca trees, a kind of palm tree with a slender trunk attaining a height of twenty-five to thirty feet. This craze was stopped by nailing little crucifixes to the trunk of each tree. There were fugues which could not be remembered later. But the presence of the Devil was clearly evidenced by the knowledge of languages and of secrets which it would have been impossible to discover in any rational way. It was finally decided to proceed to exorcism. There were no less than fourteen possessed persons, which reminds one of the historic case of the Ursuline Sisters of Loudun in the seventeenth century. The battle was long and hard. The Devil departed but returned in even more terrifying forms. Finally, however, he yielded to the exorcists. In December 1925 the novices of Phat-Diem found their peace assured. In 1949, whilst telling the story of these events, Mgr. de Cooman pointed out that since then an atmosphere of tranquility and piety had never deserted the convent of the Amantes de la Croix. Three of the formerly possessed novices had become the most admirable Mothers Superior. Marie Dien herself, the first to be persecuted, had later become an excellent Mistress of the Novices in the convent of Thanhoa, where she died in the greatest piety on August 6, 1944. This congregation, consisting at the moment of 300 professed nuns, has now, for the most part, taken refuge in South Vietnam, where they continue their mission.

~ 6 ~

SPELLBOUND IN PIACENZA

THE NEXT CASE takes us to Italy, and again straight into the twentieth century. A very curious case occurred in the district of Piacenza, recorded in a little book by Alberto Vecchio, *Intervista col Diavole*—An interview with the Devil.[15]

One May evening, in 1920, a Franciscan friar, Pier-Paolo Veronesi, was occupied in the sacristy of the church of the convent of Santa Maria di Campagna, at Piacenza, when a woman presented herself asking for a benediction. She asked if this could be given at the altar of the Blessed Virgin. The friar willingly granted this request, which seemed inspired by pure devotion. But he was rather surprised when the woman whose face was deeply lined with the marks of suffering, asked leave to speak to him for a few minutes in the sacristy. The friar supposed that she had some trouble, some painful task to perform, but he naturally could not refuse the few minutes' conversation she requested.

At first in a low voice, but later, as she gained confidence, with a little more assurance, she made the most astonishing avowals.

At certain times, she said, an unknown force took possession of her, and set her whole body in movement against her will. She was then compelled to dance for hours on end, until she dropped down

---

[15] Edizione paoline, Modena, Italy.

exhausted. She would sing operatic arias that she had never heard, she gave lectures to an imaginary audience in an unknown tongue. Often she felt an uncontrollable impulse to bite to pieces any object that fell into her hands. She would tear her husband's underclothes to shreds. At other times she would behave like a dog, to the great terror of all present, jumping from chair to chair, leaping on to the table, roaring, screaming, mewing, till the house sounded like a zoo. After such terrifying scenes in her own house, she would collapse with fatigue, and for days her body would be bruised and swollen, enough to inspire pity in all who saw her.

A final characteristic was that when she was having one of these crises, she would discover shortly afterwards that her parents, although they lived a long way off, had also suffered some disturbance, as though some mysterious fluid flowed between them.

"Believe me, Father," she concluded, "my life is a veritable hell. I have two little children, but in spite of them, I think only of death as a means of deliverance."

The friar was considerably astonished by this story, but as he was almoner of a mental hospital, he came to the simple conclusion that he was dealing with a mentally unbalanced person. He contented himself with a few questions:

"Is all this quite correct?"

"Yes, there are many people who can vouch for it."

"And how long has it lasted?"

"Seven years."

"And what have the doctors said?"

"I have been to all the doctors in Piacenza, all the doctors I know, and they have all said, more or less plainly, that it was a case of hysteria."

The friar felt reassured, for this was precisely the conclusion he had come to himself.

"Well then, you know the cause of the trouble?"

"No, because I know perfectly well that I am neither mad nor hysterical."

"Well then?"

"Well," replied the woman,

Seeing that I could get no help from men, I felt the need to take refuge in God. In spite of much repugnance on my part, I have been into all the churches in the town, to pray and receive a blessing. Each time I have received the benediction I have felt better for a few days. But I have visited them so often that I began to be afraid that I should be taken for a madwoman, so I didn't dare to go any more. But something else happened.

I had been told that up in the hills there was a parish priest whose blessings were particularly efficacious. I thought I would go and see him. One Sunday after lunch I set off with my husband and some relatives, in a carriage which the commune of St. Giorgio had lent me. The horse was a good one, and we covered the ground quickly. Suddenly he stopped and refused to go any further. They whipped him till they drew blood. He reared and kicked and struggled, but would not move forward. Then, without knowing what was happening to me, I jumped down from the carriage, although my relatives tried to hold me back, and I began to *fly*—it's the only word I can use to describe it—about two feet from the ground, right across the fields and up the hill in the direction of the church spire in the parish we were going to. The congregation was just coming out from the evening service. They all saw me coming toward the church: dogs were barking, hens scattering in every direction. I reached the square, and everyone left it. With bowed head I slipped through the half-closed door of the church and threw myself down at the foot of the high altar, on which was a painting of St. Expedit. The priest, followed by the crowd, rushed in, and seeing what had happened, gave me his blessing. Then I came to myself, and for days afterwards I felt better.

The story only served to confirm Fr. Pier-Paolo's suspicions.

"Yes, it's all very strange," he remarked uncertainly, "it's all very strange." Then he bade his visitor goodbye, saying "Listen, since the benediction helps you, don't hesitate to come here whenever you feel like it. If I am not here myself, one of my colleagues will always bless you."

A SIGNIFICANT EPISODE

Several days passed. The woman came back for a blessing. But whilst Brother Pier-Paolo was in the course of pronouncing the benediction before the altar of the Madonna, the woman, who was leaning against a pillar near the choir, began to whimper, with closed mouth, like a dog having bad dreams. Then, with closed eyes, head pressed back against the pillar, and hands clasped, she began to intone a tremendous chant. Her voice was rich, passionate, brilliant in tone, and all the children of the neighborhood crept in to listen. When she had finished, she began to speak in an unknown language, and although she did not change her position seemed to be struggling against some invisible power. Her voice rose to a pitch of fury, like that of a maniac in a paroxysm of rage.

At this particular moment another priest was passing through the church, Fr. Apollinare Focaccia. He listened first to the chant, and then to the imprecations in the unknown language.

That evening he remarked to his colleague:

"You noticed that woman?"

"Yes. Why?"

"Weren't you impressed?"

"To tell the truth, not particularly. As almoner in a mental hospital, I've got used to that sort of thing."

"I think you should pay attention. I'm certain that woman is possessed."

"Don't let's exaggerate," replied Fr. Pier-Paolo. "One shouldn't go looking for the Devil everywhere, like the people who use the Devil to explain things which have a perfectly normal explanation. And in any case, what we can't explain today science will no doubt explain tomorrow."

"I can't agree with you," answered Fr. Apollinare. "Just think it over. How can you explain her being able to talk in an unknown language? We can see for ourselves that what she is doing is very mysterious, and this mystery comes from the Devil."

"Dear Father Apollinaire, come and pay a visit to the psychiatric ward, and I will show you some very interesting cases which are not yet amenable to scientific explanation."

"I shall be glad to do so, but tell me, have you ever seen a case that resembled this one, even distantly?"

"Frankly, no."

"Then, with all respect to science, we are entitled to suppose there might be demonic intervention. This person seems quite normal. But there is a personality within her quite different from her own. You heard her sing. There isn't a single singer alive today who could sing like that. And what about all that strange torrent of abuse in some unknown tongue? Nothing will stop me thinking that she is possessed. I don't mean we've got to be positively medieval: we don't have to see witchcraft and sortileges everywhere. But I don't see why we should claim to know more about it than the Evangelists, than Jesus Christ, or St. Peter and St. Paul, who were extremely precise when they said the Devil was an actual being. You remember how St. Paul, in the Epistle to the Ephesians, declared that devils were 'in the air.' We have known about this phenomenon of possession from remote antiquity onwards. That is why the Church created an order of exorcists. Take our own missionaries, who say the Devil is very active amongst peoples still living in the darkness of idolatry. Can we doubt that he also operates amongst the peoples of Christendom, now that so many of them have abandoned the faith of their fathers?"

Fr. Apollinaire continued to develop his argument. Fr. Pier-Paolo was a little shaken, but not yet convinced.

"All that is very true, dear Father, but I am not arguing about doctrine, only about facts, and I am not persuaded that this woman is truly possessed."

THE BISHOP'S OPINION

The following morning Fr. Pier-Paolo, troubled by some scruples of conscience with regard to the previous evening's discussion, asked for an interview with his bishop, Mgr. Pellizzari, and told him the story in full detail.

After thinking it over for a moment or two the bishop replied simply:

"My dear Father, have her exorcised."

"Excellency," replied the priest, hastily, "is that really necessary?"

"Yes," replied the bishop, without hesitation.

"And I have to do it?"

"Yes, you."

"You couldn't perhaps find someone else?"

"Either you or Mgr. Mosconi [the Vicar-General], but it had better be you, since you know the woman."

"Forgive me, Excellency, but I have heard it said that during the exorcism the Devil turns against the exorcist and invents all sorts of disagreeable stories about him. If this woman is really possessed."

"But who will believe in what the Devil says? Don't you know that he is the father of lies?"

At last Fr. Pier-Paolo had to give way to the bishop's wish. Returning home, he was considerably perturbed. He felt it was a dangerous adventure to confront the Devil. He was an excellent priest, but somewhat timorous, and not a little frightened at having to engage in a conflict of which the outcome was most uncertain. But the bishop's order was explicit. He submitted, he prayed, he slept little and began to prepare himself for the task which had devolved upon him. In the morning he went to see Dr. Lupi, superintendent of the mental hospital, to whom he explained the problem at length. Dr. Lupi was so interested in the story that he asked if he could be present at the exorcism, which was precisely what the priest had hoped.

THE FIRST EXORCISM

The first exorcism took place on May 21, 1920, in a room on the first floor above the chapel. The possessed woman was accompanied by her husband, her mother, a friend of the family, and two ladies. The friar was assisted by a colleague, Fr. Giustino, whose duty it was to take note of the proceedings, and by Dr. Lupi, the medical superintendent.

On their knees in front of a small altar the two priests first recited the litanies of the saints, as laid down by the ritual. The possessed woman, seated on a rush-bottomed chair, stretched herself like a wild beast waking from sleep. Suddenly there resounded the Latin text of the first words of the exorcism:

"*Exorcizo te, immundissime spiritus, omne phantasma, omnis legio.*"

At these words the possessed woman took hold of the points of her shoes, rose in the air with a leap of extraordinary agility, landed in in the middle of the room, relaxed her grasp, and stood upright. Her whole body was totally transformed. Her face had taken on a hideous aspect. She began to scream insults at the exorcist, in a harsh, piercing, and totally unfeminine voice:

"And who are you, to come and fight with me? Do you know I am Isabo, that I have great wings and strong fists?" Then another string of abusive epithets flowed from her lips.

The priest, dazed, astonished, and quite disconcerted, was for a moment reduced to silence. But soon he recovered strength, without knowing how, and called out loudly:

"I, priest of Christ, I command you, whoever you may be, I command you in the name of the mysteries of the Incarnation, of the Passion and the Resurrection of Jesus Christ, and by His coming for the Last Judgment to hold your peace, to harm no creature of God, and particularly none of those present, and to do everything I command you."

Then, in an atmosphere of intense emotion, the following dialogue began:

"In the name of God, who are you?"

"Isabo," cried the woman, her eyes flaming and her face flushed.

"What does this name mean?"

Instead of replying the woman began to bite at her hands and arms, and tried to catch hold of the priest's robe. Finally she said: "The name means that he is so properly spellbound that no one can resist him."

"How great is your power?"

"As much as I am given."

"How much are you given?"

"A great deal."

"Where do you get it from?"

"From the person who knows how to cast spells."

"What sort of Italian is that?"

"I am not Italian," screamed the woman, or rather the spirit that possessed her, with an expression of contempt, spitting out a new stream of insults, something that she did repeatedly in the course of the exorcism.

"Where do you come from?" asked the priest, unperturbed.

"You are talking to me as if I were your slave."

"Tell me where you come from."

"No."

"In the name of God, of the God you know so well, tell me where you come from."

At the mention of God the woman turned her face away, like a bull which has been hit on the muzzle, and for a moment she remained motionless, refusing to reply. The onlookers were holding their breath, overcome by the solemnity of the scene.

"In the name of God, by the Blood of His Crucifixion, tell me where you come from."

"From the distant desert."

"Are you alone, or are there companions with you?"

"I have companions."

"How many?"

After a momentary hesitation the Devil replied: "Seven," and gave their names, as strange as his own.

"Why did you enter into this body?"

"Because of a violent love which was not returned."

"Not returned by whom?"

"You are a fool."

"Answer me! Who did not return this love?"

"This body!" screamed the woman, beating her breast violently.

"And why did you not return it?"

In a proud and disdainful voice the woman replied:

"Because it was not right."

"So this body became your victim?"

In sole response to this question the woman screwed up her face into an expression of animal ferocity and from between her thin, tightly compressed lips there came a burst of terrifying laughter, which made the bystanders shudder.

"When did you enter this body?"

After many contortions there came the reply:

"In 1913, on April 23, at five in the evening."

The exorcist plied her with questions, until the spirit was obliged to admit that on that day he had entered into her, by means of a sortilege contrived by a wizard, in the form of a bolus of salt pork, washed down by a glass of white wine.

In the course of this exorcism the friar asked if it was true that the Devil had equally invaded the rest of the family, and the reply was that he had done so.

"A case of telepathy," suggested the priest.

"Idiot!" retorted the Devil.

But when the exorcist ordered Isabo to leave the body he was possessing, he shouted: "No!"

"Leave!" thundered the priest.

"Never!"

"I command you to go!"

"I am not going: I am Isabo!"

In a paroxysm of rebellion, the woman freed herself from all constraint and with wild cries and outstretched hands flung herself at the priest, caught hold of his gown, tearing at his stole and screaming like a beast in torment.

"It took seven days to get me into this body, and you want to get me out with a single exorcism!"

It was a critical moment. The doctor, impassive, kept his eyes fixed on the possessed woman. The friar sprinkled her with holy water, and she threw herself twisting and writhing on the ground, as if she had been sprinkled with burning embers.

"When will you leave?" asked the priest.

"What can I do?" asked the spirit, on a note of profound sadness, "since whilst you are working to get me out, others are working to keep me in?"

"Leave!" cried the priest, putting one end of his stole on the woman's shoulder.

At contact with the stole the woman leapt to her feet like a gazelle and began to shout in terror: "Take that weight off me!" and she ran toward the door.

The exorcism continued. The Devil had declared that he would only leave if the mouthful of salt pork which had constituted the sortilege were thrown up. But although they brought her a basin, the woman could not do so. Several times she seemed to throw up something, and it was never the food taken at her last meal.

To the question as to which words made him suffer most, after many refusals and continued pressure from the exorcist the Devil finally replied, in obvious terror, whilst the bystanders waited in hushed silence: "*Sanctus! Sanctus! Sanctus!*"

It was, in fact, observed in the course of subsequent exorcisms that these three words, which we call in the liturgy the *trisagion*, always produced a devastating effect upon the demon. Whilst he was uttering these words, the Devil interspersed them with wails which filled everyone with terror. Even Dr. Lupi stood pale and trembling.

This first exorcism lasted until the evening. The poor woman was utterly exhausted and Friar Pier-Paolo hardly less so. He pronounced a final adjuration to the Devil, that he was to do no harm either to the possessed woman or to her family. Having promised this, with a sulky, furtive look at the priest, his eyes seemed to travel round the room in pursuit of some invisible cavalcade of specters; there was one convulsion, and his manifestations ended. The woman appeared to emerge from a profound sleep. She was pale, but normal. She was no doubt suffering from great lassitude but remembered nothing of what had taken place.

The session was over.

"Well, Brother Pier-Paolo," asked Fr. Apollinaire, "what happened?"

"This woman is truly possessed," answered the exorcist.

He could no longer doubt, but he was alarmed at the power of his adversary.

"It is incredible," he added, "the extent to which the forces of evil can resist the influences we can bring to bear on them." And with bent head he returned to his cell, in the hope of finding a little of the repose he so badly needed.

His colleague, Fr. Giustino, had taken note of all that happened, and it is from his shorthand record that Alberto Vecchio derived the story.

FURTHER INFORMATION

We are indebted to this same excellent guide for details of all the battles that were waged, from the first exorcism on May 21 to the last on June 23. There were no less than thirteen sessions in between. Later we shall relate the way in which the unfortunate woman was finally released. For the moment we should consider some of the information which was obtained in the process, as a result of the interrogation of the evil spirit.

In the first place the initial possession was due to a malefice contrived by a sorcerer of the district. The sinister power of such malefices could therefore hardly be questioned. Sorcery is a fact. And it is a fact still present in the country districts of France and Italy and no doubt elsewhere. It was discovered, incidentally, in the course of the exorcisms, that there were seven sorcerers in the district of Piacenza alone.

Secondly, we learn that sorcery makes use of something in the form of an infernal liturgy, in which certain magic formulae are able, by God's permission, to establish control over evil forces, compelling them to obey and to enter into this or that person, and possess them. This is one of the aspects of demonic reality that is still little understood.

Thirdly, we have efficacious means of resisting the assaults of the Devil, these being above all prayer, the Sacraments, the sacramental usages, the invocation of saints and angels, the protection of the Blessed Virgin, and the like.

In the next chapters we shall have evidence of the immense power God has granted by His Grace to Mary the Immaculate. In the very significant account of the life of Antoine Gay we have already learned, from a devil's own lips, that Mary is in every sense of the word our Mother in Heaven, and that is, in itself, everything.

Finally, it would seem that the names ascribed to the devils are completely arbitrary. If Isabo is to be credited, in the case of the woman of Piacenza it was the local sorcerer who had given her seven devils the more or less bizarre names of Isabo, Erzelaide, Eslender, etc. And each of these demons was different from the others, and they appeared, moreover, to have little sympathy for each other.

But the most impressive fact of all lay in the ravages and destruction caused by possession when it was working at full strength in a human being. As to this, we have the testimony of the unfortunate woman's husband.

THE HUSBAND'S COMPLAINT

One day, when Fr. Pier-Paolo was preparing for the exorcism, and Fr. Giustino was occupied in replenishing the supply of holy water, which would be so indispensable to the ceremony, the husband of the possessed woman was heard to sigh:

"Let us hope it will soon be over!"

"I can well believe," answered the friar, "that you must have passed through some very difficult times."

"Difficult? Terrible times, dear Father. I could tell you hundreds of stories, but one or two will be enough. Sometimes when I came home from work in the evening. I would find the fire had gone out, and the whole house was upside down. My wife would be hissing or mewing, growling, or dancing on chairs or table or any of the furniture. At other times I used to find her tearing up clothes and linen in a fury. Then, when she saw me, she used to cry: 'Quick, give me something to tear up. I've got to tear something up, spoil it, destroy it!' And she would be scratching and biting like a mad woman!"

"If that's the case," interrupted Fr. Pier-Paolo, "there can't be much linen left in the house."

"There's nothing left at all. She's destroyed everything. A little while ago I still had two shirts, the one I was wearing, and the other at the washerwoman's. Now the only way I can keep anything is to leave it with the neighbors. But it isn't as if that were all. Sometimes I used to find her under the table, all huddled up, her head sunk on her shoulders, like a beast caught in a trap, and yet all tense as if she was about to spring out on an enemy. If I called to her: 'Thérèse!' she would answer in a hoarse voice: 'I am Isabo, and it is I who give the orders!' At first I thought it was a joke: 'Thérèse, I'm speaking to you,' and she answered in the same deep voice, 'I am Isabo, and I wear the trousers.'"

"Then she would come from under the table and start bounding toward me, fists forward, as if she were going to plant them in my face. And, of course, the usual stream of abuse. One day, when I was very tired and fed up, I told her straight what I thought of her Isabo, and then she threw herself at me, like a cat in a rage, and caught me by the throat. I had a lot of difficulty in getting free. She seemed to have a hundred times her normal strength."

"And what did you do when you found your wife in such a state?"

"I used to drop all my tools," the husband replied, sadly, "get myself a piece of bread, and then I'd stay there sometimes until eleven o'clock at night, sometimes until midnight, trying to help the poor woman to come back to her senses."

"And the children?"

"At first, they used to get frightened and start crying, but they soon got used to it, as children do. If it was in the morning, they would go out and play in the street. If it was in the evening, they would say: 'Mummy's beginning to dance: let's go to bed.' And to bed they went."

"And you had lost all hope of its stopping?"

"Yes, all hope. All the doctors said the same thing, if they knew what to say, at all. I had got so discouraged that I was afraid of losing my head and doing something desperate."

"But now," suggested the friar, "we have replaced the prescriptions of the doctors by the authority of the Church, our Mother, and we can be sure of the result."

"True, my Father. Now I feel confident and at ease."

It was surely an achievement in itself to have given this good man fresh hope. But his very justified complaints indicate the dangers we might incur without the divine protection which keeps demonic activity away from the majority of men, and only permits the specific phenomenon of temptation, from which none is free.

THE TWELFTH EXORCISM

We come now to June 21, the day of the twelfth exorcism. Three days before, the Devil had declared that he would not leave before June 23, at five in the afternoon. But he was already much weakened, as was clear from the beginning of the exorcism. During the litanies of the saints and other preparatory prayers, the possessed woman behaved quite differently from former occasions. Instead of stretching herself like a wild beast preparing to spring, instead of casting sinister glances at the bystanders, and particularly at the exorcist, she remained seated, with sunken head, her chin on her breast, her hands clutching the arms of her chair, in an attitude of weakness, shame, and remorse.

At the first words addressed to her by the exorcist she rose slowly, then stretched herself painfully on the mattress which had been placed on the floor in front of her. Then she stiffened and waited with closed eyes. All who were there were deeply moved by the sight of this poor woman, reduced almost to a corpse, and waited for her to leap up unexpectedly, as had so often happened before, or make some terrifying cry. The exorcist, a little uneasy at this calm, cast his eyes on the crucifix placed on the little altar, and made sure the holy water was close at hand in case of sudden attack. Then he began the usual exhortations:

"I command you to stay still and do nothing except answer my questions. Do you understand?"

No reply.

"Answer me, do you understand?"

Still no reply.

"Are you silent because you cannot or because you will not answer?"

Complete silence.

The exorcist was at a loss as to how to compel the silent demon to speak. He had an idea.

"If you *cannot* answer, lift one finger; if you *will* not, lift two."

At this injunction there was a hushed silence all around, and the woman was seen slowly and painfully lifting a single finger. She *could* not answer.

Everyone present was deeply impressed. The spectacle of the being whom the Devil had so often rendered violent, authoritarian, and imperious, and who was now so tired, humiliated, and impotent, showing signs of such profound depression, was one that no one could forget.

The dialogue between exorcist and possessed went on, the woman replying solely by lifting either one or two fingers. Finally, the exorcist commanded her: "Stand up! Throw it up!"

He was referring to the malefice which she had swallowed seven years previously, and which she had to throw up to secure her deliverance. Many times already had he ordered her to do this. Although she had often vomited something, and although this was never anything she had just eaten, she had never thrown up the sortilege.

Once again she rose slowly, very slowly, leant over the basin and tried to obey, but in vain. The exorcist then had recourse to the *trisagion*, that powerful *trisagion: Sanctus! Sanctus! Sanctus!* The onlookers echoed the words after him. The possessed woman obeyed, and threw up something, but not the sortilege. And it proved impossible to get anything more from her.

THE FINAL DAY

The great day finally arrived. Isabo had said June 23, 1920. One would see. Dr. Lupi was the most curious of all as to what would happen. Everyone arrived punctually for the final test. Dr. Lupi, more than ordinarily nervous, kept tapping on the floor with his stick. The preparatory prayers were more than usually fervent. The possessed woman dragged herself into the room, paler, more exhausted, more shamefaced than ever. She slumped down into her chair, her head lolling forward, in the position of a man in the electric chair. At the first words of the exorcism, she rose and lay down on the mattress, quite rigid and with closed eyes. Dr. Lupi was paying the closest attention, anxious not to miss any detail of the experience.

"In the name of God," cried the exorcist, "I command you to obey me in everything. Do you understand?"

Silence.

"If you have understood, raise one arm: if not, raise two!"

Slowly, and as if devoid of strength, the possessed woman raised one arm.

The tense dialogue continued. It was learnt that one of the devils who had left her the evening before, to torment a third person, had not returned. It was also stated that all the other members of the family, who had been more or less obsessed, were now free.

There were further discussions between Isabo and the priest as to whether all the devils would leave together. Then the exorcist, wishing to make an end, gave the long-awaited orders:

"Stand and throw it up!"

At these words the woman, with some difficulty, keeping her eyes fixed on the ground, went and knelt close to the basin. She bent forward and with terrible efforts which shook her whole body, tried to vomit. The priest insisted, commanded, urged her to obey. The poor woman was looking like a corpse.

"Throw it up!" said the exorcist.

Her elbows resting on the back of two chairs, she tried, with pitiful spasms, to obey the order. Nothing happened.

"Let us recite the *Sanctus*," said the priest.

At these words she succeeded in bringing something up, but nothing much. Her face seemed to be caving in, and she had to be supported to prevent her from collapsing.

The exorcist looked at his watch.

"It is thirty-five minutes past four. By all the authority given to me by God, I command you, foul spirit, to come out of this body immediately. If you come out at once I will send you into the desert, into the center of the Sahara: *if not, I will send you back to Hell!*"

A tremor ran through the little group. It was a moment of tragic drama. There is nothing that the Devil dreads so much as being sent back to Hell. This is a little-known aspect of demonology. Even in the Gospels we find the devils preferring to pass into a herd of swine than to be sent back into the Abyss. At Piacenza, therefore, everyone was on the alert. Every person present held his breath, listening to the beat of his own heart.

Then, as she heard the priest's words, the obsessed woman slowly pushed back her thick mass of hair which fell almost like an immense wig to below her shoulders. Her eyes filled with tears. She looked stupefied and bewildered. The muscles of her face were slack, and her lower lip drooped listlessly downwards. There was nothing human left in that disfigured face, in the eyes brimming with tears, the half-open mouth, and the sunken cheeks. There was not one of those who saw her who did not weep with her.

Then came a voice, mournful, low, and hesitant, saying: "I am ... going!"

The woman lowered her head to the basin and vomited up a large number of unmentionable things.

"Go! Go!" cried the exorcist in a wave of emotion.

At the same moment the obsessed woman no longer felt the crushing weight of the stole nor the imposition of hands. Suddenly, in a fresh, young, happy voice she cried out:

"I am cured!"

Her eyes travelled round the group with a smile of triumph.

"And the sortilege Isabo spoke of?" asked Fr. Pier-Paolo.

"No doubt it is in the basin," answered the doctor, stirring the contents with his cane. "Look!" he cried; and then suddenly he lifted all the contents of the basin up on his stick like a piece of material. Indeed, it spread out before the astonished eyes of the spectators like a beautiful veil, shot with all the color of the rainbow. And once the veil was lifted, at the bottom of the receptable they could see the famous bolus, so often described by the demon during the exorcisms. It was a little ball of salt pork, about the size of a nut, with seven horns.

CONCLUSION

The spirit had kept its word. Even the doctor, at first so incredulous, was now convinced. The proof was there, beyond any shadow of doubt.

The possessed woman, now cured, was crying softly, but her tears were now tears of joy. There were also tears in the eyes of all present. The doctor was still busy investigating the basin. The friars turned toward the image of Christ Victorious.

The exorcist invited all present to kneel before the altar. The woman delivered from her evil spirit offered up her convulsive sobs. She had emerged from the most terrifying of all ordeals. Her initial error, no doubt, lay in consulting a sorcerer who claimed to be a healer, and who had been attracted by her. When she rejected his advances, he had cast a spell on her, and we have seen what came of it. In the next chapter, curiously enough, we shall be dealing with an exactly parallel case, which occurred in a different country, and thirty years later.

In Piacenza this exorcism is vividly remembered by those witnesses who are still alive. It should be added that the bishop who ordered the exorcism died shortly after its conclusion. There are certain facts which suggest that it might have been an act of demonic vengeance but, if so, such vengeance is in itself an admission of defeat. The bishop had done his duty and even death cannot rob him of that merit.

MAGIC IN THE
TWENTIETH CENTURY

A CURIOUS ENCOUNTER

BEFORE STARTING ON the subject of this chapter I should like, if I may, to relate a purely personal incident. While I was engaged on the present book, I received a letter from a priest whom I did not know, and who was completely unaware of the work I was doing. He had just read another book on the same subject and had written to offer me his documentation.

"Suppose I had some material?" he said. "Well, I have. Come and have a look at it."

Since it was difficult for me to go to him, he came to see me. His material was of immense interest. For the last six years he has been engaged in a constant struggle with Satan, and we have seen, in the case of the woman of Piacenza, just what a struggle that can be. If our century is inclined to question the existence of Satan, as of so many other things, this priest has evidence enough of his existence, his power, his activity, the means he uses, subject to God's permission, and the terrible state to which he can reduce a poor human being.

I am authorized to give the name of this contemporary witness to the struggle against Satan. It is Fr. Berger-Bergès, from Chavagneen-Pailler, in the Vendée.

Although he has published nothing himself, I am authorized to say on his behalf, that he is prepared to meet any audience to discuss the exorcisms which he has carried out during the last six years, some of which are still continuing.

Naturally we shall only be able to take a glimpse at his vast material, from which the following facts are derived. Discretion requires that the persons concerned should only be indicated by their initials, and the places in question will not, of course, be mentioned.

Some of these exorcisms were relatively easy and yielded a rapid success. Others were more complex, very laborious, and much slower in producing a result. In these latter cases, as in the case at Piacenza, it would seem that whenever the exorcism brought any perceptible relief to the victim, it was immediately nullified by new sortileges operating from a distance.

Amongst all of the case histories I was offered, I have selected one only, which appeared particularly significant. It is the case of Mme. G., a married woman with one daughter. The file in question contains no fewer than 145 documents, covering the period of September 14, 1953, to February 5, 1959, and is not yet closed.

We should first give some indication of the way in which the case began, and for this we shall rely on the notes provided by the victim's own husband. Although the present writer has put them into narrative form, the incidents are, in every detail, exactly those provided by the husband, retaining as far as possible his own words.

A Deadly Fatigue

"It begins," says Mr. G., "in September 1950. Our two-year-old daughter Annie was sleeping badly. Ever since she was born, my wife has had to spend many nights almost without sleep herself. She began to suffer from a general and disquieting sense of fatigue, so we consulted a doctor. The doctor noted the following evident symptoms: no interest in work, continual lassitude, loss of weight, vertigo, etc. He was, however, reassuring. The case, he considered, was not alarming. All that was needed was quiet, good food, and sleep. In other words, three weeks in a convalescent home or rest house.

"It sounded quite easy. But we were not covered by any social insurance. My wife had never left home. A stay away from home would mean a big expense. So we decided to disregard the doctor's advice. Three weeks passed. My wife's health remained the same. One day, when I was in town, I met one of my wife's friends, who enquired after her. When I said she was no better, she said: 'Why don't you go to B.? He cured my son when he was suffering from nerves, and I was very satisfied. My son is eating and sleeping well now, and his nerves give us practically no trouble.' I was impressed by her confidence, and asked for B.'s address. He was, in fact, a healer, apparently very well known in the district.

"'He comes to S.J. every Saturday,' she said, 'and he sees people all day. Go and see him: it doesn't cost anything to try!'

"But the good woman added a remark without appearing to think it was important:

"'The chap rather frightens me. When I went with my boy the first time, he cut off a lock of his hair, took it between his fingers, and rubbed it, saying: "Yes, it is his nerves which are causing the trouble," but whilst he was saying this, I could see a sort of blue smoke rising from his fingers.'"

"When I got home, I told my wife all about it. The story of the blue smoke and the lock of hair did not worry her. She didn't believe in that sort of thing. It was therefore agreed that we would go and see him the following Saturday. By chance he did not come to S.J. that week for his usual consultations. My mother was still alive at that time, and she said to us: 'My children, I don't want to stop you going to see this B. But, you know, I don't trust him. All his family are swine [*sic*] and he'd kill off half the population of S.J. if he had his way.'

"But this warning did not stop us.

"The following Saturday we presented ourselves at the famous healer's."

A Session with the Healer

"His wife opened the door to us and received us in a friendly way. We waited for our turn, and when the healer called us in, he asked us to sit down and began the consultation.

"'Your name and Christian name, Madam, and your date of birth?'"

"When he had noted these details, B. cut off a lock of my wife's hair. He held it between the thumb and first finger of his left hand, and with his right held my wife's wrist. There was a moment's silence. He rubbed thumb and finger together, and, without a word being said, there was suddenly a puff of blue smoke rising some inches above his hand. It was just like a cigarette which goes on burning on the edge of an ashtray. After a moment he opened his fingers and, strange to say, there was not a trace of hair left. 'There's something wrong with your nerves,' B. declared. 'But don't worry. That's my specialty. Two or three sessions will put you right again.'"

"Then he took a flask containing some unknown substance, stuck his thumb into the flask, for not more than a few seconds—he was watching the time carefully with his watch in front of him—and then hastily withdrew it. Then he took hold of my wife's wrists and became suddenly tense, and as red in the face as a tomato. This lasted a few minutes, during which time he kept his head lowered. All of a sudden, my wife shut her eyes and began to go to sleep. Thereupon the healer let go of her wrists and began to wake her up. B. declared that he had a pain at the back of his neck, for what he had been doing, he said, was very exhausting. He seized an ampoule of ether and squirted some down the back of his neck to restore himself. Then he squirted some down my wife's neck. She seemed a bit stupefied, and she said that her head felt heavy after those few minutes of peculiar sleep. The session was over. My wife felt a little better than she had done an hour previously. The healer gave her his private address, in case we wanted to go and see him there. But he also said he would be back at S.J. in a fortnight's time."

UNCANNY SLUMBERS

"We left feeling that there was a good chance of a cure. But that very evening whilst we were having supper, my wife suddenly dropped her fork and, laying her head on her plate, went to sleep. I could not make out what was happening. Two minutes passed, two very long minutes. Then my wife came to and said: 'What does it mean? Everything suddenly faded out and I couldn't see anything. And now I feel quite dazed and worn out.' A few moments later she felt better and declared: 'Now I am hungry.'

"The next day, and the following days, the same thing occurred. My wife would go to sleep during the meal. In the evening, just when she was going to bed, at about 8:30 or 9 p.m., she began jabbering strange words and sniggering in a strange way at the ceiling, as if she saw something there. She would walk round the table in a crazy way, pointing at things as if she were a dumb person trying to make herself understood. I used to try to stop her, but she would push me away as if I had become an unpleasant stranger.

"I could not make any sense of it, and I began to wonder what that person had done to my wife, by his 'magnetism,' as he called it. It couldn't go on like that. So, the Thursday after our first visit, we went to his house."

FURTHER TROUBLE

"When we explained what was happening, the healer made the very strange excuse that he had been mistaken in the month of my wife's birth, and that with people born in that month one had to go very gently, although there was nothing to be alarmed about. We could go home again quite happily, because everything would go much better.

"As he said this, B. was radiant. We understood why, later. Satan had carried out his orders. Our return was his first victory. Then my wife went to sleep again, on the spot, in the presence of the healer. He made light of it and contented himself with saying: 'You will eat well, when you leave here, you will see, and you will sleep well tonight.'

"And to tell the truth, on the way home my wife did eat, I think it must have been a whole hand of bananas. When she went to bed she slept like a log, which we understood later, because Satan had a hand in it. When she woke up in the morning, once more she felt completely dazed. Days passed and her state grew worse. She suffered terribly from headaches, which she had never had before. Sometimes she felt a terrible shock and began to cry at the pain it caused her. Then suddenly she would calm down, become tense, standing distraught, her eyes haggard and wide open, fixed on the ceiling, and with her arms outstretched. She would often say: 'I think I am going mad.' At other times she would be like one dead. I could not move her, for fear of breaking a bone. She neither saw nor heard me. This would last for an hour, sometimes an hour and a half, sometimes just a quarter of an hour. And there I was, quite helpless, not knowing what to do.

"Naturally the following Saturday, when B. came to S.J. for his consultations, we went to see him and complain. So we had another session, during which he held my wife's wrists. Then he gave her a bottle of tonic, which he said consisted of oxblood and hemoglobin. He added some crystals which he said were also tonic, and stated that he would make his influence gentler still, although he assured us he was not forcing her in any way. But still my wife showed no improvement. Once more, on the Saturday before Christmas, 1950, we went to S.J. to tell him that he must, at all costs, do something. We were persuaded that it was all his doing, since he was using his magnetism.

"'My poor friends,' he replied to our complaints, 'I can't do any more than I am doing. But with you' — turning to my wife — 'I really don't understand. It seems as if I were faced with a blank wall. When I try to do something, there is some force which stops me from treating you. I've treated lots of others, but I've never met such a wall! I can only make one suggestion: come and stay in the neighborhood, then I can treat you more easily.'

"This was the way the scoundrel was drawing us unconsciously into his net."

IN THE NET

"My wife was very undecided on the way home that day. But an hour later, at her request, we went back to B. at S.J. and she asked him to take her that very evening to the hotel, which was about a mile and a half from S.J. No doubt overjoyed, but showing no signs of it, the healer immediately telephoned the hotel to say that he was bringing two persons who wanted accommodation. That evening, at 9 o'clock, we set off. We stopped at the hotel from Saturday until the following Thursday without any improvement in my wife's condition. Christmas was approaching and my wife wanted to spend it at home. Her state of health was becoming more and more critical. She seemed lost, she didn't recognize me anymore, and she would say to me: 'I don't know you [and she said *vous,* not the familiar *tu*], I don't want to see you.' What was worse, she seemed to have lost all her affection for Annie, whom she used to adore. If she had a knife in her hand when she was cooking, she would go up to the little girl, as if to do her an injury. She felt she was being driven by some inner force. However, she resisted. But once the idea came into her head that she should strangle the child. She was still being driven by this strange force. Fortunately, again she was able to resist. But she began to cry. She suffered intolerably from knowing that she was harboring such terrible intentions against her daughter.

"In January 1951, one day when she was still in bed, she said: 'Go and see B. Tell him he must come and see me. I'm fed up with the whole business. He's got to stop it.' I did as she wanted. In the evening, after his consultations, B. came to our house. He asked to speak to my wife alone. Then he told her to come to his house, alone. So I took her to his house, and left her there alone with him, for about half an hour.

"When she came out, she seemed a bit confused. So I said: 'What's the matter? You're looking very queer.' 'Oh,' she said, "it's that idiot of a B.; he wants me to be his mistress.' I replied: 'Don't talk nonsense. Let's hear no more of it.'

"The healer had not pressed her, particularly since the house was full of people, though his own wife was not there. But, as we shall see, the scoundrel had not given up hope.

"'The month of January passed. My wife was still in a bad way, and she was particularly antagonistic to little Annie. It became such a terrible obsession with her that she could not hold out, and at the beginning of February she said to me: 'You know, I must go to S.J. for treatment. I shall be closer to B. so that he can treat me, and I shall tell him to get me out of this. I can't stand it anymore and *I must get away from my daughter, because I'm afraid of doing her some harm.*'

"We realized afterwards, of course, that this was just the cunning of Satan, working to B.'s orders, in making use of her fears for her daughter to throw her back on B., who hadn't swallowed my wife's refusal of his first proposition.

"'Do you really think it will do any good to be near him? I don't trust him.'

"But since she insisted, I took her back to the hotel where we had stopped before, and I left her there alone, because I had to get back to my work. There was a great deal of coming and going until the following Thursday. My wife had been there since Friday. On Tuesday morning B. came into her room while she was still in bed and made some quite shameless propositions. My wife was indignant, and told him so in suitable terms, then she added: 'Leave me alone! I shall tell my husband everything!'"

THREATS

"At this renewed rebuff B. became threatening: 'If you tell your husband, you will regret it. I don't like resistance, and you'll be sorry for it.'

"'What have you done,' cried my wife, 'to make me so ill?'

"'Look here,' he replied, angrily, 'I haven't made you ill; some fool must have done something to you.'

"'Oh,' said my wife, 'well, that fool is you!'

"His only answer was to sneer: 'I suppose I've just cast a spell on you, that's all!'

"My wife did not really understand and went on: 'I am going to telephone my husband this afternoon and tell him to come and fetch me.'

"'Well, I tell you you are not to phone, and you are to stay here.'

"Thereupon he left the room in a towering rage and went down into the restaurant café. At about 2 o'clock in the afternoon he came back and said: 'Well, have you thought over what I said to you?' And then he offered her some nougat which he had got out of a sweet-machine. My wife took the nougat and flung it in his face, saying: 'You're revolting! There's your nougat: I'm going to telephone my husband.'

"'Well,' replied B., 'we shall see! You'll be sorry you refused.'

"As a matter of fact, my wife had tried in vain, the whole afternoon, to get to the telephone booth, which was only about five or six yards away from her room, in the hotel itself. But it was only late that evening, when I rang up as usual to get the latest news, that she managed to drag herself painfully as far as the telephone and say, in a low whisper: 'Come quickly and fetch me.'

"It was all she had strength to say, but I understood what it meant. By 10 o'clock I was there, and I found her in tears. On Wednesday morning, in spite of her exhaustion, she managed somehow to put on her clothes. With some difficulty I managed to get her to the station, much to the helpless indignation of B. who happened to be taking someone to the station himself at that moment.

"In the train my wife told me what had passed between B. and herself, his humiliating persistence, his threats, and his audacious remark:

"'I can't do without you anymore! I think you must have cast a spell on me!'

"There had, indeed, been a spell, but it came from him, and not from my wife, who had no idea of what it was all about."

EFFECTS OF THE SORTILEGE

"But after our return we were soon to understand. He had said: 'I don't like resistance: you will be sorry for it!'

"Indeed, my wife began to feel the effects of his revenge immediately. She suffered more and more and had to take to her bed. This was in the first fortnight of February 1951. Her ill-health became a real torture; she could not get up, she could neither eat nor sleep and was slowly wasting away. I kept her alive with orange juice, and even that she could hardly swallow. I sent for the doctor, who gave her some injections, but we could see he thought she was in a bad way. I got four doctors in all to see her, but with no better result. One of them suggested sending her to a psychiatric hospital. But she announced, quite definitely, 'I don't want to go there, doctor, I'm not mad, but I feel there is some force inside me which makes me suffer. You may think I'm going to go mad, but I'm not mad now.'

"Toward the end of February, however, we both decided she should go to the convalescent home at Saujon, which was run by a psychiatrist, Dr. Dubois. There she was given all the usual treatment for nervous disorders: douches, electric shocks, and so on. But nothing happened. At the end of two months' treatment she had, however, gained one pound. The crises were less acute. This very relative improvement lasted until the month of August. But one evening, as she was going to bed, everything changed. She dropped the book she was reading, opened her eyes very wide, and cried out: 'My head! My head! I'm going mad!' The crisis lasted about an hour. Then she said: 'It's started again. That B. is up to his tricks: he's trying to drive me mad. It was like shocks inside my head.'

"Her state suddenly grew worse; she could eat nothing and I felt quite helpless. We went to a woman healer who quieted her down for a time, but an hour after we got home it began again, only worse. It seems that there had been a series of attacks and counter-attacks between the woman healer and B. Finally, we were so convinced of his responsibility that we decided to ask for a summons.

"We did so in September 1951. October and November passed without our hearing anything more about it. But in December we had notice to appear before the court, to be confronted with B. But on that day my wife, who had been ill all night, could not get up. So I went to the court alone, and explained everything to the judge. All he said was: 'If your wife cannot attend, we will postpone the hearing.' I didn't feel inclined to accept this. The same thing might happen every time, and our action might go against us. I met B. in the corridor, and I said to him: 'She *shall* come here, in spite of you!' And I managed to make her get up and I brought her in a taxi to the court, which was about a quarter of a mile away. In the presence of the judge, my wife made her deposition. The judge asked B. if he admitted the facts. He had gone white as a sheet and seemed completely at a loss. He admitted all the facts, *including the casting of a spell,* and signed the statement. Even his lawyer had the wind taken out of his sails. B. obviously expected a prosecution, not so much for casting spells, with which the law is not concerned, but for the illegal practice of medicine. A policeman had, in fact, called at our house shortly after I had lodged my complaint. He had found my wife in one of her crises, with a haggard expression and her arms in the air. He confiscated some medicines B. had given us. 'That'll be enough,' he said, 'to let us run him in for illegal medicine.'

"B. suspected as much, for as we left the court he came up to me and said: 'You don't realize what you've brought on my head: they'll sting me for 200,000 francs in fines.' And without worrying about the way he was betraying himself, he went on: 'Listen, withdraw your complaint, and for my part *I've no reason to continue.*' So he was openly admitting what we had always believed, namely, that all my wife's troubles stemmed from him.

"Yielding to his entreaties, we both went back into the court-room and told the judge we were withdrawing our complaint, in the interests of my wife's health.

"'Right,' said the judge, 'you are withdrawing your complaint, but the court reserves the right to prosecute B. for the illegal practice of medicine.'

"When we got home we wrote a letter the public prosecutor, saying we withdrew our complaint, and notified B. of our action."

FRESH ATTACKS

"The healer had achieved what he wanted. My wife passed a whole month without pain. But in January 1952 it all began again, worse than ever. My wife, exasperated, wanted us to go and see B. who was visiting his mother that day. It was his mother who received us, but since my wife insisted on seeing B. in person, he suddenly appeared. A violent dispute then took place in his mother's presence. Finally, since he could not get the last word, he tried to make my wife leave by taking hold of her arm. But she shook herself free and hit him on the nose. Then, as he caught hold of her again, she struck him once more, straight in the face. This time she drew blood, and his nose began to bleed violently. Then I intervened and, taking B. by the arm, I told him to be quiet and leave my wife alone. He obeyed, pulling out his handkerchief, which was soon red with blood. He himself was scarlet with rage. As we were going to leave he came after us, saying: 'I've been attacked in my own home! It's unheard of! I'm going to the police!'

"'All right,' said my wife, 'we'll all go together. You can lodge a complaint and you can also explain why I struck you.'

"Still holding his handkerchief to his nose B. began to threaten: "'As for you,' he said, '*you'll end up in a madhouse.*'

"By so saying, he revealed his plans for revenge. We soon reached the police station. The inspectors were smiling to themselves to see what had happened to him. He even had the audacity to ask the superintendents tell my wife to leave him in peace.

"'Well,' said my wife, 'why don't you make your complaint? Then I will tell them why I hit you.'

"Thereupon he collapsed ignominiously, and merely said: 'No, I'm not making a complaint, but for heaven's sake, leave me alone.' And as we left, he fired this passing shot: 'I must say, for a sick woman, you can hit hard.'"

THE HEALER'S REVENGE

"We were to discover later the plans the healer was cherishing in order to take revenge on a woman who had not only resisted him, but had publicly defied and humiliated him. She was to end her days in a madhouse. He had a servant ready to hand to carry out his threats. This servant was Satan. And the sorcerer's work was made considerably easier by the fact that nowadays there are very few people who really believe in Satan. For most doctors, and for most other people too, possession is quite simply the same thing as madness. So, by casting a spell over my wife, and sending a devil to take possession of her, B. could pretty well count on her being quickly shut up as a lunatic. That would be his revenge, lying ready for him to use.

"The violent dispute I have described took place on January 12, 1952. We went home not suspecting what was in store for us.

The first months were, of course, months of suffering for my wife, but there was nothing to indicate that her state was getting worse. But one night in August 1952 she woke up with a start, terrified and in tears. She seized me by the arm, as if terror-struck, and with a haunted look cried out: 'I'm frightened. He's here. He's coming toward the bed; drive him away!'

"'But what are you afraid of?' I asked, trying to calm her down.

"'There! He's there! A beast with claws and the body of a serpent, but with B.'s head!'

"And she kept on calling out: 'He's coming close to the bed. I'm frightened!'

"She was shouting in her terror and distress, and that lasted all night. In the morning she was exhausted. Her suffering continued. Two or three nights running the attacks went on. She was seized by a sort of delirium. She seemed to collapse into herself and suddenly, as if in a trance, she began to speak in foreign languages, laughing distractedly, and moving about restlessly for three-quarters of an hour or more. Then, when the crisis had passed, she would come to herself and say: 'What has happened to me? I thought I didn't exist anymore. I couldn't see anything. Oh, how my neck aches!'

"And I, her husband, still not knowing it was Satan, I was miserable at my own helplessness. B.'s threats kept echoing in my ears: 'You'll end up in a madhouse!'

"I kept turning the words over and over in my mind, wondering what would happen to us.

"There was naturally no lack of advice from friends and neighbors but, of course, none of them thought of the presence of a Devil. Various people persuaded us to go and see different healers. But none of them could help us, and they gave up the case when they learned they were dealing with B."

THE DOORWAY TO SALVATION

"While all this was going on, another daughter was born to us, in December 1952. In spite of her mother's terrible ordeal during the year, the child did well. One thing I should mention is that after those terrifying nights my wife could no longer endure the sight of a crucifix, or religious pictures, or a rosary—particularly not a rosary—in the house. During her crises she would talk of nothing but of throwing them all out. But this sudden aversion to blessed objects did not open our eyes to the satanic element in these new developments.

"One day in February 1953, Providence—for it was surely an intervention of Providence, without any merit on our part—brought us to Fr. Berger-Bergès. We told him our story, just as we had done to so many others. He received us with great kindness but told us we would first have to get a medical opinion, to see if there was any natural cause or not; he said he could not take action until this had been established, but that he would be very ready to help us if it should prove necessary.

"A fortnight passed after this visit. At the end of February we decided, at a friend's suggestion, to consult the priests of Belief.

"Strangely enough, we had trouble with the journey, both coming and going. The taxi had one breakdown after another, something that had never happened to the chauffeur before.

"At Belief ... we told our story again. After half an hour the almoner handed us a little book, advising us to read it and follow its instructions. He, for his part, would do what was necessary. But, he pointed out, that it might take six months or more. It would all depend on the will of God, who had His reasons for sending us these trials."

RELIGIOUS CONVERSION

"All that we had suffered since 1950 had, unknown to us, been preparing us to accept what we were now asked to do. We listened to the priest's advice. We went home determined to follow it to the best of our ability. On the way home we again had one breakdown after another, and the chauffeur declared that this was the only time in his life that he had had so many.

"But for the first time for many, many days my wife felt calmer. The priest who received us had, we discovered later, performed a most effective exorcism at a distance. It was Satan himself who told us about it later. And yet, in these February days of 1953, we were still not thinking about his presence. But an astonishing transformation soon took place in us. Up to then we had hardly considered ourselves believers, and certainly not practicing Christians. All at once, under the influence of a grace which we only learned to appreciate later, we formed the decision to go to Mass every Sunday, to partake of the Sacraments, and to communicate frequently. The advice we had been given was beginning to bear fruit. The divine action was one of prodigious strength. Our conversion took place very rapidly. We began to understand things we had not hitherto known about. And yet, when my wife wanted to attend Mass, there was enormous difficulty. One has to have lived through something like that to have any idea of what it was like. But we stuck to it. Prayers were said for us. It was like a battle which had started between two conflicting armies, without our being aware of it."

In the next chapter we shall deal with the most striking episodes in this battle, which was to last for many years.

❧ 8 ❧

THE EXORCISMS

BEFORE THE CEREMONY

THE MOMENT HUSBAND and wife began to experience the effect of divine grace, Satan made his final effort to prevent the exorcism taking place. The reader will have perceived a certain similarity between this case and that of the woman of Piacenza. As with her, Mme. G. had displayed symptoms which suggested an unbalanced mind. The intention of the sorcerer—for there were sorcerers in both cases—was to get his victim certified as a lunatic, in revenge, in both cases, for an unrequited passion.

There was, in the case of the G. family, some considerable delay. The bishopric showed little understanding. The Curé of S.J., who will reappear later, did not believe it was a case of possession, neither did a Benedictine almoner, and the bishop was naturally influenced by them.

After many hesitations, insistence on the one hand and rebuffs on the other, the bishop was informed that there was no competent priest available to perform the exorcisms, and the couple was advised to apply to Bordeaux. They did so and went to Bordeaux in the hope of finding a solution to their problems.

Progress was very slow. Once in Bordeaux the couple was directed to a religious community of great experience where, after a very scrupulous investigation, it was decided that exorcism would be justified. There were, in effect, several exorcisms, without any decisive result. But since he could not stay any longer in Bordeaux, the husband renewed his appeal to his own bishop, asking for help in his own locality. After much discussion, Fr. Berger-Bergès was officially entrusted with the exorcism. He is a former superior of the Grand Seminary, and thus a theologian, a competent and zealous priest, who understood the full gravity of the task allotted to him. He was prepared to draw on all the resources provided for him by the Church in such cases: prayer and mortification, a boundless confidence in God, in Our Lord Jesus Christ, in Mary Immaculate, in the Communion of the Saints, and in the power of the formulae of the ritual itself.

In order to follow the way in which he discharged his duties in so delicate and serious a task, we could have drawn on his personal notes of each exorcism, but we are authorized to make use of an invaluable document provided by the husband of the possessed woman, in the form of notes taken by himself at each session. We reproduce them, in this case, verbatim.

THE FIRST SESSION

"On September 14, 1953, we arrived at the presbytery in F. M. le Curé invited us into his office. Fr. Berger had arrived a few minutes before. Just as we were going into the office, my wife began to dance around on tiptoe, frantic at the sight of Fr. Berger, for the 'foul beast' that possessed her knew that the decisive moment of exorcism had arrived.

"We went into the sacristy and then into the church, but as we came and stood in front of the altar of the Blessed Virgin, the 'foul beast' tried to turn away, for it made him feel uncomfortable. But I tied my wife to a chair, and Fr. Berger ordered the Devil to be silent. Then, having prayed to the saints,[16] he began his interrogation:

"'What is your name?'

"'It's none of your business.'

"'In the name of God and of the Church, I command you to tell me your name.'

"'I am Satan! I am great! I am Someone!'

"'When will you leave this woman?'

"'When I want to.'

"'Why did you come into this woman?'

"'Well, I didn't come of my own accord. I was sent.'

"'Who sent you?'

"'It's none of your business.'

"'Once more I command you to tell me.'

"'Well then, that other fellow.'

"'Who is he?'

"'He has forbidden me to tell you.'

"Then the priest took some holy water and sprinkled the Devil. He cried with pain and immediately gave the name of the man who had sent him. It was W.B. [This was the magnetist-healer, whom his wife had consulted, and who was well known in the district.]

"'Did you make a pact with him?'

"'Yes,' answered Satan.

"'Well, you are to fetch this pact and bring it here.'

"'Where?'

"'To the altar of the Blessed Virgin.'

"Whereupon the terrified Devil began to stammer: 'No, no ... I ... I ... can't.'

---

[16] That is to say, after having recited the litanies of the saints which, according to the ritual, begin every exorcism.

"'Why not?' asked Fr. Berger.

"'Because B. doesn't want me to. We work together, and he told me to stand firm.'

"'No matter,' said the father, 'I want this pact and if you don't get it between now and tomorrow, you shall suffer until you do bring it.'

"'You're a good-for-nothing scoundrel,' declared the Devil.

"'Maybe,' replied the priest, 'but you are to go.'

"'I haven't done anything to you. Leave me in peace!'

"'We shall see,' said the exorcist.

"Then he made Satan look at the crucifix, and Satan cried out: 'And that too! As if there wasn't enough already. And you bring out that puppet!'

"'That's enough,' said the priest. 'Now we shall see. You shall suffer, I promise you.'

"And the priest began the prayers of the exorcism. The Devil cried out, screamed, twisted, wept, and begged him to stop. The priest did not relax. He commanded the Devil to kneel down and worship God. This made the beast furious, so that he made his victim rise and stand on tiptoe. He would not give ground. But the exorcist took some holy water and ordered him to fall again to his knees. The rebellious spirit had to yield and kneel down, shouting abuse and swearing to be revenged. But the priest told him to be silent:

"'I am in command here. Will you leave?'

"'Only if I want to,' replied Satan.

"'In the name of the Virgin Mary, I command you to leave!' This time the Devil answered calmly: 'Madam! O Madam!' Then the exorcist went on: 'And in the name of C. [the possessed woman] who has overcome you, the would-be lover!'

"At that the Devil became enraged and answered: 'I forbid you to speak of that. You've no right to.'

"'We shall see,' said the father, applying the crucifix attached to which was a little medallion belonging to C.

"The Devil screamed with pain and called out: 'Not that! Not that! It hurts!'

"'So much the better,' said the priest. 'May it destroy you!'

"As he continued to press the Devil more and more closely, the latter vented his pain and rage on the priest:

"'You wanted to take her from me!' [meaning C.]

"But after another moment of suffering the Devil collapsed. Thereupon the exorcist reminded him that he must depart, or his suffering would become more and more terrible as the days went by.

"'Do you understand?' asked the priest. 'Lift one arm as a sign that you understand.'

"And Satan, at the end of his strength, raised the right arm.

"The first exorcism was over. My wife came to herself, a little confused, but soon she became normal. The session had lasted an hour and a half.

"I must say that at this first session Satan was violent and wanted to play the master, but he had to yield to someone stronger than himself—God's representative, Fr. Berger."

COMMENT

It is hardly necessary to comment on this report which is so completely straightforward. We should, however, note that the husband makes a clear distinction between the times when his wife is perfectly normal, and the times when what he calls the "Devil," or the "foul beast," is speaking or acting through her. From the beginning to the end of the exorcism the Devil is speaking solely for himself when he tells of the pact made with the "magnetizer" and the constraint this man, whom he names, can exercise on him to make him possess the woman. The fact of possession is demonstrated chiefly by the convulsions, the screams, and the suffering which appear to be inflicted by the contact with holy water, with the crucifix, and by the sight of the Blessed Virgin.

It would be unnatural for a person suffering from any normal illness to be so violently affected by such intrinsically inoffensive objects. According to the monks who carried out the exorcisms at Bordeaux, it had already been noted, particularly on August 31, 1953, that in similar circumstances the obsessed woman had had violent spasms, and the Devil—the Enemy, as he is called in the exorcists' report—reacted in various ways, with pride, trembling supplications, and fallacious promises. Further, the possessed woman's countenance had taken on a hideous cast.

We should also note the very striking resemblance between this exorcism and the one at Piacenza. We are again in the same environment, engaged in the same struggle, with the same failures and successes. The similarity will become even clearer in subsequent sessions.

Each session is such a tense and exhausting conflict that it cannot be prolonged indefinitely. For this very simple reason the exorcism has to be interrupted and postponed to the next session.

SECOND EXORCISM

"September 16, 1953.

"We arrived at the Cure's house. Fr. Berger was already there. Suddenly my wife began dancing in his presence, first on one leg and then on the other, as usual. I had difficulty in bringing her to the altar of the Blessed Virgin, because she tried to hide behind a cupboard in the sacristy. But I took her in my arms and set her down in a chair, strapping her to it, because the 'foul beast' was up to his tricks, at his first sight of Our Mother in Heaven.

"Father Berger commanded him to be silent, and whilst he was praying to the saints and reciting the litanies, the Devil, looking at him askance, began to shower abuse on him:

"'Old rogue! Old bandit! It's not true! You're a liar! I'm the one, I am!' and so on.

"Then the priest repeated the question of the previous session:

"'When, on what day, at what hour, will you leave?'

"After some hesitation, Satan replied:

"'It doesn't mean a thing to me. I'm quite comfortable.'

"The exorcist asked him:

"'And B.? Did you ask him for the paper?'

"'Yes,' replied Satan.

"'Where is it?'

"'Over there, under your good wife!' pointing to a little angel. The priest looked:

"'There is nothing there.'

"The Devil chuckled at this trick, but the father came back and said:

"'You are going to get the pact for me, for there is a pact, signed with his blood, isn't there?'

"'Yes,' replied Satan, 'but he doesn't want to give it to me, and he says I'm a good-for-nothing if I don't hold out to the end.'

"'I must have this pact, do you understand!' said the priest, 'and you know where it is. In his desk?'

"'No,' said Satan. 'He's taken it out and put it in a briefcase.'

"'No matter. I must have it tomorrow: you will place it under this little angel. Do you understand?'

"'Yes, yes,' replied Satan.

"'And meanwhile, you are going to suffer,' said the priest, beginning the exorcism.

"'Eh, eh, he's even worse than the other,' cried the Devil, looking at the priest. 'It's ... it's ... beyond a joke ... what he's up to with me!'

"'I shall be up to still worse,' said the exorcist, 'if you won't leave. And with or without that bit of paper, you will leave, I can tell you that! Why don't you leave this woman?' he went on, 'and how long have you been there?'

"'Three years this September,' replied Satan. 'She came for treatment. At first it was all right, but then something went wrong.'

"'Why?' asked the exorcist.

"'He has forbidden me to say.'

"'I command you to tell me, although I know why. He wanted to get possession of this woman's body?'

"'Yes,' replied the Devil.

"'And when he didn't succeed, he sent you, and you dare to obey him: you are his slave! You are not ashamed? You, Satan?'

"'O, but I do the commanding! I'm the one,' replied Satan, for he was so proud that he did not like to admit that he was obeying orders. He was impudent enough to say to the priest:

"'You! Get down on your knees and worship me!'

"'What?' exclaimed the father. 'You'll see. Down on your knees immediately and worship God!'

"And Satan obeyed. Then he began to suffer, howling with pain, tearing at his breast, yapping like a puppy, until the priest ended his prayer and presented him with a little image belonging to C. by applying it to the forehead, so that he howled again, at the end of his strength.

"The priest reminded him that he was to bring the pact, or he would go on suffering as long as he was in the woman. Exhausted, he murmured: 'Yes, yes.'

"Then the exorcist said to him: 'Good. Till tomorrow, then. We shall see.'

"Thereupon the priest left the sacristy, the Devil declaring: 'I can't stand anymore.'

"My wife came to herself. Then we went, all three, into the sacristy, together with M. le Curé, and the father explained the meaning of the session to M. le Curé, saying that the 'foul beast' was under orders from B.

"At these words my wife started up, and the Devil declared: 'It's I who give orders, not he!'

"But the priest silenced him, and I drew my wife away. This session lasted forty-five minutes, and the Devil was much calmer and less rebellious than at the first session."

Later battles followed more or less the same pattern, although varying in detail.

An interesting point about the third session was the admission by the Devil that he had been greatly helped in the first period of possession by the incredulity of a priest who would not believe in the presence of a devil in the possessed woman and was therefore opposed to exorcism.

THIRD SESSION

Again, we quote the husband himself.

"September 18, 1953.

"The weather was appalling, and the rain never stopped, but we decided to set out, and the exorcist never hesitated: he left in the pouring rain, for he wanted Satan to see that nothing would stop him when he had to do battle with the foul fiend.

"We reached the church and, as in earlier sessions, the Devil began to play up, but that day he spoke German.[17] He tried to turn back, but the priest brought him to order.

"But during the prayers to the saints — the litanies — the abuse began again:

[17] Needless to say, the possessed woman, a simple country woman, did not know a word of German.

"'Old rogue! Old bandit! Just listen to what he's saying! Won't he ever stop? What's the matter with him?'

"Then the father began the prayer of exorcism: then the Devil howled and begged him to stop. Whereupon the exorcist asked him:

"'Haven't you brought the pact?'

"'What pact?'

"'The pact you had to get from B.'

"'Oh, I'd forgotten all about it,' said the Devil. 'You've got a good memory!'

"'Yes,' said the priest. 'So, you haven't brought it. Well, alright. Now, are you going to leave this woman?'

"'No,' answered the Devil categorically.

"'So, you won't go? Well, just wait, and you will see. You will understand.'

"The father sprinkled him with holy water and repeated the prayer which made the Devil suffer so much. When he brought out the crucifix, the Devil was still mocking:

"'Well, here's the puppet again!'

"'Wait a minute: you'll see! We're not done with you yet,' said the priest, continuing his prayer.

"Suddenly Satan called out: 'Ah, your D. [mentioning a local priest]. He didn't believe in anything like that. He prevented it as long as he could. As for me, I could see what was happening. He helped me a lot, he did: he didn't mean to, but he did.'

"(This statement, says the report, which we reproduce textually, refers to D. in the parish of S.J. and the words were heard by three witnesses: Fr. Berger, the Curé, and myself.)

"But after Satan had made this statement, the exorcist silenced him by saying:

"'That is not my business: what I want is for you to leave: in the name of the One who bruised your head, in the name of Our

Mother in Heaven, who commands both in Heaven and on earth, and everywhere, you must obey!'

"Once more the priest placed the crucifix on the woman's breast, and added:

"'And in the name of C. [my wife], who also rejects you, go!'

The Devil howled, and twisted, and shouted at the priest:

"'I shan't forget you, trust me! You are making me suffer, you old sack of coals, but I shan't forget you!'

"The exorcist prayed, asking the Blessed Virgin to drive out Satan. Satan became enraged and declared:

"'Oh, he'll do it ... he'll do it yet! He knows what to do to make me leave, the swine. Oh, you swine! I know I shall be forced to leave. And I didn't want to go!'

"Satan began to snivel:

"'I haven't done what I was told to do and now I've got to leave. I know I'm beaten, and it's all because of this scoundrel of a Berger, who's found out everything: why did I have to run across him? I've been working so hard these last three years. Just look what I've come to, me, *the great Satan, who rules over all the world!* No, it's not possible, it's not possible. It can't have happened to me!'

"Once more Satan referred to the priest who had not believed in possession:

"'Oh, D., you're not a real pal. You ought to have stopped them getting up to their tricks. D., you're a good-for-nothing: you ought to go on stopping them.'

"But the exorcist stopped him:

"'That's enough! You are going to leave, for the Virgin Mary has ordered you to: it's not from me anymore, a little servant of God, but from the Virgin Mary.'

"Turning toward the altar, the priest went on: 'Come, Virgin Mary, make Satan depart. I am counting on you, Virgin Mary:

your honor is at stake; one little gesture from you, and the Devil will go back to Hell.'

"The Devil could endure this no longer: he was listening, and stammering:

"'Madam ... Madam ... I am frightened, Madam ... We can't say anything to you, great Lady! It is forbidden to us!'

"His fears were obvious, as he himself had to admit:

"'I'm frightened! I am frightened! She is coming! She is descending from the clouds! No, no! Leave me a little while longer! Just a little while, Madam!'

"The Devil leant forward in pain, and suddenly the possessed woman had a feeling of nausea and tried to vomit. That lasted five minutes and then, in spite of his pain, Satan said: 'No, I don't want to leave.'

"Then the priest began to pray, placing the crucifix once more on the possessed woman. The Devil's sufferings started again, and he said:

"'Stop! Stop! I will go, since you want me to!'

"Then the exorcist said to him: 'It is the Virgin Mary, not I, who wishes you to go.'

"The Devil began to rage:

"'*You* don't frighten me! But I'm afraid of her, the Great Lady, of her alone, for I can do nothing against her: her will prevails.'

"The Devil was panic-stricken and could not move. He listened and answered simply:

"'I shall have to go! I shall have to! Yes, Madam.'

"Turning toward the priest he said:

"'It's all your fault, yes, it's all your fault, you old swine!'

"'I am flattered: I am proud of it, for Satan is in my hands, and I am making him suffer. You will never suffer enough, you foul fiend!'

"'Oh,' said the Devil, 'you are my greatest enemy, Berger.'

"'So much the better,' said the priest. 'I am quite satisfied. It is an honor to be called the enemy of Satan, for you know we are called "The sons of Mary." We are the community of Chavagnes, the Sons of Mary Immaculate—and Mary has bruised your head, old serpent!'

"Then the exorcist prayed to the Blessed Virgin:

"'Come, little Mother, you won't leave the last word to Satan! One word from you, and the foul fiend will go. Unless you want Satan to suffer still more: tomorrow will be *your* day, O blessed Virgin—Saturday,' and turning to Satan: 'Well, will you go now, or do you want to wait until tomorrow?'

"'I don't want anything . . . I don't know.'

"'Good,' said the father, 'well, tomorrow you'll see! You'll understand, because you will suffer more and more. Till tomorrow, Satan!'

"So the priest concluded the third session. My wife came to herself, rather tired, but more lighthearted and at ease."

This session had lasted two hours and a quarter and was remarkable both for the declarations made by Satan and for his attitude to the Virgin Mary.

In all these sessions, apart from the interrogations and the dialogues with Satan, which were in French, all the exorcisms, including those which made such a striking impression on Satan, were in Latin, which was quite unknown to the possessed woman, but which were able to affect Satan.

Fourth Exorcism

"Today the weather was favorable and the sun came out. We went to the church and after I had strapped my wife to the chair, the father began the usual litanies to the saints and, as on other occasions, the Devil began to abuse him:

"'You scoundrel, you swine, you're starting the same old game, are you? It's not true: you're a liar … it's not me, I tell you, it's not me that did it: just listen to him! He never stops talking; he won't stop. You must be thirsty, you swine. Are you going to stop? I'm here, I am … I am beautiful!'

"'Ah, yes, you're beautiful,' said the priest. 'You're an old serpent!'

"'Just listen to him,' said Satan, 'now he's insulting me! Why don't you respect me? Ah, but … '

"'What?' said the priest, 'Respect you? You, the foul fiend? Wait! You will see!'

"The exorcist said another prayer from the ritual. The Devil screamed and cried:

"'Stop him! Stop him! Don't you see he is hurting me? Didn't you make me suffer enough this morning? [Only instead of "suffer" he used a very coarse expression.] Do you have to go on? You're a swine, a criminal!'

"The father commanded him to be silent, then asked:

"'Will you go, yes or no?'

"'Yes, yes or no. I don't know. I haven't made up my mind. It isn't the right moment.'

"'So it isn't the right moment. Well, I command you, in the name of the Virgin Mary, to leave the woman immediately, for today is the day of the Great Lady herself.'

"'I know,' replied Satan, 'but she hasn't told me to go today.'

"'Liar, hypocrite, foul fiend,' said the priest, 'now you are going to kneel down at once to the Virgin Mary.'

"After several refusals, the Devil knelt down.

"'And now,' said the exorcist, 'you are to say, "Hail Mary!"'

"'Ah, no! Don't go to extremes, or I shan't say anything.'

"'You are to say, "Hail Mary!"'

"Then Satan stammered: 'H-h-hail … '

"'And now,' said the exorcist, 'you must say, "Mary."'"

"In a burst of anger, the Devil spoke:

"'Hail, M-M-Mary!'

"'Ah,' said the priest, 'he has just said "Hail Mary!"'

"'It's not true, it's not true,' shouted the Devil. 'I didn't say anything. And I don't want to go. It suits me here.'

"'We shall see,' said the exorcist.

"Then he gave me a sign, and I led my wife up to the altar. Satan was overcome with fear and began to tremble. There was silence.

"The priest showed him the tabernacle and said:

"'You see this? In the name of God and the Church, I command you to leave this woman.'

"The Devil did not reply. There was silence for about a minute. Suddenly the Devil turned to the exorcist:

"'Did you hear? Tell me, did you hear? Didn't you hear what he said? It was to you he said it! He said: "Your place is not here." Did you hear it?'

"Again, there was silence.

"Satan turned his face toward the altar: 'Listen!' He trembled as he spoke:

"'But no! It's to me that he said it! It's not possible! He said to me: "Your place is not here!"'

"'True,' said the priest. 'Your place is not here. Go back to Hell and leave the woman here.'

"The Devil began to tremble and weep. Suddenly, after a silence, an extraordinary thing happened; Satan, the proud, asked of his own accord that he should be left alone, and kneeling down before the altar prostrated himself to the ground and worshipped Almighty God. Lifting his face toward the tabernacle, he answered God:

"'Yes, yes. I hear.'

"Turning toward the priest, he said: 'Did you hear? He has told me to respect and obey you.'

"Then once more he bowed his head to the ground in adoration and stayed in that attitude for the rest of the exorcism, about half an hour. The onlookers were overcome with amazement. The great Satan, as he called himself, was kneeling in adoration of the Lord whom he must obey. And from the moment he received God's command, he did not move, but remained kneeling and listening with respect to the priest.

"This lasted for some time. Then Satan spoke:

"'Well, how long do I have to stay here? I want to go.'

"The exorcist replied:

"'Go, Satan! Your place is not here. God has told you, and I repeat it: leave this woman to God and go back to your companions in Hell.'

"'Ah, but that's not the same thing: surely I've got the right to have a woman!'

"'You have no right,' said the priest. 'Go back to Hell and leave this woman. Here she is at home, but you are not. Begone, Satan!'

"'I'm quite willing to go,' said the Devil, 'but not alone.' And addressing the onlookers: 'Are you coming? Has anyone thought about me? I can't stay here.'

"Once more the priest said:

"'Be gone you foul fiend! Hypocrite, liar, coward!'

"'Come now,' said the Devil, 'be polite. I respect you because I can't do otherwise: it is forbidden, but I'm not afraid of you, you know!'

"The priest reminded him:

"'Look on the face of God!'

"The Devil turned round and declared:

"'Ah, you know, *he* does make me a little afraid.'

"But suddenly, in spite of himself, he prostrated himself and said:

"'Yes, yes.'

"Turning toward the priest: 'Oh, sir! *He* has told me to call you "Sir." Well, well … Since that's the case, I, I the great one …'

"But he could not continue, and prostrating himself again:

"'Oh no, I cannot, I will not.'

"Addressing the exorcist:

"'Did you hear that? *He* said: "You must leave today." But it's not possible … after I've worked so hard these three years…. Ah, your D. [the priest who did not believe in exorcism] he didn't see anything! You'd better buy him some glasses. He'd see better. They said she was ill! It was I who was there! They said she was in pain! That was me, again. And you didn't see anything. Not very smart, were you? Not to see it was the great Satan who was there! Now I can tell you: it was I, the great Satan, and I'm still here! Would you like me to show you that I'm still here?'

"'I know,' said the priest, 'that you are still here.'

"'Oh, you!' retorted Satan, 'you know everything, you! You discovered everything: but I'm still here, and I'm not afraid of you. And so I shan't leave.'

"Satan raised himself to his knees, for he was still prostrate, and made hideous grimaces, pointing to himself and saying:

"'I'm still here, the Great One, the Master of the World!'

"But then, looking at the tabernacle, he was thrown to the ground once more, prostrating himself in obvious fear, his hands scratching at the ground. He twisted in pain, then suddenly collapsed on his back, gasping for breath for several moments. Then, as suddenly, he got to his knees again, but still wanted to master the situation. But in spite of himself, once again he had to prostrate himself, and the exorcist remarked:

"'You see, you, the Great One, you obey!'

"But the Devil, looking at the carpet, replied:

"'Oh, I'm just looking at the carpet: it's a good carpet. I'll make one like it!'"

"Although he still had his face to the ground in an attitude of adoration, he tried to carry it off by saying:

"'I must look at the carpet more closely. I'm getting shortsighted.' Then, raising his head, 'Well, since that's the case, I won't go. We'll soon see who's the first to have enough!'

"'Good,' said the priest, 'we shall see!'

"The prayer of exorcism, the holy water, caused Satan more pain, so that he could hardly articulate: 'I am great!'

"But suddenly the pain was too much for him, and he collapsed again, on his back, struggling, gasping, and writhing.

"Having made him suffer, the exorcist spoke to him:

"'So you will not leave! Well, we will start again tomorrow, and the day after that, if necessary. But I promise you, you will leave.'

"And the father withdrew, whilst Satan pulled himself up, saying:

"'I am the great Satan! I command the whole world!'

"Then my wife came to herself and approached the altar. Clasping her hands in prayer, she said: 'Oh God! Oh God!' Then she genuflected and made the Sign of the Cross, but Satan was still active and rebelled. She withdrew in confidence that God would save her from the power of the foul fiend.

"This session lasted three hours and a quarter. Satan was made to suffer, but the foul fiend will only leave when he is exhausted and at the end of his tether.

"During this session Satan was much calmer, he obeyed God's order to respect the priest, who allowed him no respite."

WORK IN DEPTH

For a moment we will stop quoting from the husband's notes. The Devil was obviously losing something of his strength and arrogance at each session. Often he seemed to have left, but came back again, probably as the result of new malefices operated from a distance by the man who sent him.

But the exorcist did not content himself with purely ritual intervention. As every writer on the subject recommends, he took great pains to deepen the possessed woman's piety, to reassure her, to lead her to prayer and Communion, together with the husband. He considered that the couple's piety was his greatest asset in the struggle with the Devil. Formerly the young couple had not been particularly devout, but now they were developing a deeper sense of religion. Toward the priest who had been at such pains to help them, they were full of confidence and gratitude. In fact, when he spoke of them, he was obviously deeply moved by this gratitude.

Whilst continuing with the exorcisms, which were now taking place at ever greater intervals, he had been trying to approach the problem in depth. Sometimes Satan reverted to the attack and the possessed woman displayed painful resistance. It gave her a great deal of trouble, but she was grateful for the prayers said on her behalf.

Fr. Berger considers that there are many cases in which Satan *cannot leave,* although he would like to since the exorcisms are certainly painful to him. If he leaves, he is sent back again by the magnetist on whom he depends, and whose orders he must obey by virtue of the pact they have concluded.

This is, incidentally, an established fact. Canon Saudreau has particularly stressed this point: "The spirits in possession are sometimes caught, as it were, in a trap: they are kept captive, by God's command, in the body they have entered. From time to time they express a desire to leave it, but they cannot. In such cases the purpose of the exorcism is not so much to expel them, as to keep them under control, to reduce their power and, finally, to make it almost impossible for them to do any harm."

As an example of this type of captivity we shall quote, not this time from the husband's notes but from the exorcist's own report to the bishop, dated January 1, 1955.

THE EXORCISM OF DECEMBER 31, 1954

"After fifteen months and fifteen days of relentless struggle against the Fiend, we were searching for a means of giving full weight to the injunctions of the Church, at the last session of the year. We therefore decided, the G.s and myself, by private arrangement with the Sister Superior, to hold the session in my chapel of St. Joan. I was hoping to get to the bottom of this obstinacy: if possible, to find out why it occurred, or at least to get some further details by way of confirming what Satan had already declared.

"At 9 o'clock yesterday evening, therefore, a memorable session occurred, first in an atmosphere of revolt, then in one of slow responses, respectful and profoundly disturbing.

"On arrival at the garden which surrounds the chapel, Mme. G. suddenly left her husband and, Satan taking possession, fled into the dark shadows between the trees ... a hasty pursuit. G. managed to lay hands on the Fiend after an extremely violent struggle ... the Fiend had to be dragged along ... on reaching the chapel he tried to cling to the ground. G. managed, with great difficulty, to pick up the body, weighing three times its normal weight, and carry it into the chapel. The Fiend, having been brought by force into the chapel, tried to escape between the benches.... As a precaution, I locked the door.... Then I intervened with authority, using holy water. Finally, I was able to make Satan obey the command to enter the sanctuary and to stand at the foot of the altar steps, facing the tabernacle, and close to the altar of the Blessed Virgin.... I ordered him to sit down.... He stood up for a moment in defiance....

Finally, he sat down on a chair by the side of the steps but began to protest in a loud voice. I commanded him to be silent. He obeyed and the exorcism began.

"But before reporting the exorcism, I would like to explain why I have dwelt at length on Satan's attitude of rebellion and resistance. *It was the first time for more than a year,* to be exact, since December 25, 1953, that Satan had tried to prevent his victim from entering a church or chapel or any religious establishment. For a year Mme. G. had been able to pursue her devotions without any such manifestation of violence. This sudden hardening of Satan's attitude can only be explained by the following facts: the previous evening, at my house, the G.s had been telling me how B. in his dispensary at J. had been raging against Mme. G. (Mme. G. has an inner knowledge of any conversation relating to her, a phenomenon frequently observed in demonic possession), and had been shouting 'What, isn't the bitch dead yet? I've had enough. Either she'll have to pass out, or I shall!'

"That is why Satan appeared with a sullen manner and that insolent smile you have seen yourself. This inspired me with the desire, on this last day of 1954, to conduct a very vigorous exorcism in order to bring Satan to heel, and to order him, through the exorcism, to depart. I also wondered if perhaps I had not made sufficient use of my authority to command. Perhaps the Fiend was not sufficiently afraid of me. So, turning toward Satan, who was there in front of me — Mme. G. having lost consciousness — my voice dry and cutting, but full of indignation, I declared: 'Tomorrow is the last day of the year, and for you, unclean spirit, it is your last day in this woman. Do you hear me? Tomorrow evening, in this chapel, in front of your Master, and the Blessed Virgin, you will undergo the final exorcisms, and I promise you that, willy-nilly, you will leave!' At these words Satan disappeared, and Mme. G. came to herself. It was therefore undoubtedly a feeling of fear, and an expectation of what was awaiting him, that made Satan refuse to enter the chapel, and provoked this unaccustomed resistance which the husband had such difficulty in overcoming.

THE EXORCISM

"I began the exorcism.... The husband, as usual, was standing close behind me. It was about 9.30 p.m. I admit that at the bottom of my heart I was cherishing an idea which uplifted me—perhaps it was indeed the hour of the Fiend's departure. I had decided that the only words I should say to Satan in the course of the exorcism, and delivered with such authority that no reply would be possible, would be 'In the name of God and of Mary Immaculate, I command you to leave this woman!' Theses exorcisms were to be repeated three times, ending each time with the well-known words of the ritual: *Humiliare*.

"As soon as the exorcisms began, Satan displayed a truly impressive calm and respect—and I use the words deliberately. I would almost dare to say it was a religious attitude. And as soon as the *Humiliare* was pronounced, Satan, facing toward the tabernacle, prostrated himself with his head to the ground. And then, at the end of each of the exorcisms which made Satan repeat the gesture of adoration, I pronounced in a resounding voice the single injunction: *'In the name of God and of Mary Immaculate, I command you to leave this woman!'* Satan raised his head slowly at these words, and to our great surprise, since we were not expecting any answer or any sort of statement, he began to explain his presence in the victim. Here are his exact words, uttered after each of my adjurations:

(1). After the first recitation of the exorcism (in a slow, calm voice, obviously pain-laden and imploring, so that both G. and I were deeply impressed):

*"'Leave ... go from here ... I cannot ... you know very well that
I cannot.... It's that man* [B.] *who makes me stay ... I would have
gone long ago if I could ... But that man ... won't allow me to go....
If you think I like seeing you come along with your book to torture me!
And particularly since I know there's nothing to be done.'*

"I interrupted him curtly: "'You lie! You are a liar!'

"'No, I am not lying.'

"'Yes, you are lying.'

*"'No, I am not. I know I am a liar, but not now. If I don't leave,
it's because I can't.'*

("The conviction and sincerity underlying his remarks was, for
us, unmistakable.)

(2). After the second recitation of the exorcisms (a more discouraged attitude: he spoke in a low voice, as if exhausted.... For the
second time he has heard my adjuration, pronounced in the same
authoritative manner, brooking no delay).

"'I can't ... I can't ... I can't.' (Here he leaned back slowly, head
thrown back, a gesture we interpreted as a desperate effort to quit
the body. Then his head fell forward again.)

"'I tell you I can't [louder and more firmly] *I shall leave when he
has understood.... At present he hasn't understood, but he is looking.
He'll have to be converted* [sic] *before I leave, and I know that you will
get him* [these are Satan's actual words]. *It is up to you* [the Church]
*to do what you have to do. As for me, I shall be against you: I shall do
everything I can to prevent you getting him.'*

(3). Third recitation of the exorcism, third adjuration to depart
(same calm, respectful tone).

"'Just now he [B.] *is in a state of violent agitation ... he can't understand why the spell still hasn't worked ... he's going to play his trump
card.... If there is a spell, then one or the other has to throw his hand
in, ... He can't understand why the influences flow back upon him ...*

I can't tell him it's you, that he's dealing with a priest ... [here a short pause, then] *Listen* ... *to convert him, you must recite many Rosaries, many* ... *many.* ... *You'll be the one to drive me out, but it'll take time.'*

"Satan then disappeared: it was the final exorcism of the year 1954. Mme. G. came to herself, very slowly and absolutely exhausted." The exorcist's report concludes with the following, very relevant remarks:

"Anyone, of course, is free to form his own opinion of such a session, but those who, like G. and myself, have for fifteen months been in almost daily contact with the visible presence of Satan, with his constantly changing attitudes, his methods, his lies, and his truths, with his incredible deviltry, open or disguised, for us it was a declaration made at God's command. For us it contained all necessary instructions for ending this terrible spell, as Fr. Paile has called it, through the power of the Church.

"I believe, Monseigneur, that I shall not have to write to you again. You see what direction events are taking. Time is an important factor: in fact, a constant factor in God's mysterious design. No need to add that the G.s intend to devote themselves more and more to the Rosary, and they are counting on your generous help."

The battle is still in progress. But victory now seems assured. Thanks to the exorcisms the couple have been able to resume an almost normal life. There are long periods of respite. And when a crisis seems imminent the remedy is at hand, and the violence of the attacks has enormously decreased.

CONCLUSION

We may draw certain very important conclusions from all these numerous scenes of possession and of exorcism, which are here collated for the first time.

In the first place there are striking similarities between all these diverse individual experiences. Whether the exorcism takes place at Ars, at Illfurth, in Natal, in Vietnam, at Piacenza or, almost before our eyes, at the present moment, somewhere in France, there are always the same incidents and episodes of the same character, cries, shouts, grimaces, convulsions, resistance on the part of Satan, and finally, after valiant efforts on the part of the exorcist, armed with the prayers of the Church, the inevitable triumph, often thanks to the explicit and visible intervention of the Blessed Virgin.

In the second place, it is impossible to mistake the cases of possession we have reported for cases of pure and simple mania. The reasons for this are clear. On the one hand, the prayers of the ritual are totally ineffectual in cases of natural mania. A maniac would never be relieved by exorcism, nor manifest the explosive reactions of a possessed person. And on the other, mania does not disappear overnight, as we have seen happen in the majority of the cases of possession we have described.

There is no similarity between the symptoms, the treatment, or the final result in cases of mania and cases of possession. Finally, in cases of mania we never find indications of the presence of a preternatural and obviously alien intelligence as is established in cases of possession, and which constitutes one of the indications required by the Church before an exorcism is authorized.

This leads us to an investigation into the activities of Satan in the modern world. The next chapter will, therefore, have as point of departure the conclusions we have already reached, and which we shall be able to confirm.

∽ 9 ∽

SATAN IN THE MODERN WORLD

POINT OF DEPARTURE

AFTER THESE ACCOUNTS of demonic infestation and possession, we are in a position to reject some assertions which are alleged to be scientific. Not so long ago it was unfashionable to believe in the real existence of the Devil and consequently of his activity in the world. The following is a typical example of the contempt of so-called scientists for the teaching of Catholic theology. At first glance nothing could be more decisive than this extract, yet, in our view, nothing could be more inadequate or untrue.

A certain Dr. Legué published, in 1884, a book entitled *Urbain Grandier et les Possédées de Loudun,* in which he proclaimed without hesitation:

"Science nowadays has thrown off the yoke of theology: it no longer admits explanations based on divine or diabolic influence.... Eminent teachers have, for a long time, been studying the peculiar neuro-pathological disorders which were formerly considered supernatural in origin. Thanks to their work and the stimulus they have given to contemporary research, that imaginary being, Satan, has completely disappeared; his place has been taken, by general consent, by scientific reality. Like all other patients, hysterics fall within the province of the doctor, and not of the priest or monkish exorcist."[18]

But Dr. Legué's opinion is no longer shared by all doctors. Much closer to our times, a well-known psychiatrist, Professor Jean Lhermitte, who died in February 1959, expressed a quite contrary opinion, in the review *Ecclesia* of October 1954 under the title: "Are Possessed Persons Mad?"

He stated categorically:

"Although critical and scientific enquiry has cleared up many obscurities and spoilt many a myth, *it is none the less true that in our modern world there are a considerable number of possessed persons. And I base this assertion on long personal experience.*"

It is therefore permissible to believe in the Devil and in infestation and the facts of possession without incurring a reproof from the most exacting of sciences.

For a Catholic, Satan is *someone*. Satan is not an abstraction, an invention, a character in fiction, or the hero of a novel. Neither is Satan the mythical explanation provided by ignorance for those nervous disorders which are properly the domain of medicine and have nothing to do with theology.

But we should not forget that the spectacular episodes we have recorded here are not the essence of Satan's activity amongst men. The facts of possession might be compared with analogous manifestations of a contrary nature, such as the appearances of the Blessed Virgin or of the saints. These manifestations are intended to stimulate the mind and revive faith. But the action of God, of the Blessed Virgin, or of the saints, their inner, profounder, daily, incessant action through grace, is infinitely more important. Similarly, the fact of the presence of Satan,

---

[18] Quoted by M. de la Bigne de Villeneuve, *Satan dans la Cité* (Paris, undated) 50.

in institutions and customs, in human, individual, family, national, and international life, is something infinitely vaster, more serious, and more dangerous for us all. If some unfortunate woman is possessed and subjected by the Devil to all manner of humiliating experiences, such as we have seen, it is very painful for her and impressive to us; but if whole nations are, in a certain sense, under the dominion of Satan, to the extent of undergoing a kind of *collective possession*, as seems to be the case in our time, it is infinitely more terrifying and can have far more devastating effects.

METHOD OF DISCRIMINATION

Although the ritual lays down the tests by which true possession can be distinguished from a neurosis—even though the two may indeed be found together—can we do the same for what we have just described as *collective possession*? It is difficult to be sure. Here we are left to our own conjectures. The ritual provides no exorcism for a nation nor for humanity at large. No doubt the fact that an enlightened pope such as Leo XIII felt it necessary to add to every private Mass an exorcism characterized by the invocation of St. Michael indicates that he, at any rate, believed in a demonic infestation peculiar to our age. The whole question lies in the reasons for this opinion, and our means of discovering the presence of Satan in the modem world.

There are two parallel hazards to be avoided in any solution we may propose. The first would be to attribute so much to satanic activity that human responsibility would be eliminated. The second would be to attribute nothing to him, on the pretext that human malice alone is sufficient to explain all the terrifying events we are obliged to witness. Both men and devils may well be responsible for the evils of which we complain, and which are either present or imminent.

There is a *corpus mysticum* of Christ, of which we like to feel we are a part. But there is also, or can be, a *corpus mysticum satanicum* which incorporates all the destructive will of humanity and Hell.

In a text which the Roman breviary lays down as reading for the first Sunday of Lent, for clerics who have entered sacred orders, Gregory the Great says: "Assuredly the Devil is the head of all the wicked—*iniquorum*—and all the wicked are members of his body." Then he mentions those who are "members" of this diabolic body: Pilate, those who crucified Christ, and so on.

On this head there are few, even amongst Christians, who have not run the risk, at one time or another, of becoming "members of Satan."

But the sin which is regretted as soon as it is committed, the sin for which one knows how to do penance, does not, properly speaking, entail an involvement with Satan. It is an accident, a false step, a lapse. It does not prevent spiritual progress. The *corpus mysticum* of Satan is composed of human beings who have made themselves his accomplices, who willingly submit to his suggestions, and who live by his inspiration and principles.

MANIFESTATIONS OF SATAN

Let us examine the question more closely. The means of recognizing the presence of Satan is provided by the Gospels, the source of all light.

Christ has said certain things about Satan, on which we should meditate. Speaking to the Pharisees, who never ceased to harass him, he said one day:

"You are of your father the Devil, and the desires of your father you will do. He was a murderer from the beginning, and he stood not in the truth; because truth is not in him. When he speaketh a lie, he speaketh of his own: for he is a liar, and the father thereof" (John 8:44).

SATAN IN THE MODERN WORLD

This should be clear enough.

If we wish to know how Satan manifests his presence amongst us, in our own times, we must try, on the one hand, to discern the *great lies* of our time, and the *progress made in the art of killing men*, on the other. The deeper an age is impregnated with falsehood, the more the life of man is held in contempt and overshadowed by the threat of death, the more Satan is present. It seems impossible to question that falsehood and homicide are the two indications of the presence of Satan. We shall therefore be on firm ground in asserting that he is present at the heart of the major falsehoods and the major massacres or threats of massacre we observe in our time.

THE GREATEST OF LIES: GOD DOES NOT EXIST!

If there is one falsehood above all others which has obtained more widespread currency than in any previous period, it is the negation of God, to which we may add, by analogy with a man and his shadow, the negation of the Devil.

For many centuries the Devil had succeeded, in the guise of false gods, in capturing the faith of pagan worshippers. But belief in God was not extinct. As St. Paul said to the Athenians, "Ye men of Athens, I perceive that in all things you are too superstitious" (Acts 17:22). They worshipped, in fact, many gods, even including an "unknown god", in case they had forgotten one.

But in our times atheism is growing stronger, vaunts itself, and adopts a contemptuous attitude toward a belief in God. One philosophy takes pride in believing in the Nothing rather than in Being, implying thereby that the Nothing has preceded and engendered Being.

In contemporary atheism, which we denounce as the most colossal, the most hateful and culpable of lies, we may distinguish two trends, one more serious than the other: *theoretical atheism,* the atheism of materialism, scientism, agnosticism, and certain forms of existentialism; and *practical atheism*, that of men preoccupied with their businesses, the affairs of this world, the calculations of politics, trade, even scientific research and technical invention, to the extent of no longer finding any place for God in their lives.

In many countries *theoretical atheism* is nowadays to be found in the highest circles of power and authority. It is hardly necessary to specify this or that country, this or that government, this or that national leader, for whom theoretical atheism is a law of being. We can hardly doubt the existence of a *collective possession* in such cases.

The trend started with isolated writers, with the "*libertins*" as they were called in seventeenth-century France, with the "philosophers" as they were called in the eighteenth, with the "free-thinkers" as they are called nowadays. Some protested their incredulity in the most moving terms. A page of Nietzsche is often quoted, although it is true that he puts his words into a madman's mouth. He is right, for there is much in common between madness and possession:

"Where is God," he cried, "let me tell you! We have killed him thou and I! We are all his murderers! But how have we done that? How have we been able to drink the Ocean? Who has given us the sponge with which we have obliterated the horizon? What have we done in separating this earth from its sun? Where is it going now? Where are we going? Far from all suns? Are we not even now falling headlong? Backwards, sideways, forwards, on all sides? Is there still a top and a bottom? Are we not wandering in an immeasurable void? Do we not feel the wind of the infinite spaces? Is it not getting colder? Is not the night darker? Must we not light our lamps at midday? Can you not already hear the sound of the gravediggers who are burying God? Can you not already catch the smell of God's decay?—For the gods too decay! God is dead! God will stay dead and we have killed him!"[19]

What an accent of regret, of remorse, of rage, and of terror! No doubt this is the greatest of all lies, the lie of lies!

To say that God does not exist is the same as saying *Being does not exist*. The word God means, in effect, *He who is*. In the words of Victor Hugo: *Il est, il est, il est, il est éperdûment (He is, he is, he is madly)!*

Yet we see before our eyes great peoples subject to the rule of atheists, who profess their atheism openly, who mock at religion, who reject anything which cannot be "verified" by science as they understand it, that is to say, transforming the Absolute into a pure contingency.

Things have reached such a pitch that we may well ask whether certain masters of the world—a world that with modern communications has grown so small—are not purely and simply Satan's lieutenants, even the *mediums* of Satan.

A Medium of Satan

This very word was applied to Satan by Dom Aloïs Mager in his important work, *Satan,* published some years ago by the *Etudes carmélitaines* (Desclée, 1948).

Since the man is dead, we can mention his name. In the case of the living, it is not necessary, since the reader will easily be able to supply them for himself.

To quote Dom Aloïs Mager, whose words are so vigorous and concise:

"The medium," he writes, "through whom Satan was beginning to overthrow all norms of law and morality, which had hitherto, in

---

[19] Friedrich Nietzsche, *The Gay Science.*

spite of a progressive dechristianization, been generally respected, this medium was Adolf Hitler. There is no shorter, apter, clearer definition of Hitler's character than the comprehensive epithet: *medium of Satan*. If it is characteristic, without exception, of all mediums that they are of low moral caliber, both in character and personality, this is *a fortiori* true for a medium of the Devil. No one who is not a prey to phantasmagoria can consider Hitler a great personality, from the point of view of character and morality. At the Nuremburg trials General Jodl said of him: 'He was a great man, but an infernal great man.'"[20]

Lying and homicide: we find both these characteristics fully developed in the career of a man like Hitler. Could we not say the same, or even more, of his rival, Stalin?

The presence of Satan in our age and time, and the *collective possession* of whole peoples, can hardly be doubted on the evidence of *Nazism*, which was fortunately ephemeral in Germany, and more formidably because more lasting, menacing, and arrogant, on the evidence of *Communism* in immense countries such as Russia and the People's Republic of China.

We may believe that Satan is engaged in preparing the most terrifying catastrophe that can be imagined. All the more so in that lies, nowadays, are backed by hitherto unknown instruments of mass homicide.

But before considering this second aspect of satanic activity, we should devote a little more time to considering the power of falsehood as we see it at the present moment.

LIES AND CONTRADICTIONS

The negation of God is the first, most serious of falsehoods in our present world. But it is not the only one. We are deep in falsehood,

---

[20] de Villeneuve, *Satan,* 639.

immersed in lies, so that we practically breathe falsehoods without being aware of it.

The emblem of this falsehood is contradiction. If God does not exist, who then is God? We do not say the Devil, since in his passion to secure the denial of God the Devil prefers to deny, rather than to reveal, his own existence. A modern atheist, whilst denying the existence of God, is also prepared to deny the existence of the Devil. Only man remains. We, therefore, are gods. Our science, our technics, our intelligence have sovereignty over everything. We are gods! But we have no souls, since matter alone exists. Or if we have souls, an expression meaning simply that we live and think, there is no question of these souls being immortal. When a man dies, everything dies. If God is dead, every time a man dies, it is a god who dies.

To deny the existence of God, of Satan, of an immortal soul, to deny any distinction between Good and Evil, to deny the existence of Sin, of Virtue, of Heaven and Hell; these are some of our lies by negation.

And if, after that, we glorify ourselves, if we transform ourselves into the only gods that exist, it is pure contradiction. Being and Nothing are confused. By suppressing all religion we make nihilism the only religion possible. And since that does not suppress the great speeches, the grand promises, and especially the grand illusions, once again everything, whether politics or philosophy or present-day agitation, is reduced to an immense contradiction.

Now we talk of nothing except of conquering, not only the world, but the starry spaces. And all this is only chicanery, a futile demonstration of power, it is all nothing but vanity and despair. All the time human beings are multiplying at such a rate that some statesmen are alarmed, scientists calculate the number of mouths this planet can feed, and are aghast at the "million million bowls of rice" which will be required, in forty years' time or perhaps earlier, to feed China alone. And only two solutions are envisaged: either to sterilize the source of life in the mother's body, or destroy a large part of humanity in a monstrous war. This is the outcome of the divinization of man. We should rather say, of his *satanization*.

Falsehood and contradiction, such are the first indications of the presence of Satan in the modern world.

SATAN, THE MURDERER

But the second indication, the threat to or the destruction of human life, is no less visible.

If there is one characteristic more than another which distinguishes our century from preceding ones, it is the prodigious increase in the power of our weapons of destruction.

From the first recorded history of man, even from the time of Cain and Abel, which is early enough, there have been wars. If, as Christ says, Satan has been "a murderer from the beginning," it follows that he has not only been present in all men's fratricidal struggles, but that he has also been their secret instigator. The progress in means of destruction is a satanic progress. But such progress has always been with us. Further, it is rare to find any beneficent development which has not had its origin in war. At present countries are spending more millions in preparation for the next war, which may mean the end of humanity, than they are spending on any other important purpose in men's lives. If all the money spent in preparing for the next war, or wasted in recent wars, had been used to spread the true faith throughout the world, to fight poverty and ignorance, to reduce hunger and crime, the whole face of the world would be altered. But it is not necessary for us to be at war to suffer the effects of its constant menace.

The more our means of communication are increased, thanks to the progress of which we are so proud, the more distance becomes unimportant, the more the air we breathe becomes, as it were, tainted and poisoned, every day at the same time, by news from all parts of the world, informing us, in one form of another, of hatred, conflict, impending catastrophe, and untried and fearsome means of mass destruction.

The fear of war will, in the long run, do more harm to our souls than war itself. Our lives have become strange and inhuman. Since we have killed God, to use Nietzsche's words, there is no longer any peace amongst men, yet they are condemned to a perpetual discussion of peace, as of an absent friend, a remote ideal, a dream, a chimera perhaps, since all the time men are constantly working at improvements in their methods of killing others. Some are driven by distrust, other by secret ambition, in an atmosphere of mutual recrimination, threats, and allusions to the possibility of immediate conflict, of world conflict, in the sense that it would signify the end of the world.

SATAN IN THE WORLD

In so far as indications of satanic activity are concerned, we should make some distinction between the various regions of the world, since it would not be astonishing to find that he is more present in some areas than in others.

In Giovanni Papini's strange book, which aroused so much discussion, and which contrived to combine some quite brilliant and reasonable propositions with occasional puerilities, heretical views, and sometimes unconscious blasphemy, there is a short chapter entitled: "Satan's Promised Land." One's curiosity is immediately aroused to discover which this land might be, and which people could claim the title of Satan's eldest sons. Not without amazement one learns that the promised land is France, and the people, us.

"Ever since Caesar," writes Papini, "there has been a copious literature about the 'the sweet land of France,' but no one, I believe, has made the strange discovery, as I have, that France is the promised land of Satanism."

A strange discovery indeed, but Papini insists on it. He is not, he says, writing fiction, but merely stating a fact. "A perfectly conscious indulgence in evil for evil's sake, a taste for cruel perversities, the theory and practice of revolt against God and against all moral law, particularly against Christian law."

But since Papini, throughout his book, shows a very marked indulgence toward Satan, he does not want us to take his assertion, however unflattering, in bad part. "I adore France," he explains, "I adore its art, its literature, its civilization: I have therefore no intention of slandering her. And to show that I am speaking seriously and not at random, I shall be obliged to provide a long list of authors and their publications as evidence." And he proceeds to quote a considerable number of French authors. Curiously enough, they are not those whom we would normally quote as displaying satanic tendencies. No mention of Voltaire, Diderot, d'Alembert, d'Holbach, or Condorcet. But to make up for this, he finds evidence of satanism even in Catholic authors such as Georges Bernanos and Francois Mauriac.

So far there is nothing serious. If the French Revolution, in many though not all of its aspects, may be considered as satanic, we should not forget that for many centuries it was possible to speak, in *the* Church, of the *Gesta Dei per Francos*. Unfortunately, for the last 200 years, it has been equally possible to speak of the *Gesta Diaboli per Francos!* The whole problem consists, for us, in knowing whether we have been freed from this subservience to Satan, and whether or not we wish to return to our secular tradition of truth and light informed by divine charity.

Comparative Estimate

Passing over the wild speculations of Papini, we shall try to establish more exactly the nature of Satan's activities in our present world in the year 1959.

One first point seems to be established: Satan is more active in certain countries than in others. From this there emerges a no less evident point that it is possible to distinguish between degrees of activity within a nation, somewhat in the way we can distinguish between degrees of activity in individuals. We have pointed out that Satan's activity rises progressively from *temptation* to *infestation*, and from *infestation* to *possession*. There could therefore be countries which are *possessed*, others subject to *infestation,* and those which are simply *tempted.*

So far, so good. The difficulty arises when we try to make a practical application of these logical conclusions. The following remarks are, of course, a purely personal evaluation, and do not involve anyone else.

At the present time the country in which we perceive the presence of Satan to the highest degree, that is, to the extent of creating a "collective possession" is, we must state it frankly, the People's Republic of China. All that we learn of this country, and of what is taking place behind the "bamboo curtain" is literally diabolical: a vast country, containing within its borders one quarter of mankind; a vast country, subjected to a regime of incredible hardness and power and efficiency; a vast country where falsehood and the contempt for human life, the two indications of the presence of Satan, ravage and destroy with a generalized violence greater than anywhere else.

If communist atheism is based on falsehood, on the negation of God and the soul and of all spirituality, one must admit that this falsehood is more triumphant in China than elsewhere. An American observer, John Strohm, recently paid a visit of several weeks to that country and was able to see, read, and hear many things, of which we were, indeed, aware although vaguely and confusedly. He has borne witness to the fact that the whole country is dominated by the propaganda falsehood of "American aggression" which is deliberately exploited by the ruling castes, although they know it to be a myth, in order to drive their people not merely to constructive labor, but to a feverish arms race, and to make them accept, in a time of peace, conditions suitable to a state of siege. It is further used to inculcate an aggressive hatred which might culminate in the most catastrophic action.

But this observer, although very careful in his description of economic and political problems, says nothing of the religious aspect. In matters of religion China, as is known, practiced above all the cult of the family and its ancestors, together with a certain cult of idols. The number of Christians did not exceed three or four million out of 640 million, that is, one in 200. This modest but courageous Church in China is in process of "liquidation" to use the barbarous language of Communism. Persecution has raged in the most brutal manner against Europeans, then against the best of the Christians. Its greatest triumph has been to lead far too great a part of the Catholic Church itself into schism, by the consecration of a great number of bishops, elected by the people, but detached from any connection with Rome.

The Chinese People's Republic has also revealed its satanic quality by its contempt for human life. One of its principal rulers has declared that China was the only country that could afford a war: "We can lose 300 million Chinese," he said. "There will still be 340 million left." Such a remark is surely the purest satanism.

What adds verisimilitude to the remark is the way in which the adversaries of the regime have hitherto been treated. According to

British estimates, from 800,000 to 1,500,000 persons have been executed in ten years. American estimates are even higher, ranging from five to ten, even to twenty million. The truth probably lies between the two estimates. But it is clear that the Chinese People's Republic was born in a blood-bath. What is happening in Tibet at the present moment is yet another proof.

For the last hundred years we have been accustomed to speak of the "yellow peril." This peril is now imminent. It seems very probable that the conflagration which, one day or another, will consume the earth, will be kindled in China.

For all these reasons, and bearing in mind the million millions of famished Chinese who will be born in the next forty years, considering also the present mentality of the Chinese people and the supremacy of communist atheism in that part of the world, we feel entitled to speak of the "collective possession" of that distant country.

INFESTATIONS

Second only to China, but in a very different case, is Communist Russia. But there is as much difference between China and Russia as there is between individual *possession* and *infestation*.

This distinction is, in our view, essential. China is *possessed*. Satan is master. He controls every movement of that great body. He has set up a perverse order of things, established an iron discipline, inculcated a terrible ambition, a lust for power which will, no doubt, increase with time, and a fury of destruction which our children or grandchildren will probably see at work.

In Russia the Devil is active in government circles, in politics, in education, in the directives for the future. But what was for so long known as "holy Russia" is still largely intact. Faith is alive and prayer is active. All the lies of the Devil have not modified the profound faith of the Russian people. Infestations may be violent and perfidious but are ineffective to destroy the soul of the nation. All that we know or believe about Russia leads us to trust in an essential dualism, between the demonic party in power and the great mass of the people who have remained Christian. Russia not only resists the assaults of the Devil, but, with its patience and loyalty and attachment to old national traditions is, perhaps, with the help of the Virgin Mary, to be the *Panagia*, the All-Holy, preparing a resurrection which will astonish the world. In any case, it is not certain that in a world conflict Russia would march alongside the enemies of God and Christ, or would obey the orders of Satan.

If we are moving toward some gigantic conflict, similar to that which, before the creation of man, set Michael against Lucifer, the faithful angels against the rebellious angels, it is probable it will not occur between two purely political blocks, but will be a conflict of religious nature, between Christ and Satan, between love and hate, between faith and incredulity.

LANDS OF TEMPTATION

Possession in China, *infestation* in Russia: this, if we add some other countries of minor importance, which we need not mention, covers half the human race.

It would be futile to say or believe that the other half was exempt from Satan's attacks. We have seen Satan at work in Christian countries, countries with an ancient Christian tradition. Neither individual possession nor individual infestation is unknown amongst us. But we might say that with us it is *satanic temptation* that is the general rule.

Temptation is present every day, almost at every instant. It takes on every possible form, varying according to character and temperament. Any attempt to describe it would produce a treatise on the seven deadly sins: pride, luxury, envy, and so on. But this is not what we are trying to do.

Quite recently, on February 20, 1959, an important Catholic weekly, *La France Catholique*, published an article by Maria Winowska, generally considered to be one of the most lucid thinkers of our time, entitled "The Third Temptation." The title refers to Christ's temptation in the wilderness, when the Devil offered him all the kingdoms of the earth: "If thou therefore wilt adore before me, all shall be thine!"

Maria Winowska introduces a young Hindu who has just been baptized. Together they go up to Montmartre. Before their eyes was spread the vast, magnificent spectacle of Paris. The young Hindu burst out:

"Why don't you live according to your faith? The Gospel is clear: in the first place, prayer, in the first place, wisdom, in the first place, faith, in the first place, charity. It's all there on paper, but in practice?"

Maria Winowska replied: "You are right, but all the same, there *are* people amongst us, men and women, who do follow the Gospels. That is certain. There are even a great number of them. And that pleads for us. But there are many weaknesses, deficiencies, and illogicalities." The young Hindu went on:

"European Christians, for the most part, *live as if they had no faith*. I don't mean that they haven't any, but they certainly conceal the fact." And he continued, relentlessly: "I have met priests who talked to me of pastoral techniques, of methods, adaptations, of the Press, cinema, and television. They are certainly good priests, but why don't they say what is essential? For us, wisdom is much more than that, more than anything else in the world. What proportion is there between Creator and the created?"

Naturally Maria Winowska protested that we could not judge the clergy from a superficial contact. One cannot accuse them of activism without knowing the whole of their inner life. We have already had two "revolutions" in religious matters in the last fifty years; a liturgical revolution which is still far from having borne its full fruit, and a biblical revolution which is only just beginning. We have now to achieve a *mystical revolution* which will respond to the justified longings of Maria Winowska and our young Hindu.

The great temptation for the Christians of our time, and no petty temptation at that, but the most widespread, general, and dangerous of temptations, is that of *preferring things to God*. The young Hindu maintained that he had tried to test the Christians he had met, by the test used by the Devil in the wilderness.

"Do you know," he said, "that there were very few who would not have agreed to make a little bow, perhaps just a little click of the heels, to a tempter offering them the kingdoms of the world. They would say: 'If one got all that, it would be to the greater glory of God,' or 'One has to make certain concessions to the world, in order to dominate it,' or again, 'Christianity won't be able to survive if it doesn't adapt itself to progress.' I am only quoting a few, but I can assure you that all these people had more confidence in human techniques than in faith."

In brief, out of forty-seven persons cautiously sounded by our young Hindu, *only three or four truly preferred God to things*. And it goes without saying that he had only approached good *Catholics*.

Such, therefore, is the third temptation. All these good Catholics had faith, they had even the works of faith, that is, hope and charity. They are those whom St. Paul called in his Epistles the "saints," those who have God in their souls. But they are also illogical souls — and we are all more or less illogical — those who do not follow the demands of their faith to the extreme limit, souls for whom, to use Maria Winowska's words, "having" is more important than "being."

She is right a thousand times over when she says: "All the science in the world is not worth one ounce of wisdom and the most breathtaking technical progress falls short if man does not also control it *qualitatively*. In other words, 'What shall it profit a man if he gain the whole world and lose his own soul?'"

Three centuries ago Pascal, in his own incomparable language, said the same thing:

"All bodies together, and all spirits together, and all their works, have not the value of the least movement of charity. This is of an infinitely higher order."[21]

GENERAL VIEW

We should form an entirely false picture of our present world if we were to confuse the present division into East and West with the conflict of Satan against God, or to divide the earth into absolutely separate zones: the Devil's zone, covering China, Russia, and the other communist countries, and God's zone, covering ourselves.

Let us hear what a Russian has to say. Not so long ago our papers published an interview with a Soviet engineer, who had come to Western Europe on a scientific mission entailing a fairly long stay. He said:

"All you Westerners are at heart *materialists*. With money you can obtain all the goods you want and satisfy all your desires. As a result, you think of that alone. Your life, your activities, your science, your technology, all your occupations and preoccupations, are devoted to the physical end of improving your living conditions and increasing your comfort. Cars, refrigerators, television — for the immense majority this is your sole purpose in life."

Who would dare to deny that this accusation is, in the main, justified? Materialism is not the basic flaw in Communism alone,

---

[21] Blaise Pascal, *Pensees.*

it is the basic flaw in capitalism also. According to this engineer, the degradation inflicted on man by capitalism is even greater than that inflicted by communist regimes. Here is his further comment:

"For us, on the other hand, such questions do not exist [that is, the search for comfort]. Your comfort is practically unknown to us. Since we have no such possibilities, we do not even dream of them. *This desire for a practical good*, which characterizes all your energy, *has been destroyed in us. And this destruction has liberated us.* All the energy that you squander in quest of futilities, we use for reading, for reflection, reverie, music-making. What else can we do, when in the evening we come home to our restricted living space, rather like a monk to his cell?"

And he concluded with the words, "Yes, we have still time and inclination to think, but have you?"

How reassuring it would be if amongst the occupations such as reading, music-making, reflection, and reverie, which the Russian engineer ear-marked for his own, there had been that little word "prayer." Nevertheless, it remains true that this engineer's ideals were a great deal superior to those laid down by communist leaders: to reach and surpass the level of the United States in productivity, in material wealth, in millions of tons of steel and coal, in the production of electricity, cars, television transmitters, and so on. The aims which the Soviet engineer despised—and which we also despise, in so far as they militate against the spiritual development of humanity—are precisely those which the leaders of his people, and of other communist countries, have laid down as their objectives. Communism in China has been defined as: "To each according to his needs," and our needs, in this formulation, are to be interpreted exclusively as *material needs*.

But it is not for us to set capitalism against communism. Both are inspired by Satan, to the extent that they are a negation of God and the soul. Communism, in fact, has done no more than develop the so-called "bourgeois" philosophy, of which it is the end-product. If it is true that there is neither God, nor Devil, nor spirit, and that all is matter, then neither capitalism nor Communism is any more true than the other, for there is no more truth, in the strict sense of the word, for all is falsehood, all is satanic.

It is therefore without any particular satisfaction, but without diffidence, that one may declare that there are certain undeniable proofs of the presence of Satan in our contemporary "civilization": proofs which few can refuse to admit:

(1). The mediocrity of our great media of communication such as the wireless, cinema, and television: not mediocrity in technique or in propaganda, but in the beauty and nobility of their influence on people's minds;

(2). The erotic atmosphere exuded by our novels and plays, in popular songs, in all that can be summed up as "show business"; and

(3). The degradation of modern art, which seems to have lost all feeling for beauty, and to be concerned only with ugliness and obscurity.

To conclude this chapter, which could easily have been extended, what do we see in the world around us?

Satan everywhere at work. Opposed to him one single authentic force: Jesus Christ. On the one hand atheistic materialism, lies, contempt for human life, the blood of Abel shed by Cain. On the other hand, faith, charity, the immeasurable power of love, adoration, the rejection of satanic hatred; the longing for the universal acceptance of the Kingdom of God, the power of the constant aspiration of the human heart: "Thy Kingdom come!"

The vision of world history has not changed: the City of God against the City of Satan—the City of Love against the City of Hatred. There are two banners flying: that of Satan and that of Jesus Christ!

Strangely enough, the Christian who avowedly despises our present life because he knows that there is another which is eternal, nevertheless practices the most absolute respect for human life and human personality. Satan, on the contrary, persuades his followers that our present life is the only one, and that therefore this life is man's supreme good, yet he manifests his contempt for this same life by concentration camps, by the nightmare of the vast crematoria, by massive executions and degrading tortures. In other words, falsehood and murder are akin.

But the greatest reproach that can be levelled against the Devil's disciples is their mutilation of man's stature, by denying his infinity and refusing him immortality.

The most deplorable thing about the incredulous is their narrowness of mind. They deserve the reproach flung by Tertullian at the heretics of his day: "*Parce orbis unicae spei*" (Spare the sole hope of the world). If we indeed wish to possess one day this universe, which is not of the same value as our souls, we must first, by faith and love, save our souls!

How much is at stake in this struggle between Christ and Satan!

☙ 10 ☙

SATANISM AND THE
DEVICES OF SATAN

TO DEFINE IS, strictly speaking, to limit. The word *satanism*, which has so often been used or implied in this present book, can have many meanings. One may, in fact, take Satan in his aspect as master and prince of this world. It is the description used three times by Christ. We have just been considering this aspect and asking to what extent Satan is present in our modern world. We find that this varies according to the country, race, civilization, or political structure. The word *satanism* may also mean the imitation of Satan through sin: Gregory the Great said, as you will remember, that all those who sinned, so long as they were under the influence of this sin, were members of the mystical body of Satan. We are not allowed to know the number of those who are in a state of grace, that is to say, removed, *hic et nunc*, from the power of Satan. But we are entitled to believe that their number is much greater than might be supposed, particularly if one agrees that sinners are often only men who have slipped, or taken a false step, without wishing to remain in Satan's power.

Finally, satanism may mean a *deliberate cult of Satan*, not an occasional sin quickly repented and atoned for, but a formal and deliberate adherence.

TWO FORMS OF SATANISM

In the latter sense we can distinguish immediately between two rather different forms of satanism: there is the satanism of those who do not believe in Satan any more than in God, and who cannot be properly said to be making a cult of satanism, although their lives are in strict conformity with his principles and purposes.

It is to this form of satanism that we can most appropriately apply that well-known phrase: "Satan's deepest wile is to make us believe that he does not exist." On the subject Papini quotes the words of the philosopher Alain in 1921: "The Devil has suffered the same fate as all other apparitions.... Even the war, as far as I can see, has not revived the Devil and his horns."[22]

But this form of satanism need not detain us long. It is purely negative. It can be found, incidentally, among well-intentioned Christians, without any suspicion that they are in conflict with orthodox opinion and the testimony of the Gospels.

What we have to study is, above all, satanism in its active forms. We use the plural deliberately, for it would seem that throughout the ages, and even down to our own times, there have been at least two very distinct forms of satanism: *satanism as religion* and *satanism as magic*.

SATANISM AS RELIGION

As soon as one considers this question one is not a little astonished to find that the history of this particular satanism is interwoven with the history of religion.

This very important conclusion requires some explanation.

[22] Papini gives the following reference: Alain, *Propos sur la Réligion* (Paris: Rieder, 1937), 64.

The study of the history of religion has reached a very advanced level. In general, Satan does not figure in it to any great extent. Demons are relegated to a relatively restricted role. The historian of religion is trained to describe religious beliefs objectively and to enumerate the gods and their attributes. He explains the rites by which the various gods were served. It is not his concern to put forward judgments of their value. He is not a metaphysician, and certainly not a Christian theologian.

Yet some appeal to the latter aspect seems almost inevitable. Since we are speaking of Satan and his presence in the world, we must ourselves adopt a Christian standpoint, the only standpoint from which Satan can be assigned his true place in the general framework. We must therefore consider what is said on the subject of pagan religions by the Gospels, the Fathers of the Church, and by Christian theology.

We cannot stress too often the fact that in the Gospels Satan is given the incredible title of *Prince of this world*, yet the title must be justified, since Christ himself accords it. Yet such a title could not be given to Satan if the pagan deities were not purely and simply devils. The Fathers of the Church were unanimously agreed that this was so. The pagan oracles of Delphi and Dodona, and others that were less celebrated, were demonic oracles and manifestations.

Christian theology has naturally adopted this point of view. The historical description of paganism, whether ancient or modern, is not, for us, an intellectual amusement, a form of literary curiosity, but the unhappy observation of Satan's dominion over men.

The process by which Satan and his devils were able to get control of the prayers and adoration of human beings seems to have been imperceptible. There was a sort of unconscious transition, attributable to a certain primitive realism. All historians of religion are, in fact, agreed that all religions postulate the existence of a supreme and sovereign deity, all-powerful and all-good. But such a god, they say, is usually relegated to the background, worship being reserved for a host of inferior divinities, both good and bad, whose subordination to the sovereign deity is admitted, but who are considered to be closer to man, more involved in human destinies, and therefore more suitable as subjects of invocation or manipulation. Moreover in many pagan theologies, it is the malevolent forces that are in most urgent need of conciliation.

This primitive realism, this manner of dealing with the most urgent matters first, seems to have been at the root of all pagan mythologies and all pagan rites, and their subsequent blending into practical syncretisms, such as the Pantheon of Agrippa.

What is undeniable is that to the Jews and still more to the Christians, all pagan deities could be none other than devils. Hence the heroic struggle put up by the Jews, particularly under the Maccabees, and by the Christians throughout the most bloodthirsty persecutions. Hence the religious horror experienced by Christians when confronted with what they called "idols," that is, the empty simulacra of the demonic pagan cults.

From our point of view, it is therefore clear that the history of religion — apart from the sole true religion, that of the Patriarchs, of Moses, and finally of Christianity — is nothing but the history of *satanism*. It is only in this sense that one can understand the term "Prince of this world" used by Christ of Satan.

When one compares the exiguous cult of the true God, first of Jahwé, then of the Incarnate Word, with the vast domains of the false gods, one is indeed compelled to admit that if Christ is the one true King, he had every cause to say: "My Kingdom is not of this world!"

We can also understand the manifold exorcisms which were and still are combined with the ceremonies of Christian baptism, in order to drive out the Devil. These exorcisms are to be found in many places in the Catholic liturgy. When a priest consecrates the holy water, he pronounces over the salt which is to be placed in it:

"I exorcise thee, salt created by the living God ... that thou mayest be for the salvation of true believers: so that thou mayest be a means of wellbeing for the bodies and souls of all they that use thee; so that, wherever thou art sprinkled, thou mayest drive out all *the wiles, the malice, and the snares of the Devil and all other unclean spirits,* by the power of Him Who shall come to judge the living and the dead, and to purge the world by fire. So be it!"

Then he does the same for the holy water:

"I exorcise thee, created water, in the name of God, Our Father Almighty ... so that thou mayest be purified water to cast out the *power of the Enemy;* so that thou mayest rout out and cast forth *the Enemy himself and his fallen angels* by the grace of this same Jesus Christ, Our Lord."

And again: "O God, who for the salvation of mankind hast joined the substance of water to thy greatest mysteries, in thy great mercy grant this our request ... so that this thy creation may receive by divine grace the power *to ward off the Devil."*

Finally, in the magnificent liturgy for Easter Saturday, the day of the blessing of the baptismal water, the same theme is repeated:

"At thy command, Lord, banished be every spirit of evil, far removed be every snare of the foul fiend. Here be no room for Satan's encroachment, ambush, or stealthy approach, or brewing of poison. Holy and spotless, Lord, be this thy handiwork, from the enemy's assaults shielded, from all his craft delivered."

Here the liturgy gives an impressive rendering of the Church's faith. But it might be objected that these are only phrases, residues of ancient beliefs which, to most people, represent only a superstitious hangover from the past. The answer is a purely factual one. In all the cases of possession which we have recounted, both exorcists and onlookers are in complete agreement on this particular point: it is impossible to sprinkle holy water on any man or woman in a state of possession without deadly effect on the possessing spirit. "You are burning me, you are burning me!" he cries. There is thus an active power in the holy water which cancels out hidden demonic activities. And this leads us to the other aspect of satanism.

SATANISM AS MAGIC

It is currently admitted that there has always been a magical form of satanism, running parallel to satanism as a religion. Many specialists in the history of religions and cults have, in fact, maintained that the magical form preceded the religions, of which it was the primary form, and that all pagan religions are derived from magic. But it seems that this view is gradually becoming obsolete, and with reason. It is highly improbable that humanity started with the practice of magic and then proceeded to derive from it religion in the true sense of the word.

It is important to distinguish carefully between magic and religion.

In religion man reveres a superior power and offers it his adoration and prayers, recognizing his own weakness and impotence. He admits his subordinate position. Among "primitive" peoples as we know them today, that is to say, among those who have evolved more slowly than others and are therefore closer to their origins — as, for instance, the Pygmies — this attitude to deity still survives. Religion is even in a purer state than amongst more advanced communities.

In magic man attributes to himself a mysterious power. Far from bowing down to any divinity, he believes that he can command it. He invents and employs formulae by which he believes he can control the superior powers to which they are directed. The mentality of the magician—or of his twin brother in modern dress, the sorcerer—is very different from that of the religious man. The way in which this mentality developed is still a mystery to us. Magic is, in our view, infinitely more satanic than idolatry. In idolatry there is a core of truth. Man is mistaken in the object to be venerated, but not in the necessity for subordination and supplication. Worship is not directed toward the true God, but there is no mistake in the belief that it must be addressed somewhere.

In magic there is a kind of sacrilege, a truly diabolic pride of power. The magician gives orders. He knows the gods will have their turn, and will make him pay dearly for their temporary submission, but he is proud of his power over them, proud of securing their obedience, if only for a day, and, until the situation is reversed, of enjoying a power which provides him with immediate advantages and inspires fear in his fellow men.

Magic is no doubt partly due to the same *crude realism* that produced idolatry. Inferior deities, that is to say, the false gods, were worshipped to the detriment of the acknowledged true Deity, because they were closer to hand and of more immediate use in invocation and conciliation; but some worshippers developed this realism still further, and passed from religion to magic, from submission to a form of implicit pact which gave them the right to command deity itself. The transition from religion to magic is a distortion, but it is more natural than the transition from magic to religion. If men had started from magic, it is difficult to see how they could have reversed their position, by addressing their supplications to powers which they considered they had put under control.

We therefore find there is a distinction between the two forms of satanism, religion, and magic. In the former Satan is the Prince of this world, since the whole world prostrates itself before his altars and offers him its sacrifices; in the latter Satan seems to consent to obey men who employ certain formulae or practice certain rites, but he loses nothing thereby for he knows that magic and sorcery give him absolute power over those who practice them, so that his final dominion is more total than that over any other of his worshippers.

SATAN IN OUR TIME

It is understandable that one cannot give a complete answer to the question as to how much of these two forms of satanism persists into our own times.

Satanism as religion, as we define it, is in the process of disappearing very rapidly. The altars of the false gods shrink and dwindle. This does not imply that the extent of Satan's dominion has in any way diminished, since we have seen it extending to cover vast empires. But the tactics have been modified and adapted to the general evolution of society, where he is not complete master in spite of his immense power.

Marxist atheism is the most recent form of satanism. It is satanic in that it denies the existence of God or Devil or soul, and only recognizes the existence of matter and of our temporal life, thereby crippling humanity by divorcing men from their immortality. Satan is indifferent to the love of men or of devils. He is hatred itself. His triumph lies in increasing the sphere of hatred. In our present age the most generalized and efficacious stream of hatred is derived from atheistic Marxism. Hatred between classes, hatred between races, between peoples, hatred everywhere, thinly cloaked by a purely materialist concern for the proletariat—such is Marxism. In this way satanism as religion is more widespread, more active and maleficent than it has ever been in the past. Its lies are more global, its negations more radical, its directives more homicidal than anything known to past experience.

That Marxism is truly a religion, most people are agreed, in the sense that it mobilizes in its followers all those feelings of enthusiasm, devotion, and sacrifice which are customarily considered to be expressions of a deep religious faith. This religion, however, cannot be described as anything but satanic, since it is radically and bitterly opposed to the idea of faith in God.

Satanism as religion does, of course, still persist in the form of idolatry amongst peoples living at a level of primitive animism, a state which leaves them peculiarly susceptible, even without any previous indoctrination, to an imminent invasion by atheistic Marxism.

SATANISM PROPER

Apart from Satanism as religion, whether in the form of Marxism or of primitive animism, there is a subtle, morbid form of satanism, much less widespread and infinitely more difficult to detect, and that is the conscious and deliberate worship of Lucifer. We cannot claim to have any exact idea of its present extent. All we can say is that it consists of sacrilegious rites, conscious blasphemies, abominable forms of worship such as the "black mass" — ceremonies in honor of Lucifer which are systematic, calculated profanations of holy things, apeing the homage paid to God by true Christians.

A brief review of this form of satanism is contained in a note in Latin published by the *Etudes carmélitaines* (p. 639).

"We cannot dwell at length," says this note,

> on all present-day satanists or pseudo-satanists. On December 2, 1947, the *English Press* announced the death of Aleister Crowley, described by a judge as notoriously the most perverted person in England.

Questioned once as to his identity, Crowley had replied: "Before Hitler was, I AM" — a studied mockery of the Biblical text. Before leaving this world, the septuagenarian wizard cursed his doctor who, quite rightly, had refused him morphine because he was distributing it to young people. "Since I am to die without morphine, you will die soon after I do." And this happened. The *Daily Express* of April 2, 1948 reported that the funeral of the black magician had given rise to protests from the Brighton Municipal Council. Councilor J. C. Sherrot stated that according to reports he had received, his funeral was celebrated with the full ritual of black magic. His disciples had recited infernal incantations, the "Hymn to Pan" composed by Crowley himself, Carducci's "Hymn to Satan", and the collects of the Gnostic Mass, composed by Crowley for his satanic temple in London.

Similarly, on March 30, 1948, the *English Press* published the obituaries of the famous investigator into psychical phenomena, Harry Price, an expert in demonology. In a report published for the University of London, Mr. Price declared that in every part of London, hundreds of men and women of good education and social standing were worshipping the Devil in various forms of established cult. Black magic, sorcery, the invocation of Satan, these three forms of "medieval superstition" were being practiced every day in London, on a scale and with a freedom unknown in the Middle Ages. Price was the founder and life secretary of the Society for Psychical Research, a society established under the auspices of the University of London.

A. Frank-Duquesne has quoted a curious modern instance of this cult, the report of a scientific expedition to Peru, written by Professor Paul Kosok of Long Island, and published in the *Yearbook of the American Museum of Natural History*. The explorers discovered, in a vast, sandy desert, a double series of designs, some representing the signs of the zodiac, others showing birds, plants, and, in particular, many-headed serpents. In the center of the serpent pattern there was a deep pit containing the skeletons of men and animals that had obviously been sacrificed. It is believed that the site has been in continuous use for 2,000 years.

If we have quoted this note in full it is chiefly for the first two paragraphs, disclosing the existence of flourishing satanist groups in London, formed around certain well-known satanists. But from all accounts this only gives a very meager survey of the present-day cult of Satan-Lucifer, as it exists not only in London, but probably in all the great cities of the world. We are, in fact, informed that there are at present more than 10,000 men and women addicted to a regular practice of satanism in Paris alone. But it lies in the nature of such practices to shun the light of day, and to assume an ever more occult character, which renders computation uncertain.

The satanists of whom we have spoken are not merely the leaders of cults, but also practicing sorcerers and magicians, which leads us to a brief account of the modern practice of witchcraft.

PRESENT DAY MAGIC

Apart from the great Luciferians, and those whom we may suspect of clandestine activities in the heart of our great modern cities, there is a countless but unascertainable number of country wizards or sorcerers, perhaps far more than one might suppose. Their bedside books are *The Secrets of Albertus Magnus, The Secrets of Albertus Minor,* and *Red Dragon.* The first two occult works owe their circulation, oddly enough, to the reputation of the saintly doctor Albertus Magnus, who was believed to have mastered all the secrets of nature. It was another of the Devil's unscrupulous wiles to use the reputation of a venerable saint as cover for his diabolic formulae. But more than one modern wizard makes use of pious images in his lucrative trade of duping the masses.

It is noteworthy that when we were discussing recent exorcisms, we found several cases of possession due to the use of incantations. If we are to believe the information supplied by the possessing spirits, under pressure from the exorcists, their entry into their victims was in obedience to the commands of a sorcerer. The same sorcerers prevented them, by repeated use of sortileges, from obeying the orders of the exorcists, or compelled them to reinhabit the person who had been temporarily delivered by the prayers of the ritual.

All this, if it is true, is still very obscure, but the most qualified exorcists are convinced on this point.

It sometimes also happens that the courts have to take unwilling cognizance of these superstitious practices, as in the recent case of an unfortunate woman who killed her husband because she believed he was either bewitched or himself a wizard. But human justice is obviously unavailing against such forms of attack, because witnesses are seldom forthcoming, and legal proof is therefore lacking.

It is, however, beyond controversy that there are men and women who really believe that by following these ancient and improbable prescriptions they can establish contact with Satan, make a pact with him, and thus obtain exceptional powers which they can afterwards turn to great profit. Sorcery and witchcraft are part of what one might call the shadow side of human life. As St. John said, there are always *shadows* accompanying the *light*. Witchcraft inhabits these shadows. It is furtive, avoiding human gaze, being well aware that it inspires in the average human being a shudder of repugnance. But it is proud of its pretended knowledge, and particularly of what it considers it can *do*.

THE DEVICES OF SATAN

In addition to satanism as religion or as magic, there are also what one might call the devices of Satan.

In a famous and fiery speech made by St. Peter Chrysologos to his diocesans of Ravenna, we find the words: "He that has played with the Devil will not reign with Christ!" He was speaking to professed Christians, but even they were sometimes tempted by the devices of the Devil, which in this case were the immoral spectacles of the circus. In our day, as in the fifth century, a Christian should know that he cannot sup with the Devil without risking his future share in the Kingdom.

But the devices of the Devil are hardly the same as in the days of St. Peter Chrysologos, or if they are they have taken on a new guise. We have already mentioned the cinema, and that is enough. Neither need we enlarge on the current tremendous abuse of the novel, the favorite reading of so many of our contemporaries, whose success seems in direct proportion to the unsavory nature of its contents.

No Christian can be in any doubt that the modern successful novel, with its morbid and perverted "realism," is more often than not satanic. It is only too appropriate to remember the prophetic words of St. Paul to his disciple Timothy: "For there shall be a time, when they will not endure sound doctrine; but, according to their own desires, they will heap to themselves teachers, having itching ears: And will indeed turn away their hearing from the truth, but will be turned unto fables" (2 Tim. 4:3–4).

Ad fabulas convertentur! The Latin word for stories or romances is just that: *fabulae,* fables.

How many of our contemporaries take their whole philosophy, their whole outlook on life solely from the novels they read, which are too often designed simply to titillate their senses and their imagination.

OTHER DEVICES

We have already described the views held by the Curé d'Ars on the subject of spiritualism.

Much more recently, to be precise, on November 26, 1955, Fr. Berger-Bergès asked a possessed woman the following questions:

(1). "Is spiritualism a science or just hocus-pocus? Are you behind it all?" The answer was a gesture, as the possessing spirit indicated that it was himself.

(2). "Table-rapping? Do you make them move?" Answer: "Yes, but I'm not alone. There have to be people round the table. We're all together."

(3). The spiritualists have messages signed by Marcus Aurelius. "Who signs himself Marcus Aurelius? Is it you, or one of your kind?" ("I insisted on an answer," said Fr. Berger-Bergès. "He did not or would not answer. But he made the gesture of pointing toward himself. I interpreted this gesture as that of someone trying to reply without attracting God's attention.")

(4). "And the fortune-tellers? *Quid?*" Satan replied: "Well, people have to earn a living," thus allowing him to understand that fortune-telling by cards is also one of the devices used to pander to human stupidity.

This leads us to a brief glance at that other curious phenomenon of our age, the popularity of various forms of prediction which recall the more childish aspects of ancient paganism.

PREDICTION: A SNARE OF THE DEVIL

The present popularity of various forms of prediction is almost unbelievable. The following figures are given for all forms of fortunetelling in France: 6,000 practitioners registered with the police in Paris alone, and 60,000 for the whole of France, with an annual turnover estimated at, at least, 60 billion francs. The ancient forms of divination, such as the examination of the entrails of sacrificial beasts, the flight of birds, the murmur of the wind in the forest, the pattern formed by the waters of a spring, have given way to the cards, the lines of the hand, the study of coffee dregs and all kinds of other methods, all equally imposing. And, as in antiquity, there is still astrology, considered to be the most satisfactory way of foretelling human destiny. The astrologers are still with us, and they assure us, somewhat rashly, that they have absolute proof of the value of their predictions.

The truth of the matter is that all these claims are not only empty, but, logically speaking, absurd. They are a form of falsehood in which the Devil has a peculiarly time-honored specialty. To the astrologers, who may be considered the most distinguished of all soothsayers, we would quote the words of G. de Vaucouleurs, a celebrated astronomer, in his book *Astronomy*, published in 1948. On the subject of *cosmic influences on human beings* he writes: "Not, of course, those imaginary influences on which astrologers try to base their pseudo-scientific theories." And a little further on he points out that in the past, astronomy "was, even up to modern times (and unfortunately, even today, in many limited minds), closely linked with astrological superstition." This very clearly expresses the contempt felt by modern astronomers for astrological prediction, even though dignified by the famous Nostradamus, who has retained so many fanatical supporters right up to our own time.

If astrology is thus discredited, what are we to make of the still more unreliable auguries of human destiny, such as the fortuitous juxtaposition of cards, or the more or less bizarre patterns of the tea leaves? What makes the falsehood self-evident to the believer is the certainty that God alone knows the future. How does He know it? How can that which has not yet occurred be an object of knowledge to God, since human freedom is at stake? How is this divine prescience compatible with human freedom? Everyone knows that this constitutes one of the most formidable problems of general metaphysics. There seems to be only one conceivable answer. Our world is not the only possible world. There is an infinity of possible worlds, each different from the other. But this possibility is solely due to the fact that they have existed from all eternity in the mind of God. And in this mind, that is to say, in the divine *Logos*, these worlds exist ideally, behaving according to their natural laws, which include the free play of certain created freedoms. When God decrees that such and such a world shall *come into existence*, that is to say, shall be created by Him in preference to other worlds, the conditions in this particular world are by no means changed, otherwise it would no longer be the world desired and envisaged by God. Thus, a free act will remain free, yet God will have seen it, and does see it, at the moment it occurs. It is in this sense that God knows the future. Yet since He is the only being to carry all these worlds in His mind eternally, He is clearly the only one to have foreknowledge of the future. To try to foretell the future, except in certain cases of divinely inspired prophecy, is therefore necessarily satanic, in the sense that it is an encroachment on the divine. It therefore follows that no power of prediction has been vouchsafed to the Tarot, to tea leaves, the lines of the hand, the lines formed by salt in the white of an egg, any more than to the conjunctions of stars and planets at the birth of a human being. What, in astrology, is called a *fatum*, and which used to be known as a *horoscope*, is therefore either swindle or superstition.

This does not mean that we are suggesting that the thousands of fortune-tellers and "wise women" who follow this apparently lucrative trade in Paris and other great cities are so many witches or wizards in the pay of Satan.

Probably the majority of them have merely adopted what seemed to be a profitable occupation without the least idea that it is immoral and probably diabolic. We are none the less entitled to consider that the Devil is well satisfied with such aberrations, and that prediction, in its contemporary forms, is one of the devices of Satan to ensnare humanity. It is therefore one of the forms of satanism as magic, as distinct from satanism as religion.

ᴄ 11 ᴄ

LUCIFER AND HIS ALLIES

BOULLAN AND THE MARTAVITES

THIS CHAPTER WILL be devoted to some recent examples of *Luciferianism*, of which the first example is provided by the Abbé Boullan.[23]

Jean-Antoine Boullan was born on February 18, 1824, at Saint-Porchaire (Charente-Maritime), and died at Lyons on January 4, 1893. Little is known about his career, except that he was ordained priest round about 1848. He frequented occult writers and spent his life in circles composed, as he himself said in his "Confession," of "women who were either mad or demonic, according to whichever way you look at it." One of these women was, incidentally, epileptic. In the same Confession he himself admits that he "had no aptitude" for the spiritual direction of women.

It seems much more likely that he was directed by them. He was, however, intelligent. But he was governed by a curiosity verging on morbidity, and a sensuality bordering on obsession. He explained his

[23] This account is largely drawn from passages devoted to the subject in the *Satan* of the *Etudes carmélitaines*, amplified by details supplied by the *Enciclopedia cattolica*.

feelings in the following way: "My sins," he writes, "had a threefold source and origin and foundation: in the first place, the weakness and fragility of my corrupt nature; the illusions of the Devil, all too effective in deceiving and leading me astray; and finally, my own form of understanding which led me into many things deserving of blame and reproof."

Such a confession has all the hallmarks of sincerity. The Abbé Boullan recognized his errors and his faults. He presented a curious mixture of good intentions, by which he deceived himself, and of blameworthy actions, which he tried to conceal from himself. He claimed that he wanted to cure possessed persons, and with that in view he tried to study the effects of sin, and the limits of demonic activity, through his experiences with perverse women. He was so far misled by Satan as to believe himself John the Baptist returned to earth. He followed in the footsteps of the heretic Vintras, who claimed to be a reincarnation of the prophet Elijah.

In the Gospels John the Baptist appears as a new Elias, so a successor to Vintras would naturally be John the Baptist. The moment he realizes this, he has a mission. He is a born reformer. He has to form a group of adherents to raise "the sword of God" against the Roman Church. According to him the Roman Church had delivered itself unto Satan. Catholic priests, he declared, were the "Horned Beasts" of the priesthood.

Money played an important part in his life. His Confession reveals him as "earning a great deal of money" in Paris before starting on his mission. He never says where this money came from, but it intoxicated him. He bought a château and lived in great style. The confusion in his mind between good and evil became so pronounced that he was brought to court for fraud in 1861 and sentenced to three years' imprisonment (1861–1864). The trial brought to light the fact that he had been using his alleged preternatural knowledge to exploit credulous souls and extract money from them. Yet he never kept the money, since he derived a strange pleasure from taking money from some in order to distribute it to others.

His Confession is full of thunderous denunciations of the "Horned Beasts of the priesthood" for denouncing him to Rome in order to secure his condemnation, together with that of his friend, the former nun Adèle Chevalier, a participant in the miracle of La Salette but now fallen into vice, dragging the Abbé Boullan with her in her fall.

He was summoned to appear before an ecclesiastical court in Rome and was held in the prisons of the Holy Office, from which he was delivered by the Piedmontese invasion in 1870.

The Abbé Boullan condemned all who had attacked him, to the pains of Hell, either eternally or temporarily, to imprisonment in the Tower of Babel, and to the payment of his own debts. His conduct became so outrageous that even the followers of Vintras excluded him from their circle.

The story of this unfortunate, wayward priest, the victim of occultism and eroticism, would be merely one of fairly banal misfortune if he had not been part of a specific trend, and if there had been no aftermath.

His share in this trend sheds a distressing light on a whole world of sinister manifestations and intrigues: the occultism of Eliphas Lévi, the "illuminism" of Vintras, that reincarnation of Elijah, the Theosophy of Mme. Blavatsky, the creations of Guaïta, then of Sâr Peladan, under the name of Rosicrucianism. Perhaps it even includes, on a still larger scale, the mysterious rites of "catholic" freemasonry—set up in opposition to the atheism of the French Grand Orient. But these are only a few of the esoteric doctrines and practices which ferment beneath the surface of modern society, and which can reasonably be said to be one of the forms of present-day satanism.

The Abbé Boullan left behind him one offspring: the Mariavite schism.

THE MARIAVITES

The Mariavites are a pseudo-mystical sect, founded in Poland in 1906 by an excommunicated priest, Jan Kowalski, and by a visionary, Félicie Kozlowska (1862–1922).

These two had been in close contact with the Abbé Boullan. They had taken part in his work and shared in his illuminism. Kowalski and his colleague Procnievski had both been Franciscans. Marie-Félicie Kozlowska had been a Franciscan nun. They had been amongst the adherents of the Abbé Boullan and his prophetess, the ex-nun, Adèle Chevalier. Between 1888 and 1893 they were often to be found in these more than doubtful circles. In 1893 the Abbé Boullan died, and the Poles returned to their own country. In 1894 Marie-Félicie began her prophecies, which soon earned her the title of Matouchka — little mother.

This new movement professed a particular devotion to the Virgin Mary. The constant theme of their pious exhortations was "to imitate the life of the Virgin Mary," *Mariae vitam imitare*, hence their name of Mariavites. Marie-Félicie Kozlowska was soon announcing that the Blessed Virgin "dwelt within her." In 1903 they were excommunicated by the saintly Pope Pius X. Far from submitting, the Mariavites left the Church in great numbers. The total of their adherents was estimated to be in the neighborhood of one million. The number of priests and nuns who formed the fanatical leadership of the group at the time of the official launching of the schism in 1906 was put at 300. Kowalski became patriarch of the sect. In 1909 he obtained, for himself and some of his colleagues, a valid episcopal consecration from the Old

Catholic and Jansenist episcopate at Utrecht. In December 1920 the papal condemnation by Pius X was confirmed and published in *Acta Sanctae Sedis.*

Scandals, however, soon arose. The sect authorized, and even boasted of, the practice of "mystic marriage." These marriages were intended, they explained, to ensure "procreation without concupiscence" of children who would therefore be born without the taint of original sin. But the "mystic marriage" soon developed into "mystic polygamy" or "spiritual polygamy." The old Catholics became indignant and expostulated. At the International Congress of the sect held at Berne in 1924, they excommunicated the whole of the Mariavite Church, which still numbered, at that time, 600,000 adherents. Since then, the patriarch and several of his bishops have been prosecuted in their own country on serious charges of immorality and have been heavily sentenced. According to the *Enciclopedia cattolica,* Vol. 8, 1952, their number has fallen to 50,000, with an archbishop, three bishops, thirty priests, and five hundred nuns. The Mariavites observe the rule of St. Francis: or at least, so they say, the priests observing the first rule, the nuns the second, and the faithful that of the third order.

Here again satanism is content to imitate orthodox organizations, and to sully the name of the Franciscans, for lack of better opportunity.

THE DISTURBING CASE OF LÉON BLOY

Not so long ago it would have seemed almost sacrilegious or, at least, an intolerable affront, even to suggest a possible connection between the ex-Abbé Boullan and the frenzied exaltations of the Mariavites, and the well-known author, Léon Bloy.

But in 1957 there appeared an astonishing work by R. Barbeau under the somewhat aggressive title: *Léon Bloy: A Prophet of Lucifer.*[24] For more than three years, says the author, he was a member of the "Cercle Léon Bloy," of Montreal, which was led by Fr. Guy Courteau, S.J. Fr. Courteau considered that Bloy was the most suitable person to startle the "bourgeois" from their apathy, and to lead the intellectuals back into the arms of the Church. We know of course that at the beginning of the century Bloy's influence was considerable, and that persons of the intellectual quality of Jacques Maritain (and his wife), Pierre van der Meer, Léopold Levaux, Walcheren, and others, publicly proclaimed that their conversion was due to him. Amongst his friends—his very generous friends—were Pierre Termier, René Martineau Jacques Debout, and many others. His admirers included men like Hubert Colleye, who wrote *L'Ame de Léon Bloy* (1930); M. J. Lory, *La Pensée Réligeuse de Léon Bloy* (1951); Stanislas Fumet, *Mission de Léon Bloy* (1935); Albert Béguin, *Bloy, Mystique de la Douleur* (1948), etc.

To give a brief summary of his life: Léon Bloy was born at Périgueux to an atheist father and a very pious mother; he displayed from early childhood a violent, compulsive, unadaptable temperament. In Paris he recovered his faith under the influence of Barbey d'Aurevilly, who also encouraged him in the pursuit of the powerful, elaborate style and the unusual and expressive vocabulary which is so characteristic of his writing. It is undeniable that Léon Bloy is a great writer, and that his sense of rhythm and musical phrasing is of the highest order. He maintained a close relationship with Ernest Hello and the Abbé Tardif de Moidrey. He had the greatest admiration for the writer Blanc de Saint-Bonnet of Lyons. But R. Barbeau's book has established beyond doubt that he frequented

---

[24] *Un Prophète luciférien Léon Bloy* (Paris: Aubier Montaigne, 1957).

occult circles, and lived in the expectation of grandiose revelations and surprising catastrophes, and in the belief that he himself had a signal mission to perform.

With his arbitrary temperament he was bound to come into head-on conflict with contemporary society. "I am perfectly clear," he writes on May 29, 1892, "that everyone deceives himself and is deceived, and that the human mind has fallen into utter darkness."

His own illumination was derived, not from the Catholic Church as such, but from a poor woman, a prostitute by the name of AnneMarie Roulé, the Veronica of his novel *Le Désespéré*.

He lived with her and affirmed that he had converted her. She had supernatural visions before becoming completely unbalanced and ending her days in a mental hospital. Relying on this woman's faith, and on the revelations he believed to be contained in the Secret of Melanie Calvat, the mystic of La Salette, he declared himself convinced of the imminence of the *Parousia,* the end of the world. And this end of the world would consist of the coming of the *Paraclete,* who would be *none other than Lucifer in person.*

Such extravagance falls little short of the most intolerable blasphemy. Yet the whole of Barbeau's book tends to show that this was the central and dominant concept in Bloy's mind, a concept which he considered as his own "secret," which he therefore dissimulated, although it secretly inspired all his writing.

Constantly disappointed at not being able to be present at the event for which he felt it his mission to pave the way, he wrote in his *Biography* (published for Joseph Bollery by Albin-Michel, 1947): "All that I can find in myself is a bitter, savage resentment against a God who has shown himself so cold and ungrateful.... I should be ashamed to treat the mangiest of curs in the way God treats me" (1. 428–429).

He believed, in fact, that God the Father was an imperious and pitiless master, that God the Son could do no more than make good the work in which the Father had so lamentably failed, and that the Holy Ghost alone would inaugurate the reign of universal love.

Léon Bloy was, after his own fashion, remodeling the fantasies of Joachim de Flore (*circa* 1145-1202), but it is his identification of Satan with the Holy Ghost which is so shocking.

Léon Bloy's Satan

Léon Bloy is immensely proud of having been the only one—he was so often in this unique position—to have understood Satan's true nature. From the moment he realized that Satan was the Third Person of the Trinity, it is not surprising to find him crediting him with enormous powers. In his book on Christopher Columbus, *Le Révélateur du Globe* (1884), we read:

> Of all modern concepts, the concept of Satan is the one most lacking in depth, by dint of having become purely literary. We may be assured that the Devil of most of our poets would not frighten the youngest child. I only know of one poetic Satan who is truly terrible, and that is Baudelaire's Satan, *because it is sacrilegious.*
>
> All the others, including Dante's, leave our souls unperturbed, and their threats would make even the little girls of the catechism class shrug their not too literary shoulders. But the real Satan, whom we no longer know, the Satan of Womanhood, the Tempter of Jesus Christ, he is so monstrous that if this slave were allowed to show himself as he is—in all the supernatural nakedness of Non-love—the human race and

the whole animal world would utter a cry of horror and fall dead.

So far, we can be in complete agreement with Léon Bloy. But then
he begins to exaggerate:

> He, [Satan] is between our lips and in our cups;
> he takes his seat at our banquets and feeds us full
> of horrors in the midst of our triumphs; he lurks
> in the obscurest depths of the marriage bed; he
> ravages and sullies every feeling, every hope, all
> whiteness, all virginity, and all glory. His chosen
> throne is the golden calyx of love in flower, and
> his sweetest balm the purple hearth of love in
> flame. When we do not speak to God or for God,
> we speak to the Devil and he listens ... in a for-
> midable silence. He poisons the rivers of life and
> the founts of death, he digs a precipice athwart
> all our paths, he arms all nature against us, so
> that God has had to entrust each of us to the care
> of a guardian spirit, lest we should perish at the
> moment of our birth. Finally, Satan is seated on
> top of the world, his feet on the five corners of
> the earth, and nothing *human* is done unless he
> intervenes, or has intervened or will intervene.

And he concludes: "Such is the boundless empire of Satan. He reigns
as patriarch over the swarm of hideous offspring of human liberty."

Time and again Léon Bloy would revert to the same ideas, which
might have been endorsed by Luther, the pessimistic theologian of
original, ineradicable, irrevocable sin. He takes it up again in his

books *Belluaires et Porchers* (1905), *l'Ame de Napoléon* (1912), and elsewhere. He wrote one day to Pierre Termier, "Everything modern springs from the Devil. That is the key to my books and to their author." And in *L'Invendable* (1909) we read (p. 219), "It could be that tomorrow we shall find ourselves confronted with a case of *universal possession.*"

It remains to be seen how Léon Bloy, after having so violently exaggerated the maleficence of Satan, will be able to identify him with the Paraclete. How can the being who is, for us and for Bloy, the incarnation of Non-love, become the personification of Love?

This is Léon Bloy's deepest secret. He loses himself in the most impenetrable symbolism, in which he attains a pitch of ecstasy peculiar to him alone. On October 14, 1889, writing to his fiancée, the daughter of the Danish writer Molbech, he says:

> Remember ... that which was revealed to me formerly, and which I alone have announced, that is, that the Sign of suffering and ignominy—the Cross—*is the most expressive symbol of the Holy Spirit.* Jesus, Who is the Son of God, the Word made flesh, and who represents humanity, must therefore carry this Cross, *which is greater than He, and which overpowers Him,* Simon of Cyrenaica has to help him bear it. When I think of this great, mysterious person, chosen from all eternity from amongst millions of his fellow creatures to help the Second Person of the Trinity to carry the symbol of the Third, I am overcome by an infinite awe which resembles terror.
>
> The name Simon means Obedient, and it is Disobedience which has imposed the Cross, that

is, the Holy Ghost, on the shoulders of that other obedient figure, Jesus Christ. Observe, Jeanne, that that gives us two figures of Obedience to carry the terrible burden of Disobedience, and that this suffering trio is on its way to triumph over death. What an abyss!

In another letter, dated December 2, 1889, he sheds some light on his concept of the Fall and our final restoration:

"This," he writes,

is the way in which I understand at the present moment the great drama of the Fall. The serpent, the *dark image of the Holy Spirit*, deceives the woman who is its *light image.* The woman accepts, and eats death. Up to then the human race had not fallen, since if the woman has exchanged her marvelous innocence for the modesty which is only the lamentable reflection of innocence, the man, that shining image of the Second Person of the Trinity, has not yet lost that same innocence by using his freedom. Such is the unimaginable, almost inconceivable situation. Now pay attention! The man and the woman are together, in conflict, and they are alone, for the serpent has passed into the woman, has become one with her: light and shadow have melted the one into the other for all time. The man and the woman, that is to say, *Jesus* and the *Holy Ghost,* are there, facing each other, under the terrible authority of the Father.

The woman, image of the Holy Spirit, represents all that is fallen and will fall. The man, image of Christ, represents universal salvation, by the deliberate assumption of every fall, of every possible evil, and by the miracle of infinite tenderness he consents to the loss of his shining innocence, in order to share in the fruits of death, in order to triumph one day over death itself, when his freedom shall have been so greatly enlarged by suffering. Then both of them perceive that they are naked, since the Redemption—which has already begun—must be achieved one day on a tree of which the tree of Eden was only a prefiguration, and on that day the victim, the universal holocaust of Freedom and Modesty, must be contemplated in all its nakedness on the Cross of universal expiation. I should have fifty other things to tell you, if I were not dying of cold!

Never mind! Love, in one ineffable, incomprehensible movement, falls to earth: the Word, from which it is inseparable, falls after it, and the Father lifts them up, one through the other, man first of all having to make the terrible sacrifice of his liberty to save the woman, and the woman thereafter having to make a still more terrible sacrifice of her modesty to deliver her husband. When you write that perhaps the woman is the only one who is truly *rich* and the man the only one who is truly *poor*, you are expressing—do you realize it?—one of the most adorable formulae of transcendental exegesis. But the formula is not perfectly true

except in the sense of this exegesis, and that brings
me back to the subject of my letter.

If we understand this ambiguous and pretentious language aright,
the serpent, that is to say, Satan, the shadow side of the Paraclete,
deceives the woman, and not only Eve, but the woman who is to
become the Virgin Mary, the radiant side of the same Paraclete.
The serpent has "become one with her" which means that "Satan
and the Light and Woman" are melted into each other for all time.
"The serpent and the Woman now form a single being, who is the
Paraclete. But after the Fall, the rehabilitation. Love, in one ineffable, incomprehensible movement, falls to earth: the Word, from
which it is inseparable, falls after it, and the Father lifts them up,
one through the other." The Paraclete is synonymous with Lucifer.
His most striking image is that of the Prodigal Son. The Father
anxiously awaits his return. Lucifer will return. He will be received
with joy by the Father. His elder brother will be dissatisfied. This
means that the Church will persecute the Paraclete-Liberator, who
is to bring Christ down from the Cross at the end of time. This
will be the inconceivable Second Coming, the triumph of the Synagogue and of Satan.

It is time to conclude this farrago of nonsense. When one has
studied Barbeau's indictment of Bloy, the least one can do is to place
him amongst the neo-Gnostics who have been proliferating for the
last two centuries. Eighteen hundred years ago the Gnostics were
heretics who considered themselves superior to the ordinary run
of the faithful. They claimed on examination of the Scriptures to
have discovered mysterious meanings inaccessible to other mortals,
and erected improbable systems based on a theory of "aeons" which
were a bridge between matter, identified with evil, and God, who
was remote and almost inaccessible.

Like the Gnostics, Léon Bloy considered himself the depositary of a *secret* known only to him and a few initiates whose revelations he alone understood. He tried, by making use of his own peculiar interpretations, to find support for this secret in the Scriptures. He lived in the wild expectation of a catastrophe, of which he would be not only the witness but the most active agent. He felt it was his role to be the prophet, the privileged harbinger of the *Parousia,* which would take the form of Lucifer's re-entry into Heaven, where he would reassume his title and his glory as Paraclete, the Third Person of the Trinity. To secure this restoration, it would be sufficient that he who is Non-love should revert to his earlier form, which was Love, by invoking the Father: "*I appeal to thy Justice and to thy Glory!*" In other words, if God keeps Satan in Hell, together with other damned souls who have fallen with him, this may be an act of justice, but does not redound to his glory. Creation, which is his handiwork, is incomplete. Not to mince words, if Hell is eternal, creation is a failure. There is a blot on it, an intolerable slur. God, "for His own glory," is obliged to pardon Satan, and all the other damned. He cannot allow the continued existence of the horror called Hell.

This seems to have been Léon Bloy's "secret." The author of the book which we have briefly analyzed makes the following important declaration:

> This present work forms only a part of the text submitted to the Sorbonne on June 1, 1955. The full text will be published later, together with correspondence and unpublished documents relating to a number of important questions, such as the reincarnation of the "Poor Woman," Bloy's belief in the reincarnation of several of his friends, his unshakeable conviction that he himself had been

reincarnated, the non-existence of Time, the angelic nature of man before the Fall, the auto-divinization of man, the themes of the Earthly Paradise, Atlantis, the sex of woman, incest, the celestial paradise of the Gnostics, the language of occultism, Luciferian art, the Septenary, the climacteric year, the Holy Grail, necessity and freedom, the two Abysses, anagrammatism and other occult allusions, and finally, two complete studies of the magnetic luciferianism of Eliphas Lévi, and the mythological luciferianism of H. P. Blavatsky, which establishes the connection between Léon Bloy and the initiates.

With Léon Bloy we passed into the realm of pure fantasy. We shall stay there awhile with Giovanni Papini.

PAPINI'S SATAN

The connection between Léon Bloy and Papini is established by the fact that both writers had a leaning toward illuminism, and both were staunch partisans of Satan's final rehabilitation, which is necessitated by the "justice and the glory of God." If Papini indulges in fewer neo-gnostic elaborations, he does however revive in a very curious way an ancient heresy, that of the "Theopaschites," who considered suffering to be part of the nature of God. But whereas the Theopaschites of old explained God's suffering by the death of the Son of God upon the Cross, a theory which embodies both legitimate and heretical interpretations, Papini ascribes God's suffering to one of the most essential characteristics of His nature. He has no hesitation in declaring:

> If God is love, then He must necessarily also be pain. If love is a perfect communion between the lover and the beloved, it follows that all the pains, all the trials undergone by the beloved must cast a shadow of pain over the one who loves. If God loves His creatures as a father loves his children—and He loves them infinitely more than an earthly father loves the children who are his own flesh and blood—God must suffer, and He assuredly does suffer, for the sufferings of beings whom He has created out of nothing. If God is by nature infinite in everything, we may believe that His suffering is as infinite as His love.[25]

The theological ignorance betrayed by these lines is truly distressing. One must lack all understanding of the nature of God to be able to speak of him in such improper terms, and it shows an unpardonable degree of anthropomorphism to attribute to God the deficiencies in love as we conceive and practice it.

God is beyond all our classifications and all our concepts. His infinite love has its principle and its end in Him, and in Him alone. The creative act which resulted in the institution of finite beings such as men and angels can only be an act of love, because God can perform no other acts. But the love of creatures who demand their freedom cannot exercise any influence on the divine essence, nor cause any modification of this immutable essence. To think otherwise would be to confuse the finite with the infinite, the creature with the Creator, beings with Being. Love as it is in God, is God Himself. We personify it in the Paraclete, or Holy Ghost, just as we personify

---

[25] Papini, *Le Diable*, 74.

the Wisdom that is God in the *Logos*. But the substance and infinity of this love can only be infinite beatitude, and it *excludes forever* all suffering and all pain. Papini therefore plunges into complete theological absurdity when he continues:

"We do not pay sufficient attention to the infinite suffering of God. We have no pity for His torment. The greater part even of those who call themselves His sons are not concerned either to understand or to console this measureless affliction of God. We ask our Father for presents, intervention, pardon, but there is no one who shares, with the tenderness of enlightened filial affection, the eternal agony of God."

He admits that the saints have meditated a great deal on the Cross of Christ, that they have tried to associate themselves with His suffering as a man. But he reproaches the saints for having restricted themselves to a "physical epiphany"—the words are his—of the suffering of God. According to him "the Cross is only the finite and tangible symbol of a Crucifixion which both preceded and followed it."

Papini is unaware that, in so writing, he goes much further than the old Theopaschites, who were condemned as heretics. They were above all *monophysites* or *eutychians* and, starting from the belief that in Jesus Christ human nature was so immersed and lost in the divine nature as to form *one single nature* with it, they felt entitled to say that it was His divine nature that suffered on the Cross. But Papini considers suffering to be the very essence of God. He not only revives the heresy of the Theopaschites but also that of the Patripassians or Sabellians, who, in virtue of the unicity of the divine substance, taught that the Father died on the Cross together with the Son.

Papini's romantic imagination is in full flight. He wants us not only to believe in God: he wants us also to *pity God.*

It is a strange, and unexpectedly blasphemous reversal of roles. God, Who is infinite beatitude, since He is infinite love, has no need of our compassion. He desires it from us for His Son dying on the Cross. He desires no vain and sterile compassion but a necessary repentance for our misdeeds, since it is these misdeeds and not solely the fury of Satan, the treachery of Judas, or the hatred of the Pharisees, which are the cause of his suffering. But all this is in the domain of the finite, the created. Nothing that is finite or created can affect that which is infinite and uncreated.

Thus Papini only succeeds in becoming absurd when he asks us to pity God.

PAPINI AND LUCIFER

He is no less absurd when he suggests it is our duty to pray for Satan, to implore God's forgiveness for him, and reminds us that Satan is not only a great sinner but also a deeply unhappy being.

This concept alone is sufficient to cast a different light on the problem. A guilty Satan we have the right and duty to blame, but an unhappy Satan is one whom we must pity, praying to God to forgive him.

In fact, according to Papini, if God loved Satan greatly before his fall—which can be considered self-evident, since he was God's most beautiful creation—"will He not love him still more now that he has become the most desperately unhappy of all unhappy spirits?"

The sophistry of the argument is obvious. God loves the unhappy. Satan is the most unhappy of all, thus God must love him above all others.

To which ordinary common sense suggests the answer: God loves those who are unhappy through no fault of their own, who have not sought their own unhappiness, who know how to transform their sorrow into an act of love, and of supreme love, like that of Christ on the Cross. It is indeed true that God has infinite love for Christ crucified. But it is impossible and inconceivable to think of God loving someone who has chosen hatred instead of love, revolt instead of obedience, pride instead of humility.

IS THERE HOPE FOR SATAN?

Papini requires us to pity Satan, because of the chastisement he suffers. He imagines that we, the orthodox theologians, teach that there is on the one hand an implacable and irritable God, inflexible in His justice, and on the other a poor, unhappy Lucifer, who would like to be pardoned, but to whom God refuses pardon, unless we intercede in his favor.

This is, as we said, pure fantasy. It is much simpler than that, as Papini himself knows very well, since he describes Satan's misfortunes as follows:

"Satan's punishment is the most terrible that human or divine mind could conceive: *he no longer loves, he is no longer capable of loving, he is swallowed up and held fast in the endless darkness of absence and of hatred....* There is no malefactor on earth so accursed that he can never have even a temporary rush of feeling, a confused gleam of hope. These meager but priceless gleams of light are denied to Lucifer."[26]

Papini has thus laid his finger on the basic reason for the eternity of Hell. It is sometimes asked: "How can we accept that a momentary fault should be followed by an eternity of punishment?" But this is a misunderstanding of the Church's teaching about Hell. A *momentary* fault is never punished by an eternity of Hell, since it is a fault

[26] Papini, *Le Diable*, 77. (The italics are ours.)

which is immediately regretted and obliterated by the contrition of the offender or, rather, by the infinite mercy of God. It is the eternal fault which suffers eternal condemnation. Lucifer can do nothing but hate. He not only *cannot* but *will not* do anything but hate. It is this hatred which is his boundless crime and the cause of his boundless damnation. Even more, it *is*, itself, his boundless damnation. Hell is not *superimposed*, so to say, on his crime, it is inevitably part of it. It is as impossible for Lucifer not to be "unhappy" as it is for him not to hate. Not being able to love, he has forever closed the door of return. We found the same error in Léon Bloy. We asked how someone who was, according to Bloy, Non-love, could become again the essence of Love, the Paraclete, who is none other than the Holy Ghost. It was a reversal of roles that could only occur to a completely unbalanced mind. Papini is less fantastic. He does not go so far as to identify Lucifer with the Paraclete, which is an abominable blasphemy, but he wants to see the chastisement of hatred in Lucifer to be felt as much by infinite love as by the guilty being himself. Whereupon he insists that we shall pity God by feeling pity for Satan.

At least one of the devils interrogated by an exorcist cried out: "Above all, I don't want anyone to be sorry for me!" Satan certainly does not desire our pity. Papini's book must have caused him the worst of torments: that of being an object of compassion to mortals like us, who are so much his inferiors!

The solution put forward by Papini is therefore without the least foundation. It relies solely on a false concept of angelic nature. Just as Papini has a radically mistaken concept of divine nature, since he does not hesitate to say that it is open to suffering, so he is equally mistaken about angelic and, consequently, diabolic nature, since he assumes it to be as subject to modification as human nature in its decisions.

To end this discussion of the *apocatastasis* or the *final redemption of the damned*, which is frequently discussed nowadays, and which many

Protestant theologians have settled by assuming the limited duration of Hell, let us quote some recent remarks made by Jean Guitton:

> The idea which inspires and justifies the Christian belief in the eternity of punishment is that the defeat of the wicked must be total. What I mean by *wicked* is the man who has lucidly and deliberately chosen a radical evil, persevering in it until the last moment. Now any shame, any punishment, however great, is blotted out if it is temporary. If the evil man were not riveted for eternity in his evil, to him would be the real triumph. At the end he would have the right to say to God: "You see, I have managed to survive. It is I who am the most courageous, most patient of beings. I have exemplified the grandeur, the poetry of suffering—I, and I alone, throughout my long passion, which has lasted for such an age. When all is said and done, I was right to choose this evil, which has brought me so many moments of infinitude. I am the cleverer and the nobler. My expiation is over. I shall be right for all eternity, which makes us all equal before Thee!"[27]

What is said here about the evil man is all the more applicable to Satan.

All that remains for us, in our last chapter, is to consider the character of Satan, and to try to give an indication, for what it is worth, of what we may call his *mentality*.

---

[27]   Jean Guitton, "La vie éternelle," *Revue de Paris*, (December 1958).

∽ 12 ∽

THE MENTALITY OF SATAN

NECESSARY DISTINCTIONS

WHEN SPEAKING OF the Devil we should bear in mind that Satan is unique, whereas devils are innumerable. In the course of this book we have treated Satan as if all devils were like him — as if the master and his servants were more or less interchangeable. Yet in cases of possession, we have observed devils calling themselves by various names, such as Isacaron, Isabo, Asmodeus, and so on, names which are not altogether synonymous with Satan. The first point to make in this brief survey of demonic mentality is that devils may differ as much from one another as men do. There are no two alike, and they are not always even in agreement amongst themselves. There was the case at Perpignan, for instance, where Isacaron, who possessed Antoine Gay, quarreled furiously with the Devil that possessed Chiquette.

In the case of the woman of Piacenza, it appeared that Isabo was accompanied by six other demons, with equally exotic names, toward whom he displayed an acute indifference.

When outlining the mentality of Satan, the first task therefore is to distinguish between master and servants, if this is at all possible.

SATAN AND OUR FIRST PARENTS

There is no doubt that the serpent that tempted Eve was Satan in person. The serpent is the Dragon of the Apocalypse. And the Dragon is either Satan or Lucifer.

We can deduce something of Satan's mentality from the language of the serpent.

The first trait is "of all the beasts which the Lord God had made, there was none that could match the serpent in cunning" (Gen. 3:1 Knox Bible). There is no doubt on this point. Satan is distinguished by his *cunning*. Cunning entails the use of "wiles to deceive." The use of cunning implies evil intentions. If a cunning person speaks, it is not to tell the truth, but to deceive, to incline toward error, toward non-truth. Satan is *false*. He cannot be trusted. What he chiefly lacks is what we call uprightness, loyalty, frankness. He is shady. He is deliberately obscure and a dissimulator. If we meditate on his dialogue with Eve, we are struck by the simplicity and ingenuousness of the woman on the one hand, and the subtlety, audacity, and cynicism of Satan. He has his own way of interpreting the divine command.

He *denies* that the command is just, and that the woman might incur dire penalties by violating it. Eve says that God has forbidden anyone to eat of the fruit of the tree, under pain of death. What is the serpent's reply?

"No, you shall not die the death. For God doth know that in what day soever you shall eat thereof, your eyes shall be opened: and you shall be as gods, knowing good and evil" (Gen. 3:4–5).

Satan not only gives God the lie, but accuses Him of acting as the enemy of man, like a tyrant who does not want anyone's eyes to be opened. But Satan's own hidden ambition is betrayed: "*You shall be as gods.*"

By these words Satan gives away his secret, the cause of his revolt, the reason for his fall. "*To be as God!*" This act of pride lies at the very heart of Satan's mentality.

One may wonder how a being of high intelligence could have yielded to such insensate ambition. We know nothing of the life of the angels before the fall of Satan. The fact that he dragged down "one third of the stars," that is, of the angels, with him in his fall, suggests that he had a great many admirers in the angelic world. This admiration was his testing point. He succumbed, by reason of his own admiration for himself. All that we know of human minds supports this conjecture. Pride inspired his words to Eve: "You shall be as gods!" He regards himself as a god, even in his fall. His pride is still alive.

It is pride that keeps him separated from God and turns him into the Adversary. In Sirach the consequence of pride is made perfectly clear: "The beginning of the pride of man, is to fall off from God: Because his heart is departed from him that made him: for pride is the beginning of all sin: he that holdeth it, shall be filled with maledictions, and it shall ruin him in the end" (Sir. 10:14–15).

Thus, in this separation from God, we find the clue to the mentality of Satan the Tempter, and his hatred of mankind cloaked by the semblance of friendship.

He hopes to deceive the woman and through her to deceive the man. He offers his interpretation as an alternative to God's, holding up to the woman that fatal, preposterous dream: "You will be as gods." Yet he knows full well that he is thus bringing death into human destiny.

We see why Christ, the Way, the Truth, and the Life, has defined Satan as the *Father of Lies, a murderer from the beginning*. And yet even this epithet is, for us, only one aspect of the total truth. *Satan not merely guilty of homicide, but of deicide.*

Satan, having tempted Christ in vain, pursues Him even unto death. By entering into the heart of Judas, he became the principal agent of the drama consummated on Calvary.

THE TEMPTER OF CHRIST

All this is confirmed in the threefold temptation of Christ. What insane pride in his words when he shows Christ, in a moment of time, all the kingdoms of the world: "If thou therefore wilt adore before me, all shall be thine." The ultimate basis of satanic ambition lies in the desire to entice worshippers away from God and to draw all the adoration of man toward himself. A fantastic project indeed, yet the history of religion has shown that Satan in a large measure succeeded in replacing God as an object of worship.

Even today, though worship may no longer be directed toward Satan in person, he has succeeded in diverse ways in withdrawing men from God. Men no longer worship the gods of ancient mythologies, but the gods of human pride: Science, Progress, Technics, Matter. Man is about to conquer the whole world and lose his own soul. This is Satan's great triumph, the greatest solace to his hatred of God and man.

In short, pride, the desire to be God, cunning, jealousy, and hatred toward man, all leading to falsehood, murder, and deicide: such is the portrait of Satan.

If we seek for him today, we shall not find him among the secondary and more or less obscure devils appearing in cases of possession, but in the greater field of world politics. Satan will be in the center of the global murder which could be unleashed by a third world war. It is he, beyond a shadow of doubt, who has inspired the Cold War, sowing discord amongst nations, setting one against the other, provoking the persecution of Christ's disciples, imposing his inhuman yoke on the communist nations, and stealthily preparing the bombs perfected by modern techniques for the final catastrophe.

The mentality of Satan has its own satanic grandeur owing to its planetary range: it is tragic since it tends to universal destruction, and infernal since it withdraws man from God, who is the Light and Life of the world.

Léon Bloy, for once, was not overshooting his mark when he said, that if men could see Satan as he really is, they would be struck dead with horror.

THE DEVILS IN THE GOSPELS

But if it is impossible to render a full portrait of the perversity and the power of Satan, it is not the same for the lesser devils at his command. Within their teeming swarm one can find every degree of intelligence, in so far as its evil purposes allow.

Mgr. Catherinet, analyzing the data we have concerning the number of possessed persons healed by Jesus, mentions the following characteristics:

"Timid, obsequious, powerful, evil-doing, versatile, and even grotesque—all these traits are clearly portrayed in the Gospel account of the miracle at Gerasa, and are to be found in varying degrees in other accounts of the casting out of devils."[28]

The same author adds, in a footnote:

> This ridiculous, vulgar, and malevolent aspect of demonic possession also appears in Acts,

---

[28] *Satan, Etudes carmélitaines*, 319. This passage has already been quoted, but is still relevant to a general survey.

particularly 19:13–17, describing the situation in Ephesus: "Now some also of the Jewish exorcists who went about, attempted to invoke over them that had evil spirits, the name of the Lord Jesus, saying: I conjure you by Jesus, whom Paul preacheth. And there were certain men, seven sons of Sceva, a Jew, a chief priest, that did this. But the wicked spirit, answering, said to them: Jesus I know, and Paul I know; but who are you? And the man in whom the wicked spirit was, leaping upon them, and mastering them both, prevailed against them, so that they fled out of that house naked and wounded."

The characteristic of these devils, other than of Satan himself, seems to be *contradiction*, for they are both menacing and subservient, proud and timid, and at all times cynical, coarse, and banal.

THE DEVILS OF JOHN CASSIANUS AND IN MODERN TIMES

Even the most summary description of the demonic world would be incomplete without mentioning John Cassianus and his account of the views on this subject of Serenus, one of the greatest of the Desert Fathers. Serenus speaks of his own experiences, and those of other Fathers, in their encounters with devils.

"There is no doubt," writes Cassianus, quoting Serenus, "that these foul spirits are as diverse in their habits as men themselves. There are amongst them those whom people call 'the vagabonds,' who are above all seducers and clowns. They are constantly to be found in the same places or beside the same roads. They delight in deceiving, much more than in tormenting those whom they meet. They are content to weary them by their mockery and illusions, without troubling to do them great mischief."[29]

Serenus continues with a lengthy enumeration of their characteristics, of which the most essential is surely: "They delight in deceiving."

But they also delight in insulting, threatening, and intimidating. They have their own form of "cold war" waged in cases of infestation, although they are not permitted by God to do great harm.

Such was the Devil who appeared at Ars and at Lourdes. The *Grappin* was not dangerous because, as St. Augustine said: "the dog is chained." He may bark, but he only bites those who approach too closely. Men like Boullan were cruelly savaged, perhaps Léon Bloy also, but it was their fault. Neither the Curé d'Ars nor Bernadette suffered great harm from demonic infestation.

For the common run of mortals, the tempter has indeed the established traits: he is cunning; sophistical, obsessive, at any rate at intervals, but he is impotent against faith: *Cui resistite fortes in fide*—resist him in faith, says St. Peter.

THE DEVIL AND THE EXORCISTS

To conclude this chapter, we cannot do better than quote the following letter from Father Berger-Bergès, who is still active as an exorcist:

"You ask me," he writes on February 17, 1959, "to explain the mentality of Satan under exorcism."

> Whatever may be the cause of possession—and it
> often seems an unfathomable mystery—we might

[29] See Jean Cassien, *Editions de Fontenelle* (1946), Vol. 2, 139, *et seq.*

sum up the mentality of Satan by these three words: *pride, contempt* for his victim, and *tenacity.*

Pride, that will be subjected to the humiliation and terrible suffering imposed by the exorcism of the Roman Ritual. Hence this conflict of attitudes, terrified, insulting, disconcerting, all appearing in turn in the course of the exorcism; hence the violent convulsions, in an effort to escape, so that those present have to tie down the possessed person, or hold him down with all their strength; hence these furious exclamations, when Satan is thrown to the ground, twisting impotently before the tabernacle:

"I didn't want anyone to see this—I didn't want anyone to see me like this!"

Hence the arrogant blasphemies: "I'm not afraid of you, God! ... I am the master.... I am the Master of the World."

And when he tries to break the crucifix which the priest lays on his breast, he has to declare: "I will not bow the neck to Jesus!"

And with the demonic laughter which the exorcists know so well, he will pour out abuse: "The Puppet on the Cross! The Hanged Man on the Tree!"

It is always impressive to see how this hatred of anything religious, provoked by the thwarting of his pride through exorcism, is rendered impotent by the person and the name of the Blessed Virgin. Many a time Satan has had to confess:

"She is the most powerful!... I can do nothing against you, Great Lady!... I can't manage anything, because of her! And something makes me say so.... Something ... that is, God."

Never, never, has Satan been known to insult the Blessed Virgin, but he never fails to try to get rid of the book of exorcisms, of the ritual which, as he has often told me, makes him endure a second Hell. He tries to lay hands on the ritual which the priest is holding, and if he does manage to snatch it away, it burns his hands; if he could, he would get rid of the exorcist too, unless Satan is compelled, to his great fury, to declare: "There's nothing to be done about you! *It's those up there ... who protect you ... but for them, I should have strangled you long ago.*"

You will appreciate, Monseigneur, as will your readers, that all these facts are fully documented in our records, with still more damaging admissions, which have more than once provoked Satan into shouting at me: "Ah, your records! ... If I could, I'd throw the whole lot into the fire!"

I have already explained that Satan's attitude, as displayed during the exorcisms, includes not only pride, but also a *brutal and loathsome contempt for his victim.* This attitude can be explained by the fact that Satan sees in the possessed person a rival, a possible supplanter in the Paradise from which he is excluded. When the exorcist calls him the "Accursed," there is an immediate and impressive reaction of silence and profound sadness, which will later be transformed into violence against the possessed person.

Then the exorcist, and whatever witnesses may be present, at these painful but always impressive episodes, see the possessed man or woman roll on the ground, writhing in pain, trying to avoid the blows which Satan showers on him with revolting cruelty, a scene so intolerable that some onlookers feel compelled to leave.

Whilst Satan is thus displaying his cruelty, the exorcism naturally is pursued unremittingly, for two hours, for three, sometimes even for four hours, imposing an almost intolerable strain on the exorcist—for the priest will not yield to Satan, until finally, overcome by the power of the Ritual as it slowly begins to dominate and exhaust him, the Devil suddenly collapses and falls down, his face to the ground, and gasps out words that seem almost unbelievable:

"Enough! Enough! Have pity! Make me leave!"

Stricken by the avenging powers of the exorcisms of the Church, Satan might then be expected to capitulate and give the signal for the release of his victim. It would be natural to expect this immediate deliverance, but alas! All too often the hope and belief of the layman is disappointed. He discovers that the possession continues, and that the tenacity of Satan compels the Church and the exorcist to renew their work at frequent intervals. Here we must have recourse to theological teachings on mysticism and demonology, both part of the mysterious ways of God:

"Who knows His unfathomable mysteries?"

As for the writer of this letter, who for the past five years has been confronting the Devil with all the weapons of the ritual, he never fails to repeat to all possessed persons, tormented by the Beast: "Have courage! Hold fast! Trust in the power, however slow, of the Church's exorcisms; trust in the power of the Blessed Virgin, victorious over Satan, and await the certain triumph of God!"

About the Author

THE REV. MSGR. LÉON CRISTIANI was a French priest who sometimes used the pseudonym Nicholas Corté. He was a prolific author of the twentieth century and wrote extensively on the reality of evil, possession, and spiritual warfare. His book Who Is the Devil? is available from Sophia Press.

Sophia Institute

Sophia Institute is a nonprofit institution that seeks to nurture the spiritual, moral, and cultural life of souls and to spread the gospel of Christ in conformity with the authentic teachings of the Roman Catholic Church.

Sophia Institute Press fulfills this mission by offering translations, reprints, and new publications that afford readers a rich source of the enduring wisdom of mankind.

Sophia Institute also operates the popular online resource CatholicExchange.com. *Catholic Exchange* provides world news from a Catholic perspective as well as daily devotionals and articles that will help readers to grow in holiness and live a life consistent with the teachings of the Church.

In 2013, Sophia Institute launched Sophia Institute for Teachers to renew and rebuild Catholic culture through service to Catholic education. With the goal of nurturing the spiritual, moral, and cultural life of souls, and an abiding respect for the role and work of teachers, we strive to provide materials and programs that are at once enlightening to the mind and ennobling to the heart; faithful and complete, as well as useful and practical.

Sophia Institute gratefully recognizes the Solidarity Association for preserving and encouraging the growth of our apostolate over the course of many years. Without their generous and timely support, this book would not be in your hands.

www.SophiaInstitute.com
www.CatholicExchange.com
www.SophiaInstituteforTeachers.org

Sophia Institute Press is a registered trademark of Sophia Institute.
Sophia Institute is a tax-exempt institution as defined by the
Internal Revenue Code, Section 501(c)(3). Tax ID 22-2548708.